Abbeys and Priories
in England and Wales

Abbeys and Priories in England and Wales

Bryan Little

HOLMES & MEIER PUBLISHERS, INC.
New York

First published in the United States of America 1979 by
HOLMES & MEIER PUBLISHERS, INC.
30 Irving Place, New York, N.Y. 10003

Library of Congress Cataloging in Publication Data

Little, Bryan D   G
  Abbeys and Priories in England and Wales.

   1. Monasticism and religious orders – England.
2. Monasticism and religious orders – Wales.
3. Monasteries – England   4. Monasteries – Wales.
I. Title.
BX2592.L53 1979   271'.00941   79-213

ISBN 0-8419-0485-5

PRINTED IN GREAT BRITAIN

FRONTISPIECE   Westminster Abbey: the choir

Contents

List of Illustrations

Acknowledgments

The Author and Publishers would like to thank the following for the illustrations in this book:

Aerofilms Ltd, for figs 7, 64 and 67

The Prior, Alton Abbey, for fig. 134

Ampleforth Abbey, for fig. 72

Hallam Ashley, FRPS, for fig. 106

Aylesford Priory, for figs 73, 114 (photos by Photo Precision)

Barnaby's, for figs 28, 57 and 58

Beacon Studios, Brecon, for fig. 31

Humphrey Berridge, for fig. 132

G. Douglas Bolton, for fig. 88

British Insulated Callender's Cables Ltd, for fig. 122

Bromhead (Bristol) Ltd, for figs 129, 130, 135 (photos)

J. Allan Cash Ltd, for fig. 18

Chartwell Illustrators, for the plans

B.C. Clayton, for figs 5, 80 and 123

Community of St. Mary the Virgin, Wantage, for fig. 68

Country Life, for fig. 84

Courtauld Institute of Art, for fig. 66

Department of the Environment, for figs 19, 23, 26, 59, 77, 81, 82, 83, 97 and 112

Farnborough Abbey, for fig. 65

Herbert Felton, for fig. 20

Fr. Ignatius Memorial Trust, for fig. 69 (photo by W.I. Davies)

F. Frith & Co. Ltd, for fig. 90

Leonard & Marjorie Gayton, for figs 6, 29 and 41

Leonard Hill (Photographer) Ltd, for figs 70 and 113

Jarrolds Ltd, Norwich, for fig. 105

A.F. Kersting, for frontispiece and figs 1, 9, 17, 36, 43, 44, 45, 46, 48, 53, 54, 61, 76, 78, 86, 95, 100, 101, 102, 107, 110, 111 and 117

Edward Leigh, for fig. 37

L. Bruce Mayne, for fig. 98

Mount St. Bernard Abbey Archives, for fig. 71

National Monuments Record, for figs 12, 24, 38, 42, 50, 56, 60, 62, 93, 103, 104, 108, 116 and 131

Photo Precision, for figs 49, 73 and 114

Pix Photos, for fig. 35

Prinknash Abbey, for figs 129, 130 (photos by Bromhead)

The Abbot, Quarr Abbey, for fig. 133

Mr. Francis Pollen, FRIBA, for fig. 135 (photo by Bromhead)

St. Mary's Abbey, West Malling, for fig. 70 (photo by Leonard Hill)

St. Scholastica's Abbey, Teignmouth, for fig. 63

Ronald Sims, RIBA, for fig. 91 (photo)

The Mother Superior, Society of St. Margaret, East Grinstead, for fig. 75

Edwin Smith, for figs 14, 32, 33, 39, 40, 47, 52 and 115

Southwell Cathedral, for fig. 51

Will F. Taylor, for figs 15 and 124

Charles Westberg, for fig. 74 (photo)

Christopher Wilson, for fig. 126

Reece Winstone, for fig. 119

C.H. Wood, for fig. 2

The Vicar, Worksop Priory, for fig. 94

A General Survey

Terms and meanings

The monasteries and nunneries of mediaeval England and Wales were numerous, and many of them were large and splendid. Yet not all of these establishments were 'abbeys', while hardly any of their inmates were monks in that word's original sense. Nor, despite the remote original setting of the Cistercian houses, were the monks of those particular abbeys 'hermits' as that word was first understood. In a book which deals, under the title of 'abbeys and priories' with the whole picture of mediaeval and present-day convents one can fitly start with a short glance at the meaning of some terms which any such work must employ.

An abbey is a religious house whose head is an abbot or abbess. The word comes from the Aramaic 'abba' which means 'father'. The abbot or abbess is thus the spiritual father or mother of the community. But many convents, some of considerable size and with many monks, canons, or nuns, were priories, their heads being priors or prioresses; the title, illogically in view of its true Latin meaning, was given, in abbeys, to the second in command. In some religious houses, notably those of the Benedictine monks and Augustinian canons, the status of a priory was held to be lower than that of an abbey, so that priories would, at various times including our own, be 'upgraded' to abbeys. Yet many important establishments, as at Malvern, or Plympton, or Christchurch in Hampshire with its well-known, splendid church, continued as priories till the time of their dissolution. But in some orders, particularly that of the Cistercians, all monasteries, however small, had abbots as their rulers and were thus as much abbeys as Fountains and other large, rich houses of their particular grouping. The word 'abbey' conveniently used in the title of this book, thus covers many establishments, in time including those of the various orders of Friars, which were not ruled by abbots or abbesses.

Nor did the word 'monk' correctly fit those who dwelt in most abbeys and priories. For the word monachus (μόναχος), from which 'monk' derives in essence, denotes one whose religious yearnings lead him to live alone. Many of the earliest 'monks' were also hermits; their title of eremites (ἐρημίτης) implies a life, true of the early hermits who retired from the bustle and noise of Alexandria and other cities and who lived under hard conditions in waste and deserted places. But the essence of mediaeval monasticism, even for the Cistercians in their wild, remote sites, and partly for the Carthusians who largely lived as solitaries in cells, was community life, with worship, work, eating, and sleeping done not alone but in well-ordered communities. Hermits in the true sense existed in the Middle Ages, while anchorites and anchoresses lived, alone in their cells, in populated areas. But the monks, nuns, and canons regular, dwelling in carefully planned, well-ordered convents, had moved far from the original notions of monasticism.

Now for the clearance of a long-standing misconception. There was, and is, nothing whimsical or romantic about monasticism. Deep, unworldly spirituality was, indeed, part of the ambition of mediaeval monks and nuns. Many achieved their ideals, combining their spiritual experience with an austerity of life which denied and reproached luxury and affluence. But this spirituality could, and did, go with practicality. Nothing could have been more matter of fact, or better conceived as an answer to the needs of a worshipping community, than the lay-out of the churches and domestic buildings of the monks and nuns; even their siting, in precise relationship to the nearest stream of flowing water, was determined by such mundane considerations as the most convenient disposal of effluents. There was, indeed, much architectural splendour in the monasteries, while both beauty and artifice went to the embellishment and fitting of monastic churches. But in the main the buildings were there because they had to be. They were not put up to humour the musings or the artistic

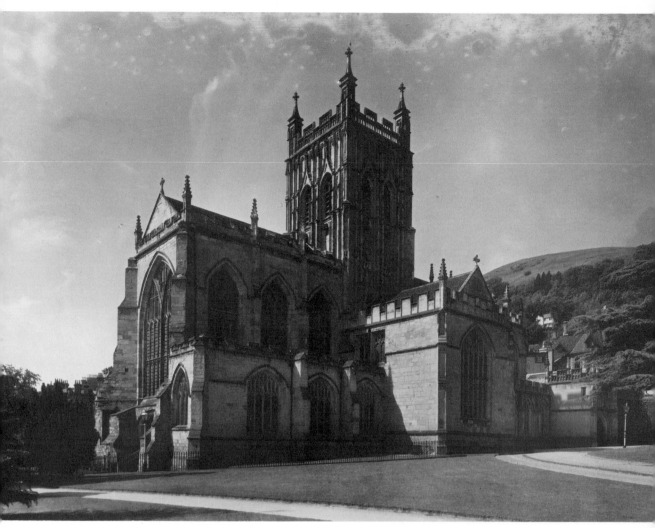

1   Great Malvern Priory: general exterior

taste of latter-day enthusiasts whose knowledge of real monasticism, except perhaps for William Beckford who had been to real monasteries in Portugal, was almost nil.

The sad fate of the English monasteries, and the picturesque, over-grown ruination of many of them by the time that the beginnings of the romantic revival joined the pseudo-Gothicism of Chatterton and Horace Walpole, cast a rosy glow over monastic ruins and was supposed, by some, to have been the true nature of the monastic life. The abbeys, as seen by the romantics, made up a vision of ivy, owls, ghostly abbots and monks and, more satirically, of the tunnels (really sewers running short distances to the nearest rivers) which were absurdly supposed to connect all too many monasteries to the nearest dwelling places of nuns. The abbeys, or mock-abbeys, of those days were the Nightmare Abbey of Peacock, Beckford's Fonthill, and the Northanger Abbey of Jane Austen who neatly satirised such places just as she laughed at such follies as Blaise Castle near Bristol and the horrific, or Gothic, novels perused by some of her heroines. Even where genuinely monastic buildings, like those of the modest Augustinian priories of Bolton and Newstead, became parts of country houses, their owners, like Lord Burlington at Bolton or the Byrons at Newstead, would, for greater effect, promote their priories to abbatial status. An age bred on such fancies was poorly equipped, in the 1790s, to welcome or understand the return to England, under the pressure of the French Revolution, of the modest reality of English post-penal monasticism.

English Origins

The Egyptian hermits, first living as solitaries but later organised, by St. Anthony and St. Pachomius, into more ordered communities, had laid the foundations of Christian monasticism. Though genuine hermits still existed, communities of monks and nuns had become normal by the time that monasteries were founded in England. Celtic monasticism, with monks living in scattered hutlike cells, but within an enclosure and worshipping in a communal chapel, flourished in the West of England. The Cornish monastery at Tintagel was such a place, while excavations have shown that this was the original pattern at Glastonbury. When, in 597, St. Augustine and his companions arrived as missionaries to a paganised south-eastern England they came from a monastic community in Rome. The life of this community, and in the monasteries first founded in Anglo-Saxon England, was much influenced by, and in part followed, the rule of St. Benedict. This was compiled some half a century before St. Augustine's time, providing for a wise blend of liturgy, study and meditation, and manual work, all under the close direction of the abbot and, in this early monastic period, with simple, unassuming buildings. Architectural modesty, replaced by the grand churches and carefully ordered domestic quarters of post-Conquest abbeys and priories, was normal in most English monasteries during their early centuries.

England's pre-Conquest monasticism fell clearly, as did most other aspects of life, into two periods. Monasteries and nunneries were founded, increased in numbers and developed in the seventh and eighth centuries. Not all were 'enclosed' in what was, to a large extent, a missionary country. For some *monasteria* – 'minsters' which gave their place names to such country towns as Ilminster and Axminster – were less the convents of men living in seclusion than missionary stations whose priests led a missionary rather than a claustral life. Others, like the monastery at Jarrow where Bede lived and worked, were more enclosed, with their life conditioned by St. Benedict's rule if it did not, in all details, follow its provisions. By later standards the churches of these monasteries were small and simple, with arches flanking some of their naves, but with those arches leading not into continuous aisles as in Continental basilican churches but, as at Deerhurst, into series of enclosed chapels (misleadingly called *porticus*) which could house the tombs of

2   Bolton Priory, Yorkshire (Augustinian): general view

benefactors and abbots. Round-ended sanctuaries would, in the basilican manner, lie beyond the naves. The 'minster' church at Brixworth in Northamptonshire, and Deerhurst Priory in Gloucestershire which became a 'cell', or dependency, of Tewkesbury Abbey were both built, before the great upheaval of the ninth century, as churches of this type, though Brixworth seems, originally about 690, to have had continuous aisles. At Jarrow and Monkwearmouth much less remains of the churches which served the monasteries founded, in the last quarter of the seventh century, by Benedict Biscop. All these early monasteries, as institutions and largely in their buildings, were swept away, some of them for ever, by the Danish attacks which sharply bisected the long Anglo-Saxon phase of English history. For the creation of the monastic system which still existed at the time of the Norman Conquest we turn to the general revival, in church affairs as in secular concerns, which followed Alfred's victories and the steady unification of England after his reign.

King Alfred himself played his part in the revival when he founded the monastery at Athelney, a thank offering for victory and sited close to the scene of his refuge in his darkest days. The abbey failed, in later centuries, to be of much size or importance. But its first church, square with apses leading out from each side, was a building, under French influence, of real architectural note. In the tenth century, with the powerful King Athelstan a benefactor to many abbeys, and with St. Dunstan the main driving force behind a great movement of monastic reform and revival, many abbeys whose life had for some decades been obliterated were revived, while others, like those of Ramsey and Thorney on the edge of the Fens, were newly founded. By now, moreover, new influences from the Continent helped to mould England's monastic rebirth. A Carolingian revival, in many Continental abbeys, had been started by St. Benedict of Aniane. The original Benedictine way of life had by now been altered, with less manual work and more emphasis on liturgical worship. Liturgical splendour was also dominant in the great Benedictine abbey of Cluny in Burgundy, founded in 910, enlarged under some able and powerful abbots, and soon the most famous monastic house in northern Europe. These historic factors were important for the three great reformers – St. Dunstan of Glastonbury and later of Canterbury, St. Ethelwold of Abingdon and then Bishop of Winchester, and St. Oswald of Worcester – who supervised the restoration, and in some cases the new founding, of the Benedictine abbeys which still

existed at the time of their Anglo-Norman transformation. King Athelstan had already helped some Wessex monasteries, in 931 for example when he made gifts to those at Bath and Malmesbury. But it

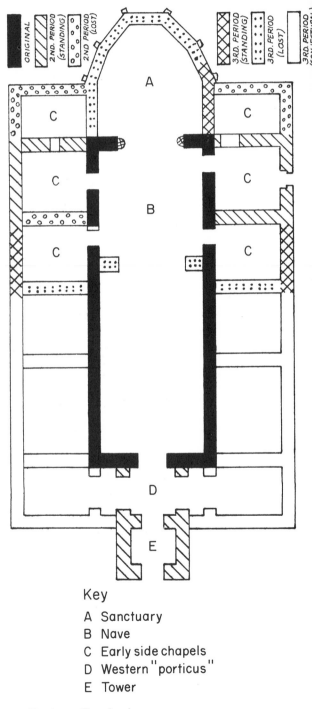

Key

A Sanctuary
B Nave
C Early side chapels
D Western "porticus"
E Tower

3   Deerhurst Church: plan

was St. Dunstan, born in Somerset, a monk at Glastonbury and its abbot before he held bishoprics and eventually the see of Canterbury, who particularly encouraged the monastic rebirth of which King Edgar (959–75) was a vigorous supporter. Many monasteries, including those in such cities as Winchester, Worcester, and Canterbury where the monastery churches (in a practice peculiar to mediaeval England) were also cathedrals, were refounded or came newly into being. Important abbeys of nuns, particularly in Wessex, also shared in the revival. About 970 a meeting of abbots and abbesses agreed to the *Regularis Concordia* which set out the Benedictine régime as it was now, in English conditions very different to those in Italy four centuries before, to be applied to the English monasteries and nunneries. An important historic point, setting a precedent in time to affect the original, withdrawn simplicity of the Benedictine life, was that in this time of slow recovery from the great Danish catastrophe the English monasteries had, inevitably, a near monopoly of literacy, learning and higher education. Now, and in the coming centuries when land was the only effective basis of endowment, the monks were the owners and managers of large estates. Their education, with no Universities yet in existence to compete in the supply of instructed talent, qualified them for important posts in politics and administration. St. Dunstan was virtually Prime Minister as well as Archbishop of Canterbury, while abbots and bishops sat in the Anglo-Saxon Witan as they later did in the House of Lords. Many bishoprics, far more than in later mediaeval centuries, were filled by men whose earlier life had been that of monks.

Of these late Saxon monastic churches even less remains above ground than of those started before the Danish invasions. A simple round-headed doorway survives at the west end of the north aisle of the pre-Conquest cathedral at Sherborne; excavations have also proved that the church had a western porch or tower. Excavation has also shown that the early Winchester Cathedral, as this was enlarged before 850, had elaborate transepts, with rounded ends, of a Carolingian type. At Canterbury the cathedral which stood in 1066 was a large, aisled, basilican building, over two hundred feet long with flanking towers and an apse at each end. But none of these Benedictine buildings were grand enough for the ambitious barons and abbots who came in with the Norman Conquest.

Norman Transformation

The transformation of England's monasteries started before the fateful year of 1066. For the church of Edward the Confessor's new abbey at Westminster, started some years before the King's death and with its eastern half complete by the end of 1065, was modelled on some Benedictine churches in Normandy which already displayed the Norman Romanesque style; it was particularly related to those of Jumièges and Bernay. New or reconstructed abbeys continued to be built during the nine decades of the Norman kings. The Conqueror's thank-offering of Battle Abbey was founded not long after his triumph. Other new foundations, as at Chester, Colchester, Selby, and Reading, increased England's existing Benedictine presence. The churches and the domestic buildings of the older monasteries were one by one pulled down and replaced. Some of the new churches, like that of the great monastic cathedral at Winchester, were on sites a few yards away from their Saxon predecessors; such a device made it easier to use the old church while its successor was being built. Elsewhere, as at Sherborne where the Saxon nave may have lasted for some centuries, the eastern half of the new Norman church, with space for the choir under the central tower or in the first bays of the nave, and with the high altar in the eastern limb, was built first so that much of the Saxon church could be used till the new work was ready. Abbots like Paul of Caen, who came to St. Alban's from the Conqueror's abbey of St. Stephen, brought with them the planning feature of the parallel apses which made up one type of Romanesque east end. A later, more complicated development, better seen in English than in Norman abbeys was the ambulatory, for processions and in some cases with projecting chapels, which ran behind the apsed sanctuary. In other respects, particularly in the length of many of their naves, the Anglo-Norman abbeys and monastic cathedrals were larger and more splendid than those which the conquerors had known, or still founded, in Normandy. In these early mediaeval decades the western parts of these naves were probably used as parish churches, being eventually replaced by separate parish churches whose existence, at the Dissolution, argued for the disuse and destruction of the monastic churches. The eastern limbs of Anglo-Norman abbeys were also, in some cases, larger and grander than those of the Benedictine abbeys in the Norman duchy. Points of planning and style also came from Continental areas other than Normandy, in particular from the 'Lotharingian'

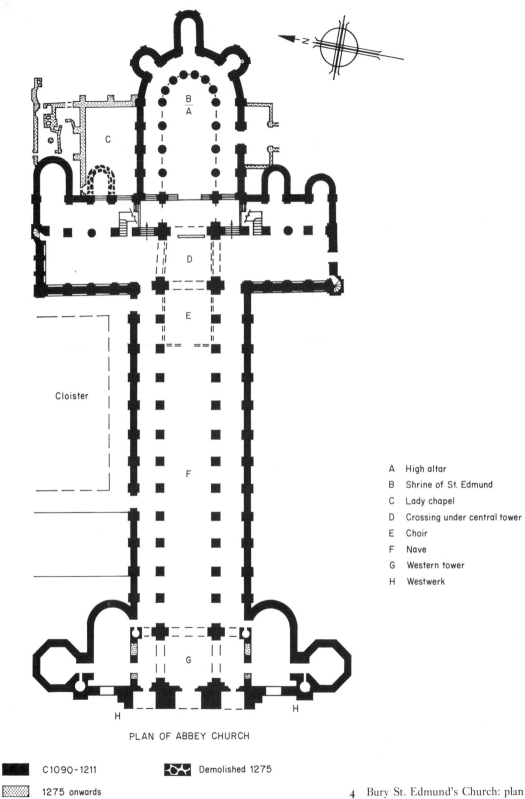

PLAN OF ABBEY CHURCH

A High altar
B Shrine of St. Edmund
C Lady chapel
D Crossing under central tower
E Choir
F Nave
G Western tower
H Westwerk

C 1090 - 1211   Demolished 1275

1275 onwards

4 Bury St. Edmund's Church: plan

territories of what is now the Rhineland and Belgium. The flanking towers of Rhenish building practice seem not to have arisen over English monastic churches.* But Germanic western transepts ended the great abbey church at Bury St. Edmund's, and were finished, in the second half of the twelfth century, at Ely Cathedral which had been started before 1100, as the church of an abbey.

The Anglo-Norman Benedictines were not confined to the historic abbeys or the great new foundations. The abbeys' estates were not all close to the actual monasteries. Benefactors would augment their endowments by widely scattered gifts of land. On some of these estates small dependent priories, or 'cells', were established; the monks who lived there supervised the running of their abbeys' property. The priors of these dependent priories were appointed by the parent abbeys; in some cases the prior of a 'cell' would go back, as abbot, to the parent house. Many of these 'cells' were far too small to run a proper conventual life. Others were of more note, built on fully monastic lines with churches of some size and splendour. Some of these 'cells', like those of St. Alban's at Binham and Wymondham in Norfolk, in time broke away and became fully independent. Leominster in Herefordshire, always dependent on Reading Abbey, was the largest of these priories, while at Bristol five bays of the nave of St. James' Priory, founded as a 'cell' of Tewkesbury, survive because in 1374 this part of the building became a parish church.

Other cells, or dependent priories, belonged to Benedictine abbeys in Normandy and other parts of northern France. The endowment of Norman churches with English estates had started under Edward the Confessor. Once Normandy and England were parts of the same realm, and as the abbeys of England were steadily being Normanised, it seemed natural to many Norman barons who had obtained large English estates that they should give thanks for their success by the gifts, to the Norman abbeys to which their families were linked, of property in the newly conquered land. Many Norman abbeys, particularly that of Bec where Lanfranc, the first Norman Archbishop of Canterbury, and his successor St. Anselm had been monks, thus became landowners in England. Some of their estates continued as ordinary

5 Ewenny Priory, Glamorgan (Benedictine): barrel vaulted Norman presbytery

manors or granges, but on others the Norman abbots and their benefactors established small priories whose inmates, seldom numerous enough to live a really full conventual life, supervised the property of their Norman superiors. The process started soon after 1066, at Chepstow for example when William Fitzosbern, the builder of the great castle which commanded the crossing of the Wye, saw to the founding of the priory as a 'cell' of the Norman abbey of Cormeilles of which his family were the patrons. The churches of these establishments were not, as a rule, large or impressive, but at Stogursey in Somerset the attractive Norman church, cruciform and with traces of its three early apses, was that of a priory dependent on the Norman abbey of Lonlay and is preserved because much of it was used by the parishioners. At Boxgrove near Chichester the church of the priory dependent on the abbey of Lessay in the Cherbourg peninsula was

*They were, however, a feature of the secular, or non-monastic cathedrals of Old Sarum, Exeter, Hereford and Llandaff. For their possible presence in the original church of St. Augustine's Abbey, Bristol, see Bryan Little in *Bristol: An Architectural History*, 1979, pp. 16–17.

larger than most of its kind. An admirable eastern limb, of four double bays and typifying a process of eastward lengthening seen in other English monastic churches of that time, was built and is still used as the local parish church. The work was done, early in the thirteenth century, at about the time when the English Crown's loss of Normandy put these 'alien' priories into an increasingly false political position.

In 1087, when William the Conqueror died, the transformation of England's abbeys had started, though many of its most spectacular achievements had yet to be seen. Some abbeys, notably Peterborough which long seems to have remained as a stronghold of Anglo-Saxon thought and letters, still kept their Anglo-Saxon churches and domestic buildings for some time to come. In others a good amount of Norman Romanesque work had already been finished, at St. Alban's for example, in the eastern portions of the priory church at Blyth in Nottinghamshire, and in the particularly fine crypt designed to lie under the eastern limb of the new cathedral at Worcester. At Winchester and Ely the massive transepts, with their simple arches and galleried ends, had been started by Simeon, at first the prior of the cathedral monastery at Winchester and then abbot of Ely. Elsewhere, as at Gloucester where Serlo, in earlier years the Conqueror's chaplain, had revived the life of the older abbey and much increased the number of its monks, work on the crypt and upper structure of a great new abbey church was soon to start. All this was being done at a time of Benedictine monopoly in England's monasticism. This, however, was a situation due to change, with a vast increase in the number of religious houses in England and in the orders or congregations of 'religious' men and women who inhabited them.

Monastic Multiplication

The year 1100, in which Henry I's accession inaugurated the most peaceful and stable phase of England's Norman régime, also marked the start of what was, in England and elsewhere in Northern Europe, the supremely monastic century. England's great outburst of monastic expansion, and of new foundations, was all part of a great movement which spread widely on the Continent. English monasticism was specially linked, as geography and political

6 Boxgrove Priory, Sussex (Benedictine): the choir limb, early thirteenth century

conditions made it likely, to new monastic moves in northern and central France. The opening years of the twelfth century also included the first arrival in England of religious communities of a type, so far new to this country, which was soon in the sheer number of its convents though not in their average size and importance, to surpass the more traditional monastic family of the Benedictines.

The new element in English conventual life was that of the Augustinian canons regular. Unlike some of the monks, all of them were in priests' orders and they lived, for the most part, in communities. The 'Rule of St. Augustine', by which they lived, was an altered, expanded version of a rule which St. Augustine of Hippo had worked out for early Christian communities in North Africa. Shorter and less detailed than the Benedictine rule it had flexibility and possibilities of adaptation so that it was, and is, used for such organisations as mediaeval almshouses and hospitals and unenclosed communities of nuns; in the coming century it was followed by the Dominican friars. A point in which the Augustinian canons differed from the monks was that some of them could, and did, serve as parish priests in the churches whose patronage was held by their priories and abbeys. But most of them led a conventual life not greatly different from that of the Benedictines, and their living quarters were grouped on monastic lines.

The Augustinian canons had, before 1100, been numerous for some time, particularly in Italy and the Empire, though less so in France. Their arrival in England seems to have been delayed by the Benedictine predominance of the eleventh century. But about 1100 the adoption of the Augustinian rule by the secular canons of Holy Trinity, Colchester (later St. Botolph's) seems likely to have seen the establishment of England's first house of Augustinian canons regular. Another such foundation was soon made elsewhere in Essex, at Little Dunmow, while in 1107 Queen Matilda founded the important priory of Holy Trinity, Aldgate. Others soon followed at Barnwell just outside Cambridge, at Merton in Surrey, and at various places in the North of England. The rest of the twelfth century saw a rush, by royalty, important landowners, and by some of the lesser gentry, to found houses of the Austin canons. With few other outlets, besides monastic houses or nunneries, for endowed benefaction, the establishment of some kind of convent became a fashionable device whereby atonement could be made for sins and also, through the requiem masses and other prayers offered by the inmates, salvation could be procured for one's soul. In the upshot too many foundations, both of Augustinian canons and other conventual bodies, were made for all of them to prosper economically or to live properly organised and observant monastic lives. But donors in the twelfth century could not foresee the widespread decrepitude of the fifteenth. Well over a hundred houses of Augustinian canons regular, and a few for canonesses, were founded in England by the year 1200; some of those for canons at first belonged (as at Lilleshall) to the more rigidly disciplined sub-groups based on Arrouais in Picardy and the famous abbey of St. Victor at Paris.

By the beginning of the twelfth century the Benedictines, with their liturgy more complex than in their earlier days, and with many of their monks inevitably caught up in landowning, learning, and high politics, had their 'ginger group' in the white-habited monks of the Cistercian order.

The great movement of reform, by monks following the rule of St. Benedict but doing so in a spirit of renewed and primitive austerity, was of threefold French origin. Its first location was at Cîteaux, a wild and remote spot in Burgundy to which, in 1098, some monks from the abbey of Molesme retired to live in poverty, with strict religious observance. Their abbey became the mother house of a large international order whose spectacular growth was much helped by the dynamic personality of St. Bernard of Clairvaux. Frequent general chapters of the Cistercians were held at Cîteaux itself. Nearly all the abbeys were founded in what are still remote, and to modern eyes beautiful scenery, but which were, in those days, considered repellent and horrific. In an order which looked so strongly to a central headquarters there was a large measure of standardisation in the lay-out of the Cistercian churches and domestic buildings. Other movements of reform, on a smaller scale than that of the Cistercians, started at Tiron and Savigny in northern France; these 'orders' of Tiron and Savigny were later merged in the larger Cistercian body. It was from Tiron and Savigny, not Cîteaux, that in 1113 and in the 1120s England's first 'Cistercian' abbeys were founded. Waverley in Surrey, in 1128, was the first English abbey planted from Cîteaux itself. From then onwards, and particularly in the North and in Wales, new Cistercian abbeys soon proliferated. The worldly involvement of the Benedictines and the liturgical complexities of Cluny were modified in favour of a more withdrawn life, with a simple liturgy rendered in severe churches in which the monks rejected such luxuries as central towers, coloured windows, statuary, and elaborate chants. A more important

element in the Cistercian régime was their great use of manual labour, with the new class of lay brethren *(conversi)* living a simplified monastic life and carrying out the heavy work needed, in the remote surroundings of the Cistercian abbeys, for the clearance of woodlands and heaths and the creation of valuable agricultural estates. Some lay brothers lived at the abbeys, while others formed small groups to manage outlying granges (like Beaulieu's estate at Great Coxwell) too far from the monasteries for direct farming.

Towards the middle of the twelfth century another important 'ginger group' had its first foundation in England. This was among the canons regular; like the Cistercians the members of the new religious houses wore white habits, and they had an identity more lastingly distinct than the subsections of the Augustinians which started at Arrouais and St. Victor. The canons regular of Prémontré in northern France were established, soon after 1119, by St. Norbert. Like the Cistercians they built abbeys in remote rural sites; their insistence on asceticism and strict observance made their lives an Augustinian equivalent to the Benedictine rigours of the White

7 Fountains Abbey, Yorkshire (Cistercian): aerial view

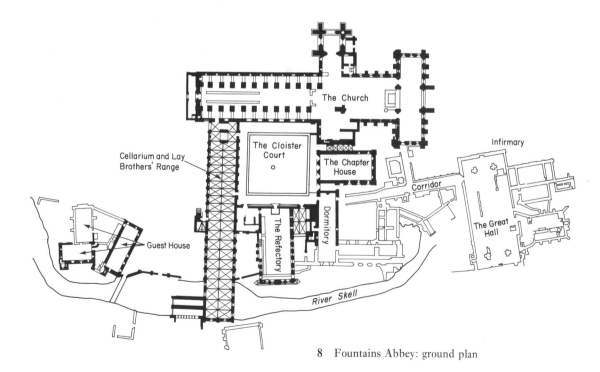

8 Fountains Abbey: ground plan

monks. Their first English house was founded, in Lincolnshire, in 1143, and although they were less numerous than the Cistercians or the main body of the Augustinians, thirty more Premonstratensian abbeys, all owing spiritual allegiance to Prémontré, followed at various dates, most of them before 1200. As the White canons' way of life, with a limited use of lay brothers and with no parochial responsibilities round the actual abbeys, had much in common with that of the Cistercians, their churches, at first, in some ways resembled those of the White monks.

Another monastic phenomenon was that of the 'double' orders, in which communities of nuns had as their chaplains groups of canons or other priests who themselves lived in community. Naturally enough the domestic buildings were separately arranged, but the churches were shared. One such body, from the 1130s, was that of the Gilbertines, founded at Sempringham in Lincolnshire by St. Gilbert and the only religious order in mediaeval England which was itself of English foundation and which was only found in England. In most of their churches, which were subdivided down the middle, the canons, who followed the rule of St. Augustine, used one side of the church, while the nuns, who followed that of St. Benedict, worshipped in the other half. Lay brothers on the Cistercian pattern completed a curious mixture of observances. All the Gilbertine priories were in Lincolnshire, Yorkshire, or the eastern Midlands. The other 'double' order, with only a few abbeys and with its nuns keeping a strict observance of the rule of St. Benedict, was that of Fontevrault. Its mother house, the great abbey of that name in western France, was under the special patronage of the House of Anjou and contained some of their tombs. It was no surprise that its English nunneries, later Benedictine on the normal pattern, were founded during the reign of the Plantagenet Henry II.

By the end of the twelfth century mediaeval monasticism, in England and elsewhere, had reached and perhaps passed its peak. Most of the houses of monks and canons regular, and of nuns which included some Cistercian nunneries, had now been founded. The first buildings of the new convents had often been simple and unassuming. But many had been replaced by churches and domestic quarters of greater size and architectural ambition. All were laid out and built, without sentiment, to meet the worshipping and domestic needs of the fully developed monastic way of life.

Life and Buildings

By the end of the twelfth century most of those in England who, in organised communities, followed the religious life were found in the two great groupings of the Benedictines and Augustinians. The Benedictines, the Cluniacs with their spiritual dependence on Cluny, their elaborate liturgy, and their marked architectural splendour, and the Cistercians all, in varying degrees of severity, lived by the monastic rule laid down by St. Benedict and altered since his time. The canons regular had their more flexible rule, allowing for a wider range of activities and for a less extreme, more liberal observance than that of some of St. Benedict's followers. It could be argued, and was often avowed by Benedictine purists, that canons regular were not actually monks. A non-monastic status certainly applied to the 'secular' canons who served some of the cathedrals, also 'collegiate' churches where the liturgy was on monas-

9 Great Coxwell: manorial barn of Beaulieu Abbey

tic lines but where neither community life nor permanent residence were enforced. But in the priories and abbeys of the canons regular a normal pattern of community life, with its ordered grouping of churches, dormitories, refectories, and other buildings, made them hard to distinguish from the monasteries, at all events those of the black monks, whose external relationships were apt to be more and wider than those of the Cistercians. Community life was the essential common factor between the monks and the canons, most aspects of that life being basically the same for both of the great groupings.

In any religious community the most essential activity was that of communal worship in a church which had no other purpose. In the various parts of that church the floor space was carefully allotted to those liturgical functions, and to the needs of movement and communication. Where churches, monastic or parochial, varied was in the height, style and decorative elaboration of their third dimension, and in the degree to which, in conventual churches, the monks or canons found it necessary, or aesthetically desirable, to lengthen the eastern limbs.

The service which most clearly distinguished the monks and canons regular from most of the parish clergy was the recitation or chanting, in choir, of the offices *(opus Dei)* with their blend of psalms, scriptural passages, prayers, responses, and hymns. Masses, said privately or celebrated with more elaborate ritual, the monks had in common with those who served other churches. But the regularly spaced, and in Benedictine and Cluniac churches time-absorbing sequence of mattins, lauds, prime, terce, sext, none, vespers, and compline, was the distinctive, treasured speciality of the religious communities. As antiphonal chants became normal in the *opus Dei* a closed-in rectangular space, with most of its seats or stalls on each side of a central alleyway, was the heart and

10 Byland Abbey, Yorkshire: tiled floor

11 Tintern Abbey: mediaeval tile, the de Clare arms

12 Christchurch Priory, Hampshire (Augustinian): the choir fittings, *c*1520

centre of a conventual church. To the East a spacious sanctuary, or presbytery, had to contain the high altar used for conventual masses. The combined effect of the two spaces was as if a long, rectangular chapel, shaped like the later, unaisled chapels of academic colleges, had been inserted and screened off within the much larger fabric of a fully developed abbey church. The churches of some religious communities, including those of several small nunneries, never grew beyond this essential rectangle. But in most of them the liturgical needs of communities wholly or partly made up of priests caused greater complexity. As all Augustinians were in priest's orders, and as more Benedictines and Cistercians proceeded to the priestly status, numerous chapels for their private masses (now largely superseded by the revived practice of concelebration) were needed. Some of these chapels were, in early days, built off the transepts or close to the sanctuary, while in the great Norman abbey church at Gloucester an ingenious 'three tier' system

provided chapels down in the crypt and up in the triforium gallery as well as those leading off the ambulatory which ran behind the main sanctuary. Other abbeys and large priories met their need by the rebuilding or lengthening of eastern limbs which had, at the start, been comparatively simple. Aisles had also to be built, not only to hold the growing number of conventual processions but as alleyways and circulating space so that all these elements of the monastic, or central and eastern parts of the church could readily be reached. Sacristies or vestries had at first been built, outside the actual churches, off the eastern alleyway of the cloisters. But in these longer eastern limbs it was sometimes convenient, as at Selby and St. Augustine's, Bristol, for the none too spacious sacristies of a mediaeval abbey to be newly built off one of the sanctuary aisles. Large chapels, for special masses

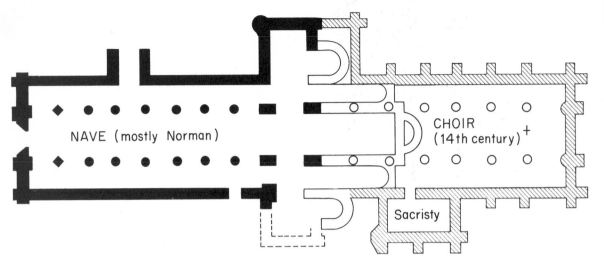

13 Selby Abbey, Yorkshire: plan
14 Binham Priory, Norfolk (Benedictine): west front, mid-thirteenth century

and choir offices in honour of the Blessed Virgin, were also common in and after the thirteenth century. A particularly English feature, they were also built, from Hereford onwards, as additions to many secular cathedral and collegiate churches. Though many were at the extreme east ends of their churches by no means all lay in that position; Peterborough, Ely, Rochester and perhaps Bath had them elsewhere. The Cistercians, all of whose churches were anyhow dedicated to the Blessed Virgin, did not think that they needed them.

Immediately west of the choir a solid screen, as a rule of stone, divided the church into two clearly distinct parts. The nave, in some of the great Benedictine churches of enormous length, was thus quite separate from the sections of the church in which the monks or canons worshipped. What purpose some of them served is not wholly clear, but it seems likely that in some such churches the western portions were at first used by the parish laity, with the heavy screen hiding the monastic parts of the church from these worshippers from outside. In later years, as the parishioners grew in numbers and wished to worship in buildings of their own, separate parish churches, as one sees in such places as Glastonbury, Tavistock, Evesham, and Winchcombe, were built not far away, a sad result being that the parishioners of such places felt no need, when the Dissolution came, to keep any part of the abbey churches. But in some places, as at Binham and Wymondham in Norfolk, at St.James' Priory in Bristol, and in the nuns' abbey of Elstow near Bedford, most of the nave was used by the parishioners and thus continued, after the Dissolution, as the local parish church. In some nunneries, like St. Helen's, Bishopsgate in London,

and in the small Warwickshire priory of Wroxhall, the parishioners used, and continued to use, one half of the church which was subdivided down the middle. But in many abbeys, where no parochial use remained for the nave, and where it had few purposes except for some burials, the marshalling of pilgrims and perhaps occasional special sermons, the long nave must, by the sixteenth century, have had little use; one notes, in such churches, that less was done to Gothicise or rebuild the naves than in what were, for the monks or canons, the more important choir spaces and eastern limbs. Gloucester, Tewkesbury, Rochester, and other one-time monastic churches remind us, in their naves or in some cases by the main structure of their presbyteries, that the Romanesque period in architecture coincided with the great monastic century.

With the Cistercians and the White canons the use of churches was, from the first, more logical. The Cistercians had no parish responsibilities, but they did, in each abbey, have many lay brethren, in many monasteries outnumbering the choir monks. So their naves, of considerable length even if their eastern bays contained the monks' choirs, were used as the virtually separate churches of the lay brothers. The Premonstratensian canons, like the Cistercians, did not share their churches with parishioners from outside and although, in their remote abbeys, they had lay brothers to work their estates their *conversi* were much fewer than among the Cistercians. Their naves did not, in consequence, need to be on a really large scale. Most of them seem at first to have been built without aisles, while some of them were also com-

paratively short. As always, the architecture of a monastic building was vitally conditioned by its convent's way of life.

The siting and arrangement of the monks' and canons' living quarters was no less carefully planned in its relationship to the life of their abbeys and priories. Most of them were laid out, for greater warmth and sunlight, on the southern side of the church. But in some abbeys, as at Tintern, Gloucester, Malmesbury, Chester and St. Radegund's nunnery at Cambridge (now Jesus College), they were on the church's northern side; what determined their position was the unromantic factor of convenient access to the nearby river or stream whose water carried away the convent's kitchen and sanitary effluents. The lay-out and the building, in one or two storeys, of the domestic quarters, brings us to some points in the practical organisation of the larger monasteries and to the officials (or obedientiaries) who supervised particular aspects of the convents' management.

As St. Teresa proved in sixteenth-century Spain, the spiritual life of a great religious mystic could well be combined with great practical and organising ability. Though the vocation of monks and regular canons was essentially to a contemplative life there had also to be some who could display considerable practical and organising ability. Such talents were not, of course, invariably to hand, and one hears, in mediaeval records, of plenty of monasteries plunged in practical mismanagement and financial distress. But even though some of the better educated and more able lay brothers could take over some of the administrative burden, and though seneschals and bailiffs could be, and were, recruited from among the laity (particularly, towards the end of the monastic period, from the landed gentry) there still remained practical tasks, within the cloister and outside it, which only the abbot or prior, and some senior monks, could perform. So one also found monastic officials of ability and organising power, proving, as do the procurators and bursars of modern convents, that enclosure and contemplation need not be inconsistent with a practical vocation.

Two of these officials were in particular concerned with the liturgy rendered in the church, and with its material setting. The precentor made the arrangements for the services and for their actual performance; as his title implied he was specially responsible

15 London, St. Helen's, Bishopsgate (Benedictine nuns): general view

for the chants and their worthy rendering; he also looked after the books and records of the monastery. The sacrist had more to do than to care for the vestments, church plate, and other apparatus of worship kept in the sacristy. He was responsible, under the authority of the abbot or the prior, for the whole maintenance, and where necessary for the repair and virtual rebuilding of the church. So when, in 1322, the central tower of the cathedral priory church at Ely collapsed, it was Alan of Walsingham the sacrist, not Prior Crauden, who shouldered the main task of arranging for the great work of rebuilding which so dramatically transformed the central section of the great cathedral.

The cellarer, corresponding to the procurator nowadays, was the officer of the convent whose special concern was the procurement of foodstuffs; in a large monastery, with lay servants to be fed as well as the monks, the amounts he had to lay in were very considerable. Some of the food would come from the abbey's own lands, close to the monastery or from outlying granges. But much would be bought from outside, so that the cellarer was one of the monks or canons who had most contact with the laity. Fuel, wax for candles, and building materials were also his concern. The refectorian, as his title indicated, was responsible for good order and cleanliness in the monks' dining hall; he had to provide, and to maintain the furniture of the refectory as well as its linen and utensils. Closely allied to the refectorian was the kitchener who, with the aid of lay servants, supervised the daily workings of the kitchen as well as the intake (in collaboration with the cellarer) of the necessary supplies. The chamberlain was the official responsible for the clothing of the abbey's inmates, and for the repair as well as the new making of the garments used in the convent. He also arranged for the baths which the monks took with reasonable frequency by mediaeval standards and he also, at intervals of about three weeks, saw to the regular shaving of the monks' tonsures. In a large monastery the chamberlain, like other officials who saw to the business side of the establishment, needed some lay employees to ensure the carrying out of his allotted task; only in a Cistercian house could he rely, at all events in the peak centuries of monasticism, on lay brothers to help him.

The infirmarian had the care of the infirmary, in which he had his own quarters. In large monasteries, including the cathedral priories, he could, at various times, have several monks under his care, as those who came to the infirmary were not only the temporarily sick, but old and infirm monks who lived there permanently when they could no longer play a part in the services in church or in the general work of the monastery. Two other obedientiaries had key posts

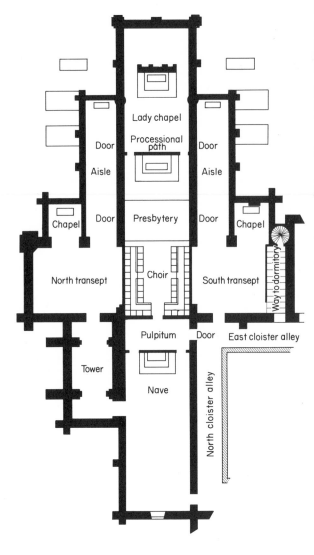

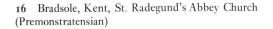

16 Bradsole, Kent, St. Radegund's Abbey Church (Premonstratensian)

17 Cleeve Abbey, Somerset (Cistercian): dormitory range, chapter house below

with a bearing on their monastery's relations with the world outside. The almoner saw to the distribution of alms, and of surplus food and clothing, to the poor. He also had a hand in the supervision of any school that might be kept for the education of boys from the town outside; the almonry would be a building suitable for both of his main duties. The guestmaster saw to the entertainment of guests, in the guesthouse or, where particularly important visitors had to be accommodated, somewhere in the actual monastery or in the abbot's more private residence.

It must have been difficult, in a small monastery or nunnery, to fill the full range of all these official posts. But all of them, sometimes with such assistants as sub-sacrists and assistant infirmarians, existed in the largest communities. A point in which the abbeys and priories varied, from order to order and within the Benedictine body, was the way in which these various activities were financed. In some large Benedictine monasteries each official had his separate income, often allocated to him from particular estates or from the income of particular church livings, and would keep his separate accounts. The system was, however, open to abuse, and a careless or incompetent official could cause much financial confusion to his monas-

tery. The Cistercians, and in due course the Augustinians, preferred that a single treasurer or bursar should, under the abbot or prior, handle each convent's complete finances.

The inner domestic buildings of a mediaeval monastery or nunnery were carefully laid out and built to serve the needs of enclosed communities whose members wanted the minimum of contact with the outside world. The *clausura*, or enclosed part of the convent, was more tautly planned, with special reference to its buildings' nearness to the church, and to convenient movement between its various parts, than the outer buildings, outside the monastic enclosure, where business of one kind or another had to be done with those coming in from outside.

The claustral buildings, including an alleyway built against the south or north aisle of the church's nave, ran round the four sides of a moderate-sized quadrangle. The eastern range, and the range running parallel to the church, normally contained the buildings most specifically geared to the needs of enclosed conventual life.

Next to the church and its sacristy the chapter house was built for the meetings of the convent at which business matters were discussed and important decisions were made. Entered from the eastern cloister walk by a trio of arches it was a room of great dignity, vaulted as a rule and often, if room was

31

needed for all the members of a large community, projecting a few feet beyond the eastern alignment of the block. Most monastic chapter houses were rectangular, with apsidal eastern projections added to a few of them, as at Gloucester and the first Llanthony. But some, mostly from the thirteenth and fourteenth centuries, were beautiful buildings of a polygonal shape. The Norman chapter house of the cathedral priory at Worcester, circular inside and polygonal without, was the earliest of these splendid structures, and as the dormitory (by an unusual arrangement dictated by the nearness of the river Severn) was here on the western side of the cloister quadrangle the chapter house abutted directly onto the eastern walk of the cloisters. But most of these polygonal chapter houses, as at Westminster and Abbey Dore, were approached by a special vestibule so that their unusual, lofty construction did not interfere with the normal planning of the eastern range.

As the infirmary and the monks' cemetery both lay to the east of the domestic buildings a passageway was cut through the ground floor storey of the eastern range to allow the monks to reach them. The rest of

the ground floor contained a parlour, the one room where the monks or canons could meet for needful business conversation, and the warming house where the comforting relaxation of a fire was allowed.

The upper floor of this eastern range contained the monks' sleeping quarters and their sanitary arrangements. A long, narrow dormitory had its beds on each side, with a narrow slit window to light each bed. At first sleeping was wholly communal, but by the later monastic years greater privacy was given to each monk by wooden partitions which divided the dormitory into cubicles. Originally the abbot slept in the dormitory along with the other monks, but here too relaxation, in part determined by an abbot's inevitable position as a landowner and social figure in his locality, came in with the provision of separate houses for abbots, or in cathedral monasteries for the priors who were the monastic heads of these communities. At its end nearest to the church the dormitory often led direct, by a special stairway, into the north or south transept which gave convenient access, in the dimly lit chill of the times of the night offices, to the stalls of the choir; the Augustinian night stairways at Bristol and Hexham are particularly well known and picturesque. At its other end the dormitory led, by a passage running at right angles to its north–south alignment, to the 'reredorter', or latrine block,

18 Hexham Priory (Augustinian): night stairway
19 Rievaulx Abbey, Yorkshire (Cistercian): the refectory

suitably cubicled and carefully planned over the stream, artificial channel (as at Reading off the river Kennett), or sewer down to the nearest running water (as at Evesham and Keynsham) which took away both the kitchen waste and sanitary effluvia.

The side of the cloister court most distant from the church contained the eating and cooking facilities of the convent. The refectory, or dining hall, was the chief building; most were at ground level but a few were raised up on undercrofts which could be used to store food. Most of them ran parallel to the church, but the Cistercians, in their early days, built them, at right angles to the cloister, on a north to south alignment; the space between the refectory and the western range could thus contain a kitchen serving both monks and lay brothers. In the Benedictine and other convents the kitchen could either be at the western end of the refectory or, more separately, on the side of it furthest from the cloister walk. Close to the refectory door one normally found the *lavatorium*, or long, narrow trough in which the monks could wash their hands before and after meals.

The western range of the buildings round the cloisters mostly contained the housekeeping side of the convent. The cellarium, or long, vaulted undercroft, was for the storage of food and other goods, while some of the other rooms would serve the cellarer as his own living accommodation, as an office (or checker) and as a room where conversation could be held with business visitors. In Cistercian abbeys the western ranges were also used, for the first two centuries of the order's presence in England, as the living quarters of the lay brothers who there had their own dormitories, refectories, and infirmaries. But in other abbeys and priories, including the nunneries, the upper floors of these western ranges eventually came to be used for the housing, away from the main dormitories and often with their own chapels and extra wings, of the superiors of the convents. All abbots and priors, and the heads of the nunneries, were landowners and had a position to maintain in secular society as well as religious circles, while the abbots of some twenty of the greater Benedictine abbeys were, like the bishops, members of the House of Lords. The entertainment of distinguished visitors, at times in large numbers at the same time, was among

20 Norwich Cathedral Priory (Benedictine): the *lavatorium*, fourteenth century

21 OVERLEAF Fountains Abbey: vaulted cellarium, twelfth century

their inevitable duties; this was more conveniently done in a separate residence than in some more public part of the monastery. Some of the greater abbots, in a worldly spirit a good deal remote from the earlier, more withdrawn idea of the religious life, preferred to have elaborate houses, like great manor houses, on sites entirely detached from the claustral buildings.

The working spaces of the convent were not confined to the main blocks which ran round three sides of the cloister quadrangle. The cloister walk nearest to the church was, in most monasteries and specially in their early days, the place for reading, writing, and general study, the recessed cupboards for books being at its eastern end not far from the entrance to the transepts of the church. In some abbeys, most notably in the fine vaulted cloisters at Chester and Gloucester, special recesses, or carrels, were built to hold the monks' desks. The western walk of the cloisters was used for the instruction of novices.

22 Muchelney Abbey: fireplace in abbot's house, c1515

23 Lilleshall Abbey, Shropshire (Augustinian): cloisters doorway and book locker

The claustral plan had, however, been worked out in the comparative warmth of the Mediterranean climate, and the open arcades or timber supports of the earliest English cloisters must often have caused great cold and discomfort. Even when many of them had been rebuilt and glazed they must, despite a degree of partitioning with curtains and other hangings, have been chilly and draughty as working spaces. So one hears, in the later monastic period, of separate rooms, in the main domestic blocks, for use as libraries and *scriptoria*.

Some of the monastery buildings lay outside the carefully planned quadrangle of the claustral enclosure. One of these was the infirmary. As it formed a part of the monks' or nuns' living quarters it was sited in a quiet, secluded position to the east of the dormitory and chapter house range. Monastic infirmaries varied much in their design and lay-out, but

a feature common to most of them was the large infirmary hall, aisled like the nave of a church and similar to the hall of a mediaeval hospital. Beyond or to one side of it was the infirmary's own chapel, while some infirmaries, like those at Thetford Priory and the great abbey at Gloucester, had their buildings grouped round small cloisters. Many of these monastic infirmaries were surprisingly large, but one has to remember that they were, in addition to their function as temporary lodgings at a time when sickness was more of a scourge than it is now, the final home of those monks or nuns whose age and infirmity prevented them from observing the normal monastic routine.

Other buildings, more haphazardly grouped and serving the needs of housekeeping and hospitality, lay west of the monastic enclosure. The great court, to which the laity had access for business reasons, would be the focal area not only for the almonry and the guest-house but for such buildings as granaries, forges, watermills, stables and bakeries. This outer courtyard must have presented something of the bustle of a small town in the secular world. It would be entered, from outside the precincts, by one or more gatehouses. Many of these survive, including two at St. Augustine's, Canterbury, while in such places as Montacute, Cerne, and Kingswood, they are now the only convincing above-ground remains of the buildings of monastic precincts put up, at the instance of the heads of religious houses, in or on the outskirts of their towns. Buildings for which the monks and nuns were responsible were by no means confined to the actual abbeys and priories; we shall see how there could also be important building ventures on their more distant estates.

One order of monks in mediaeval England had a rule, and a way of life, which made the planning of their monasteries quite different from those where life was lived wholly in community. Though most of England's few Carthusian priories were founded after the main monastic period the origins of the English Carthusians, and the career as a Carthusian prior of their greatest personality, lay back in the twelfth century.

The Carthusian order was founded, before the end of the eleventh century, by St. Bruno, a Rhinelander who held an important ecclesiastical post at Rheims. Their first monastery, from which the order itself and all its 'Charterhouses' took their name, was at La

24 Lacock Abbey, Wiltshire (Augustinian canonesses): cloisters, fifteenth century

25 Kingswood Abbey, Gloucestershire (Cistercian): gateway, fifteenth century

Grande Chartreuse in the French Alps. Like the Camaldolese Benedictines in central Italy the Carthusian monks spent most of their time in separate cells and combined the way of life of solitary hermits with that of monks living in community. They would meet in church for Mass, and on feast days for the corporate chanting of the choir offices, while each monastery had a modest sized refectory for use on special days. A chapter house, surviving intact at Hinton Charterhouse in Somerset, was also provided for the business meetings of the convent. But for most of their time the Carthusian monks lived alone, reciting their offices, eating, and working in the privacy of their cells, in which they were tended when they were sick or infirm. Each 'cell' was in fact a small cottage, with a bedroom, an oratory and a room for working, while a privy stood at the far end of the small garden in which the occupying monk could do his manual work. As each cell had to be well spaced from its neighbours the Great Cloister round which the cells were grouped had to be large and spacious. Along with its more utilitarian buildings, and the quarters of the lay brethren who waited on the monks, a Carthusian priory thus occupied a considerable area.

The first English Charterhouse was not founded till about 1179, when a priory was started at Witham in a remote area of eastern Somerset. One of the early priors was Hugh of Avalon who came over from Chartreuse and, apart from his duties as prior of Witham, was the friend, the spiritual adviser, and frequently the admonisher of King Henry II before, in 1186, he went to spend the last years of his life as bishop of Lincoln where he was duly venerated as St. Hugh. His career showed that even so strict and austere an order as that of the Carthusians could sometimes find its members called, for a time or more permanently, from the life of the cloister.

In the nunneries the buildings were arranged on basically similar lines to those of the monks and canons regular. As one sees in the surviving western range of Polsloe Priory on the outskirts of Exeter, the quarters of the prioress or abbess were, from a comparatively early period, fitted out in this part of the convent. But in many of the smaller nunneries the churches were of a simpler pattern than most monks' or canons' churches. Unless an abbey of nuns was, as at Shaftesbury and Barking, large and well endowed, it would be unlikely to have more than one or two chaplains, so that although a rectangular choir space, and perhaps a lady chapel, would be needed as in the religious houses of men, there was no requirement for many altars at which priests could say private masses. So although some large nunnery churches, as at Romsey and Barking and probably also at Shaftesbury which was England's largest and richest house of Benedictine nuns, were cruciform and basically similar to large churches of monks or canons regular, most other nunnery churches started, and remained, as simple rectangles, with single altars seen from the nuns' choirs and in many cases with a parallel nave and chancel to serve the local parish. One found it thus in the important London Benedictine nunnery of St. Helen's, Bishopsgate, at the small Augustinian nunnery of Easebourne in Sussex, and at Wroxhall in Warwickshire where the small Benedictine priory had associations with the Shakespeare family and where, in the eighteenth century, the mansion on the site of the western range was bought, for his son, by Sir Christopher Wren.

26 Mount Grace Priory, Yorkshire: Carthusian remains

Later Foundations

By the early years of the thirteenth century the monks, canons regular, and nuns of mediaeval England had almost reached their numerical peak. The late Professor Knowles reckoned that there were, at that time, some 13,000 fully professed religious in the country; his figure did not include the numerous lay brothers of the Cistercians and the smaller numbers, in this same category, in other orders. From then onwards, though but slowly at first, there was a slight drop in the numbers of the monks and canons, with nuns (in any case far fewer than the male religious) remaining at a constant strength. But it was another century before English monasticism saw a really marked drop in its numerical strength, and still more in the fervour of many of those who lived in its various communities. Monastic activity could still be said to be in its peak period, with little competition as yet from the infant Universities. Agricultural development and prosperity, by no means only under Cistercian auspices, was at a high level, with

Benedictine abbeys the sellers of much wool, where their estates were appropriately sited, as well as the Cistercians whom modern historians have particularly linked to the wool trade. Both now and in the next century architectural activity, particularly in the virtual rebuilding or at all events in the eastward transformation of churches, was very pronounced both among the monks and the canons regular; the main difference from the Romanesque period was that such vigour coincided with great rebuilding in the cathedrals and other collegiate churches, Wells for example, or York, or Lincoln and Beverley, of the secular canons. But such Cistercian churches as Fountains and Rievaulx, Tintern, and the new ones at Beaulieu, Hayles, and Netley, great Benedictine churches at Pershore, Ely, Malmesbury, and St. Mary's at York, and the churches of the canons regular at Southwark, Guisborough, and Bristol all proved that the building ambitions of the religious houses well outlasted the more specially monastic period between the Norman Conquest and the year 1200.

What did occur was a sharp falling away in the number of new foundations, though the families who had already founded houses of monks, nuns, or canons regular continued, with outright gifts and new endow-

27 Romsey Abbey, Hampshire (Benedictine nuns):
view looking east
28 Netley Abbey, Hampshire (Cistercian): general view

ments, to augment the resources of existing abbeys and priories. But no more Benedictine or Cluniac monasteries were founded in the thirteenth century, and, except for the London priory of St. Helen's, Bishopsgate, the new Benedictine nunneries founded after 1200 were of little note. A fair number of new foundations for Augustinian canons still arose, while a few more came into being after 1300, some by the conversion to 'regular' status of small colleges of secular canons. None of these new priories was of much size or importance, though some of them, as at Chetwode in Buckinghamshire, Woodspring and Stavordale in Avon County and Somerset respectively, and Flanesford near Ross-on-Wye have left important remains, mostly of their churches. Some new houses of Augustinian canonesses were also founded at this comparatively late period; one of them, the abbey at Lacock in Wiltshire, is of outstanding importance for the survival of its buildings. Three English abbeys of the White canons were founded after 1200; two of them were, by the comparatively modest standards of the Premonstratensians, of fair wealth and importance. The Bonshommes, a small order very similar to the Augustinian canons, had not existed before the thirteenth century. Their two priories in England were both late foundations, one from about 1283, the other one, whose noble church survives intact at Edington in Wiltshire, having its origin in the middle years of the fourteenth century. Both of them owed much to the generosity of the Black Prince.

One more Carthusian priory, like that of Witham in Somerset, was founded in the thirteenth century. But the Carthusians, whose fervour and asceticism remained undimmed and in no need of reform, continued, at a time well past the peak period of English monasticism, to appeal to founders of serious purpose and genuine piety. Like the small monastic family of the Grandmontines (named after their French mother house of Grandmont) the Carthusians never attracted any large number of vocations, so that their priories in England never went beyond nine. But six of those, including the London Charterhouse, were started in the fourteenth century, while that at Sheen, the largest and best endowed, was founded, as late as 1414, by Henry V. Of the other orders the Cistercians, in relation to their total numbers, had more new abbeys in the thirteenth century than most other monastic groupings. They included three in Devon, Netley in Hampshire whose ruins are an attractive feature of the country near Southampton Water, and the important royal foundations of Beaulieu, Hayles,

and in Cheshire at Vale Royal. Then in 1350 the London abbey of St. Mary Graces, with whose foundation Edward III was concerned, was in a populous location quite different from that of the average Cistercian site.

The two Universities of Oxford and Cambridge were only beginning, in the thirteenth century, to be the monasteries' serious rivals either for benefactions or by way of recruitment. The great new factor, however, was that of the friars.

Friars and Hospitals

Most of England's friaries were founded in the thirteenth century and most of them belonged to the four groupings of the Franciscans, Dominicans, Carmelites and Augustinians; only among the Augustinians were new foundations fairly numerous after 1300. Some minor orders of friars also existed, but in the early years of the fourteenth century they were allowed, by a deliberate prohibition on the entry of new members, to become extinct.

The friars were neither monks nor regular canons, though the Dominicans followed a suitably modified version of the flexible rule of St. Augustine. But their habits – greyish brown for the Franciscans, white with black cloaks for the Dominicans, white for the Carmelites, and black for the Augustinians – were similar to those of monks. Though their priories, except the few houses of Dominican and Franciscan nuns, had no regular endowments like those of the monasteries, they were laid out with cloisters and domestic buildings of a monastic type. Along with the outside preaching which was the friars' special work there was much teaching in Universities and elsewhere, while friars were much in demand, among royalty and other eminent people, as confessors. But the laity were also encouraged to come, for the hearing of sermons, to the friars' churches. Nearly all the friaries, except for some of those of the Carmelites, were in or on the immediate outskirts of towns, and the churches were so designed and laid out as to serve a dual purpose, as the private worshipping places of those friars who were resident and as buildings to which outsiders might freely resort, in large numbers, to hear the friars' preaching. Only a few of the friars' churches were cruciform like that of the Dominicans

29 Edington Priory, Wiltshire (Bonshommes): nave and choir, late fourteenth century

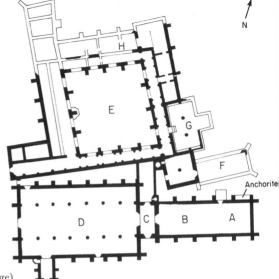

A Presbytery
B Choir
C Space under tower
D Nave
E Cloister
F Library
G Chapter house
H Cellar (Refectory above)

30 Norwich Friary (Dominican): plan

31 Brecon, Dominican Friary: choir (now chapel of Christ College)

at Gloucester, and the friars, though in priests' orders, seem not to have needed the multiplicity of altars that one found in the churches of the monks and canons regular. But the eastern part of a friary church was laid out, like the chapel of a college, as a rectangular choir, while a narrow space, crowned by a slender steeple, would divide it from a spacious nave which was designed, with aisles but often with slender pillars so as to keep visual obstruction to the minimum, like the nave of a large parish church. Many of these naves, as one sees in St. Andrew's Hall at Norwich which was once a Dominican preaching nave, were enlarged or rebuilt in the comparatively late period of Perpendicular Gothic. As nearly all of the friaries were in towns, and as their sites, after the Dissolution, were attractive to urban developers, their remains are sparse compared to those of the monasteries.

Like some of the monastic orders the friars had their problems, in the later Middle Ages, of lessened fervour and slack observance. Among the Franciscans there was thus a movement of reform and greater strictness. The Observant friars, protesting against various mitigations of the earlier Franciscan rule, came into being in the last decades of the fourteenth century. Their first English house, founded in 1482 at the instance of Edward IV, was close by the palace of Placentia at Greenwich. A few others followed, two of them as new establishments, the rest by the acceptance, in existing Franciscan priories, of the Observant régime. These Observant friaries were still in their first fervour when they had to face, with a courage which did not bar the acceptance of death for their beliefs, the trials imposed by the early stages, under Henry VIII, of the Reformation settlement.

Some of the numerous hospitals and almshouses founded in mediaeval England were akin, in the way of life of those who ran them and to some extent in their buildings, to small monastic houses. The rule of St. Augustine was a convenient guideline for such communities, and the priests and lay brethren who organised these houses of charity would wear habits, or at least cloaks with distinctive badges, which marked them off from the ordinary clergy. The fine church, which was once that of St. Mark's Hospital in Bristol and is now, under municipal ownership, the Lord Mayor's Chapel, was the church of such a foundation; the hospital itself, like many others whose monastic character was so pronounced, was dissolved under Henry VIII.

The Last Phase

The last two centuries of England's pre-Reformation monasticism were deeply marked by tragedy, by some measure of recovery in the face of new challenges, by the gradual disappearance, or transformation, of the religious houses and scattered estates which belonged to French monasteries, by competition from other devotional outlets, and by a trimming down of what was, without doubt, the excessive number of the smaller abbeys and priories.

Though no fully accurate figures of deaths have survived there can be no doubt that the Black Death of 1348–49, along with other fierce outbreaks of plague in the next few decades, dealt a devastating blow at England's communities of monks, canons, and nuns. Some religious houses escaped altogether or had few deaths. But in most of them, with their inmates living in community with every risk of the spread of infection, losses were extremely severe. Professor Knowles accepted the probability of a drop of about half in monastic numbers. Among the Cistercians the lay brothers, by 1340 already declining or deliberately restricted, suffered particularly, so much so that the system whereby they worked many of their abbeys' estates never really recovered. But among the monks and nuns, and to some extent among the canons regular, more vocations came in and numbers rose again by the end of the fifteenth century, though not as a rule to the level at which they had stood before the great plague. The Carthusians, attracting devout patrons by their high reputation for sanctity and strict observance, actually went up both in the number of their priories and in the total of their monks.

In the other orders, however, a steady replenishment of numbers was not, in general, matched by fervour like that which had prevailed in the twelfth century. In some of the larger monasteries – the 'solemn abbeys' and those whose churches were also cathedrals – a dignified and well-ordered routine of liturgy and study was still maintained. But there was, by now, a good deal of relaxation in domestic quarters much rebuilt (as one sees in such cloister walks as those of some cathedral priories, at Gloucester and Chester, and in the lovely nunnery at Lacock) and more furnished than before with such comforts as smaller and more cosy eating parlours, separate libraries, and special *scriptoria*. More than ever the heads of the more important religious houses took their places among county society; at such abbeys as Cistercian Forde and Benedictine Milton late mediaeval abbots found it necessary to build such status symbols as magnificent halls for the entertainment of notable lay guests. Parliamentary visits apart, they would also have such urban residences as the abbot of Tavistock's town house in Exeter, while much time, excessive by earlier, more austere standards, was spent, by abbots, at favoured country manors away from the monasteries whose day-to-day supervision they were supposed to maintain. Not many went so far as the prior of Bath who had, in the 1340s, to be deposed for keeping a mistress at a grange some four miles from the monastery. But periods spent 'in grange', by abbots and their spiritual subjects, were apt to go beyond the genuine needs of convalescence or recuperation from the periodical bloodlettings which were a marked feature of monastic routine. Stricter observance and fervour seem, however, to have been more pronounced, with a good effect on the local standing of the monks, in the northern counties. The best of the nunneries seem, moreover, to have been well filled, with convents like St. Mary's at Winchester of a high reputation in their own counties and keeping genteel boarding schools for the daughters of the neighbouring gentry.

The fourteenth century, and the reign of Henry V with its renewed, vigorous outbreak of war with France saw the gradual end of the dependent priories and other properties which had, from before or soon after the Norman Conquest, belonged to monastic and other churches in Normandy and elsewhere in France. The English Crown's loss of Normandy, the rise of national feeling in France and England, and the growing frequency of war between the two countries, made the position of these 'alien' priories and manors increasingly false. Difficulties also beset proper communications between the Cistercian and Premonstratensian abbeys and their mother abbeys across the Channel; this was a situation made worse, after 1378, when in the Great Schism the English Crown backed the legitimate Popes while the kings of France supported the Anti-Popes who set themselves against the better authorised heads of the Church.

For the English kings the vexation caused by the 'alien' priories was largely a matter of money. When war broke out with France they were apt to take these priories and other possessions into temporary control. This was to prevent the forwarding, to enemy territory, of money which could, from the French abbeys, get into the hands of the French kings. The abbots in Normandy often found their contacts with their English dependencies spasmodic and unreliable,

32 Forde Abbey, Dorset: abbot's guest hall, *c*1530

with their possessions north of the Channel as much of a worrying liability as were the possessions of English abbeys in turbulent Ireland. Some of the properties, including part of what the great Abbey of Bec owned in England, were sold, to private buyers or to English religious houses, in various years not long before 1400. With the Cluniacs, who had spiritual and financial links with Cluny but whose relationship with the great Burgundian abbey fell short of outright ownership, the situation was easier. Most English Cluniac monasteries which were not, like Castle Acre in Norfolk, the daughter houses of priories in England, and which had disciplinary and financial links with Cluny and other French monasteries of the order solved their problem by accepting 'denizen' status, carrying on till the Dissolution as ordinary English monasteries of a basically Benedictine type.

In 1414, the year before Agincourt, an Act of Parliament made it lawful for the Crown to take over all the English estates of monasteries in France. Not only were the numerous small or moderate-sized priories affected, but outlying manors and the patronage of English livings were also caught up in a massive transfer of ownership. So we find, in Gloucestershire, that the manors of Cheltenham, Minchinhampton, and Avening were taken from the Norman religious houses which owned them and were duly made over to an important new religious house of Henry V's own founding, while at Pauntley, the parish in which the famous London merchant Dick Whittington had his origin, the patronage of the church once held, like the priory at Chepstow, by the Norman abbey of Cormeilles was transferred, after its confiscation by the Crown, to the rich collegiate church of Fotheringhay which became the special favourite of the House of York. Some priories, like those at Chepstow and Abergavenny in the Welsh Marches, rich Spalding in Lincolnshire, and Holy Trinity at York, and Boxgrove near Chichester whose church, in large measure surviving, presents the best monastic remains in Sussex (see Fig. 6), became 'denizen' and so continued, for the most part as small Benedictine priories, for over a century. But most of these dependent priories, small monastic units and of no great fervour or distinguished observance, no longer continued as the scenes of modest monastic life. Where things totally differed now from what later happened under Henry VIII was in the disposition, after a spell of confiscation, of the massive endowments now finally removed from their owners in

33 Milton Abbey, Dorset: abbot's guest hall, 1495

34 Saighton Grange, near Chester: monastic grange

France.

The pious Lancastrian kings were the last men to countenance the spoliation of the Church. But they were not averse to the careful transfer of church property from one ecclesiastical body to another. So the property taken from the French abbeys was granted, almost at once or within the next thirty years, to monasteries, collegiate churches like that at Fotheringhay, or to the increasingly important academic colleges at Oxford and Cambridge. Some of the lands and buildings went to such existing monasteries as Bruton Priory in Somerset, Westminster Abbey, or the Charterhouses at Coventry and Beauvale. Occasionally, some care was taken to ensure that the break was, in ecclesiastical terms, somewhat modified. So when the wealthy priory of Frampton in Dorset was taken from William the Conqueror's abbey of St. Stephen at Caen it was given to St. Stephen's College within the Palace of Westminster; however much the abbot in Normandy might be annoyed, the feelings of the protomartyr would not, as a result, be unduly ruffled. Other properties went to such existing academic colleges as New College at

Oxford and at Cambridge to Pembroke Hall. But the largest pickings from this massive transfer went to four wholly new foundations. Two were conventual, one being Henry V's large Carthusian priory at Sheen. The other, not far from Sheen and on the other side of the Thames, marked the last occasion on which an order new to England was first established in this country. Originally at Twickenham but later at Isleworth, Sion Abbey was the one English house of the Bridgettine order which had been started, after her death in 1373, according to plans made by St. Bridget of Sweden. Like those of the Gilbertines its abbeys were 'double' establishments of nuns and canons. Syon Abbey, richly endowed by Henry V, is of special interest in that its community survives, without any break in its observance, at the present day.

The other two were Henry VI's great academic colleges of Eton and King's College at Cambridge. Both of them, despite the vicissitudes caused by the Wars of the Roses, drew much of their endowed wealth from what had once been the property of abbeys in France. Eton, for example, got Stogursey and much of what had belonged to Bec, while grants to King's included some more of Bec's property and the small Yorkshire priory of Allerton Mauleverer. Etonians and Kingsmen must alike reckon that their colleges could not have flourished as they did without this windfall from a monastic upheaval caused by the Hundred Years War.

The monasteries which had no ties with French abbeys, and which thus survived, faced other problems unforeseen in their earlier days. To a much greater degree than before they now faced competition from the two Universities and their component colleges. Men and benefactions both flowed in to these more recent institutions which now had the primacy, as places of organised learning, which the abbeys had held before the thirteenth century. The religious orders themselves felt it wise to keep up with the times, and to send some of their members to study for degrees. Early in the fourteenth century a papal decree had laid it down that one in twenty of the monks should attend the Universities. This proportion was not, however, invariably reached, and hardly ever by the smaller monasteries which could seldom spare enough monks from their routine tasks of worship and administration. But for some of those who did go to Oxford and Cambridge, monastic colleges, as distinct from the hostels like the one

established at Cambridge before 1350 for monks from Ely, were duly founded. Some, like the Benedictine Gloucester and Durham Colleges at Oxford and St. Edmund's at Cambridge for Gilbertine canons, had been started before 1300. Others followed later; they included one at Oxford for Augustinian canons, St. Bernard's at Oxford (most of whose buildings survive in the present St. John's) for Cistercian student monks, and at Cambridge the Benedictines' Buckingham College whose court, with some additions, survived the Dissolution and soon became that of Magdalene College. Other monks and canons regular, including the few Premonstratensians who went to study for degrees, went to existing colleges or made other arrangements for their residence.

Religious foundations of other types showed that the monastic houses had moved far from their position of near monopoly. Several new colleges of secular canons came into being during the last century and a half before the Reformation and their own almost total dissolution. Some, as at Tattershall, Fotheringhay, and Manchester, or the one at Wye in Kent founded by Cardinal Kemp the Archbishop of Canterbury, were of considerable wealth or ecclesiastical importance. For benefactors, particularly in the rising bourgeois class, who opted for a smaller outlay chantries, for the most part served by secular priests who might also keep small grammar schools, were an increasingly favoured type of endowment. Some, like the splendid chantries of Humphrey Duke of Gloucester at St. Alban's, or of Prince Arthur at Worcester, were in abbeys or monastic cathedrals. But the great majority, as with the numerous chantries in the churches of London and Bristol, were in parish churches, absorbing money and gifts in kind which might otherwise have gone to the monks or canons or, more probably in the circumstances, to the four groups of friars who were still active in late mediaeval England and who attracted much support from the urban laity.

What also happened to England's late mediaeval monasticism was its steady diminution, by premature extinction or by suppression within the pre-Reformation system, in the fifteenth century or in the years before fateful 1534.

Despite a fair measure of numerical recovery from losses in the Black Death and other severe outbreaks of plague the monks, nuns, and canons regular never fully regained the numerical strength they had known about 1300. Many small priories, especially some of the less well endowed Augustinian houses, lingered as

35 Castle Acre Priory, Norfolk (Cluniac): west front, twelfth century

mere handfuls of inmates, too small for the proper liturgical life expected in an abbey or priory. In any case, again in particular among the Austin canons, there were too many monasteries at a time, even before the new developments of the Counter Reformation, when new outlets were available both for benefactors and for men anxious to play a full part in church life and in the official positions which were still, in large measure, filled by ordained clergy. So some of the smaller priories dwindled, through deaths and with not enough power to attract new vocations, till they became extinct or were suppressed by the bishops, without severe controversy and with the bestowal of their property on other religious houses. Most of them were Augustinian, with nearly twenty priories, none of them rich and some down to one or

36 Oxford, St. Bernard's College (Cistercian), now St. John's: gateway, fifteenth century

37 Cambridge, Buckingham College (Benedictine), now Magdalene College: staircase entrance

38 Cambridge, Jesus College (at first St. Radegund's nunnery): chapter house arches, thirteenth century

two canons, disappearing between 1443 and 1534. The property of the little Suffolk priory at Kersey thus went to King's College at Cambridge, Chetwode priory in deeply rural Buckinghamshire was given to the much larger abbey of Notley in the same county, and in the sixteenth century the small priory of St. Radegund at Longleat went, for a few pre-Dissolution years, to the devout Carthusians not far away at Hinton. In Somerset the small Victorine priory at Stavordale, whose church survived as it became a house, disappeared, as late as 1533, to swell the resources of the reasonably wealthy Austin canons at Taunton.

More significant, and taking a cue from the way in which Eton and King's had been endowed, were several suppressions which made money available for educational endowment. So at Cambridge, in 1496, Bishop Alcock of Ely dissolved the small, hopelessly inefficient Benedictine nunnery of St. Radegund and refounded it, with carefully thought-out alterations to its buildings, as Jesus College. As there were only two nuns when this pre-Reformation suppression occurred they must have felt forlorn if they still bothered to use the refectory which now, with the bishop's new roof and windows, serves as a spacious hall for dons and undergraduates. Some years later the saintly Bishop Fisher of Rochester did not scruple to dissolve two religious houses, one in his own diocese, for the financial benefit of St. John's College in Cambridge University. Far more extensive were the widespread suppressions carried out by Cardinal Wolsey, using his great power as papal legate, so as to finance his proposed colleges at Ipswich and Oxford. Some two dozen religious houses, two of them nunneries but in particular priories of Austin canons, thus disappeared. Most of them were small and poor, but the endowments of Bayham Abbey (of White canons) and of the Cluniac priory of Daventry were of moderate size, while the Augustinian priories of S.S. Peter and Paul at Ipswich and St. Frideswide at Oxford (most of whose church nobly survives as the cathedral) were to provide the two collegiate sites.

These suppressions, like the conversion of the Hospital of St. Bartholomew in Bristol into a Grammar School in 1532, were reforms carried out within the discipline of the pre-Reformation church. They were soon followed, more quickly than Fisher or Wolsey could have foreseen in the 1520s, by drastic changes which lay wholly outside that system.

Though the last two hundred years of English monasticism were not its greatest period the abbeys and priories were still responsible, between the middle decades of the fourteenth century and the Dissolution, for much building activity. We have seen how much work was done, in these years, on the rebuilding, on more comfortable lines, of domestic quarters. Cloisters and guest halls apart, many monasteries now faced those who came in from outside with large and splendid new gatehouses which stood between their outer courtyards and the secular world. In some cases, as with the Cluniac priory of Montacute and at Benedictine Cerne in Dorset, a late mediaeval gatehouse, being a building readily turned over to domestic uses, is almost all that remains above ground of a once flourishing monastic complex; the same applies, in the eastern counties, at St. Osyth and Thornton. Near the abbey and out on the monastic estates new building work would be a part of the abbeys' well-developed technique of estate management. Though some estates were still directly farmed by the abbeys, yielding produce which could be sold or sent to swell the cellarers' supplies, far more manors and granges were now let to tenants whose rents contributed to the income of the monasteries. The rebuilding of such properties would increase their rent-producing capacity. With the decline of their lay brothers the Cistercians, who rebuilt many of their North Country granges, now followed a policy long normal for the Benedictines and the Austin canons, while it seems clear, from architectural evidence and from the badges of Abbot Selwood on several houses which once belonged to Glastonbury Abbey, that the greatest of the monasteries in the West of England was active in a similar way. Bridges, as at Burrowbridge in Somerset, Keynsham, Greystone over the Tamar, and, most notably, at St. Ives over the Great Ouse, were built to link abbeys with outlying estates.

Their churches were still the main buildings of the monks and canons, and though some of them, like the cathedrals at Durham and Norwich, the abbey churches at Gloucester, Tewkesbury, and Peterborough, and some Cistercian churches, remained basically Norman or transitional Gothic, without much eastward elongation, there were others which saw major rebuilding or transformation. Completely new churches, from the ground upwards, were only rarely built and then for special reasons. At Sherborne, for example, the almost complete reconstruction of the church, though with the retention of the Norman crossing arches and some other early masonry, was made necessary by a devastating fire in the

39 St. Osyth Priory, Essex: gatehouse, late mediaeval

40   Abbotsbury: Abbey Barn, west end, *c*1500
41   Glastonbury: The Abbey Barn

fifteenth century, while at Bath Bishop Oliver King
felt that he had episcopal as well as monastic dignity to
maintain when in 1499 he ordered the replacement, on
a smaller scale and only on the site of the Norman
nave, of his badly dilapidated co-cathedral. But complete halves of great monastery churches, as at Canterbury and Winchester where one nave was almost
wholly renewed while the other was totally transformed in its architectural character, could still be
great works in the Perpendicular Gothic style. What
also happened, with fourteenth-century precedents to
follow, was the transformation and re-windowing of
several presbyteries. Glastonbury and Malmesbury
both followed the example set at Gloucester whereby
earlier masonry was cased, on the inner side, with a
cage of Perpendicular stonework, while at Great Malvern there was a far more complete rebuilding of the
eastern limb. The vaulting of Norman naves, carried
out in earlier centuries, as at Blyth and Gloucester,
very largely as a fire precaution, was now done as
much for glorification as for severe practicality. Such
work is apparent in the nave at Norwich Cathedral
where similar work, in rich lierne vaulting with
numerous bosses, was also placed over the presbytery
and transepts, and in Bristol Cathedral where the

42 Sherborne Abbey (Benedictine): Norman crossing, fan-vaulted nave and choir

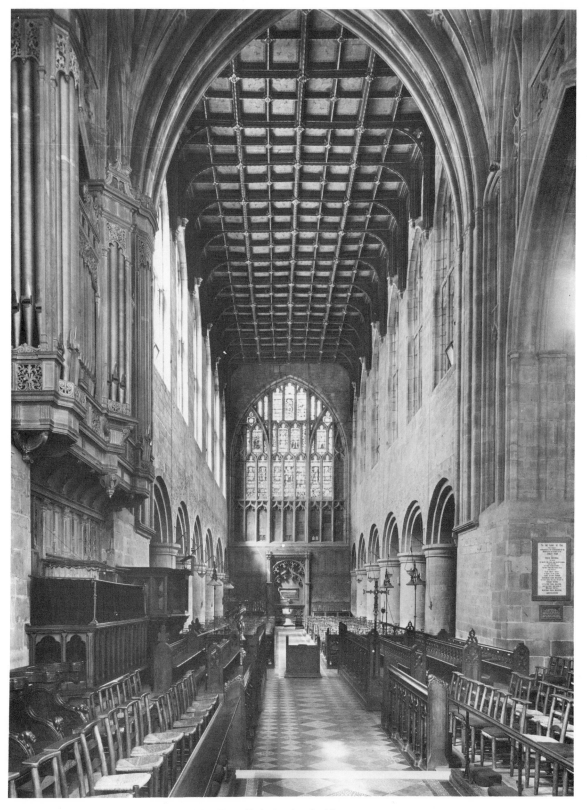

43 Great Malvern Priory, Worcestershire (Benedictine): view looking west

Norman transepts of the Augustinian abbey were richly vaulted in the 1490s. No less splendid, in another Augustinian church of only moderate size, was the vaulting placed over the 'transitional' Norman choir of St. Frideswide's priory at Oxford; similar work in the transepts was started but was nipped in the bud by Wolsey's collegiate scheme.

The building of lady chapels continued in the Perpendicular period. The chapel at Gloucester was of particular size and splendour, while in the Benedictine cathedral priory of Rochester the new lady chapel, in the Perpendicular Gothic of the early sixteenth century, was unusually placed in that it led off the southern aisle of the nave. At Peterborough, the east end was remodelled as the finely fan-vaulted 'new building' of the early sixteenth century. Other side chapels, many of them chantries, were still built as projections from the main fabrics of the churches, while the chantries of other founders, including bishops and abbots, took the form of attractive, delicately worked cages of decorative stonework, each one taking over a little floorspace without heavily breaking in on the main worshipping areas of presbyteries and choirs. Windows, especially the comparatively small, round-headed ones of the Norman period, were altered by the removal of shutters and the putting in of Perpendicular mullions and tracery. In other churches whole expanses of walling and single-light windows were torn down, somewhat harshly by modern antiquarian standards, to make way for vast windows in the mullioned and transomed Perpendicular manner. In Norfolk this happened at the western ends of the naves at Castle Acre and Norwich Cathedral; also, in a similar architectural setting, at Rochester Cathedral. In Yorkshire the two Cistercian abbeys of Fountains and Kirkstall replaced lancets by large Perpendicular windows which may well, in disregard of the earlier practice of the order, have been filled with coloured glass but which must have flooded the interiors of those churches with much additional light; at Fountains the change was made both in the eastern and western walls.

The building of splendid towers, mostly over central crossings but sometimes on other sites, was another, most conspicuous architectural activity in the last century and a half of English monasticism. Many of these noble structures have wholly disappeared. The destruction of some monastic churches has been so complete that one can now tell nothing, above

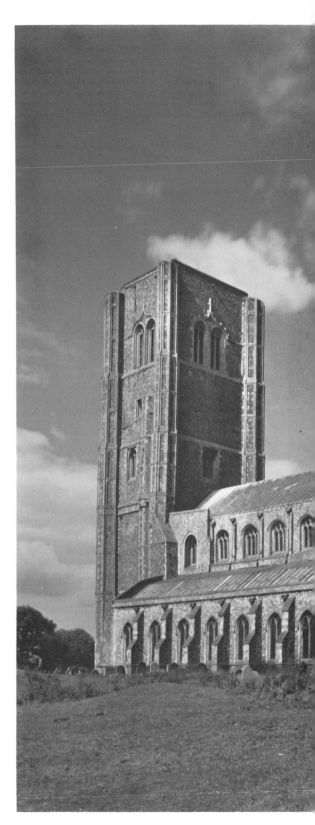

44 Wymondham Abbey, Norfolk (Benedictine): the two-towered nave

ground level where excavation has occurred, of what they may have had as their crowning features. Enough remains of Glastonbury to prove that a tall Perpendicular central tower, supported by 'strainer' arches which were, in their engineering intention, similar to those not far away at Wells Cathedral, was built above the crossing. But one can only guess about what could have been built, by the 1530s, at Winchcombe or Ramsey, Bermondsey or Merton or the great nunnery church at Barking, at Augustinian Leicester or Plympton, or over smaller priories where naves have survived as parish churches but where choirs and transepts have disappeared. In a few places a *western* tower was built to hold the parishioners' bells. Such a tower survives as a fine feature at Christchurch, also at Wymondham in Norfolk, but at Bolton Priory in Yorkshire it was never finished. The common device of a detached belfry was carried on towards the end of the monastic period, so that although, at Evesham, we can tell nothing of the appearance of the abbey's central tower the bell tower, a nobly panelled work of the early sixteenth century, survives in all its splendour. A few abbeys may, of course, have remained content with what they had. One notes, for instance, that at St. Alban's and Tewkesbury rich and prosperous abbeys allowed their Norman central towers to remain, while geological conditions prevented the building of any elaborate tower over the great Benedictine cathedral at Winchester. The Cistercians seem, as a rule, to have continued to deny themselves such vaunting luxuries, and when at Fountains Abbot Huby (who died in 1526) disregarded his order's early austerity and built a tall tower he had to do it on a site abutting his northern transept. But elsewhere, at a time when hundreds of parish churches were putting up splendid towers, great monastic churches were building them on an even more splendid scale. Worcester Cathedral, in the early Perpendicular style, had continued an existing tradition before 1400. The priory at Great Malvern, and the abbey at Gloucester on a more ambitious scale, did the same in the middle years of the following century. Grandest of all, and the last structural addition to the archbishop's cathedral at Canterbury, the Bell Harry tower was finished in the reign of the first Tudor King.

45 Evesham Abbey (Benedictine): detached bell tower, early sixteenth century

46 Tewkesbury Abbey (Benedictine): Norman tower from the north-west

Dissolution

Cardinal Wolsey was, along with his statesmanship, a worldly, self-indulgent, over-wealthy prelate. But he was also a fine organiser, with a genuine desire for more efficiency in the Church over which, in England, his Papal legacy gave him a wide-ranging power exceeding that of the Archbishop of Canterbury or any power he might himself have, in the northern province, merely as Archbishop of York. His dissolution of small monasteries and nunneries to provide sites and endowments for his two academic colleges continued, on a larger scale, what bishops like John Alcock had already done, and displayed one aspect of his activity, within the pre-Reformation system, as an ecclesiastical reformer. He also had a scheme, never carried out in his lifetime, for the dissolution of several far larger religious houses and for the endowment, from their revenues, of some badly needed new bishoprics whose cathedrals would be the churches of the abbeys so dissolved, whose territories would be comparatively small and manageable, and whose existence would end a situation whereby some English dioceses, far bigger than single counties, were too large for proper supervision even by resident bishops; Wolsey himself, as the holder, for a short time in 1514, of the see of Lincoln whose diocese stretched from the Humber to the Thames, must have personally been aware of the scandal. He proposed to do in England what Cardinal Granvella did, some thirty years later, by the sub-division of the large, unwieldy bishoprics of the Low Countries. But his political fall and death postponed another reform which could, late in the day, have been carried out within the framework of Papal discipline. It was left to Henry VIII, in a far greater upheaval in English church affairs, to carry out a part only of the Cardinal's plan.

England's Reformation settlement, ending, in 1559, with the Act of Uniformity passed under Elizabeth I, was not a sudden cataclysm but a gradual process extending over more than twenty years. Voluntary surrenders apart, and apart from the attack, in 1532, on some of the Observant Franciscans who criticised the King's relationship with Anne Boleyn, the dissolution of the monasteries, and of most secular colleges, took a dozen years from the time when the first blows fell. A crucial year, logically opening the way to almost any changes which the King might find it convenient to make, was 1534; in the previous year Anne Boleyn had been formally crowned, and the

future Elizabeth I had been born three months later. Early in 1534 the Succession Act declared Henry's marriage to Anne to be valid, adding that her children were in the lawful line of succession to the Crown; it was not then assumed that Elizabeth would be Anne's only child. Bishops, clergy, and laity were all to take an oath to observe the contents and dynastic results of the Act. Such an oath involved the denial both of Henry's marriage to Catherine of Aragon and of papal authority in England. Almost all the clergy, including the heads of the religious houses, acquiesced and swore the oath. Sir Thomas More, Bishop Fisher of Rochester, and a handful of others alone refused. Later in the year Parliament, at the King's strong prompting, passed the Act of Supremacy by which the King, and not the Pope, was declared the supreme head of the Church in England. The heads of nearly all the religious houses took an oath whereby they accepted this latest proposition. They were, of course, in a cruel dilemma, and some may have given verbal rather than mental assent. Few of them could have doubted what refusal would mean. But the action of all but a very few implied that they could hardly, in logic, dispute the fate which gradually befell them. In the meantime, swift and drastic punishment had come to those who saw what was involved in the transfer, from Rome to the Tudor court, of ultimate religious loyalty. Fisher and More, who had been arrested for opposing the Act of Succession, were kept in prison and in 1535 were executed. In the same year a terrible, and for some an agonisingly drawn-out vengeance was set in motion against the most steadfast of the Carthusian monks.

John Houghton, the prior of the London Charterhouse, and the priors of two other Carthusian monasteries, refused the oath of supremacy and were arrested, tried, and executed as traitors; three other London Carthusians and a chaplain from Syon Abbey soon met the same fate. Then, after two years of close supervision and harassment for the London Charterhouse some of its members reluctantly submitted, in 1537, to the royal supremacy. Others were imprisoned under terrible conditions of darkness, pain, and filth and were allowed to starve; the details of their deaths are among the most gruesome in the annals of Christian martyrdom. The London priory was seized in 1537 and suppressed in the following year. The remainder, with hardly any protest comparable to those made in London, awaited the main dissolution of 1539. In the meantime many of the Observant Franciscans, who had opposed Henry VIII's change of queens and his assumption of

47 Fountains Abbey: Georgian waterscape

ecclesiastical supremacy alike, were executed, exiled, or allowed to die in prison. Some of their friaries carried on as houses of conventual Franciscans, but the closure of some others foreshadowed the massive suppression which was soon to come.

The immediate prelude to the main process of dissolution was financial rather than religious; the whole episode displayed a mixture of economic and ecclesiastical motives. The King, as the chief authority in the State and, by his own urging, in the English Church, was anxious to know more of the economic and financial realities of his domain. He may also, as far back as 1533, have had in mind the 'reuniting to the Crown', by an act of fiscal feudalism, lands and goods which his royal predecessors, and their vassals, had made over to religious houses. At a time when the Church, under various guises, held about a third of the land, and much town property, in England and Wales the endowed income of bishoprics, church livings, and religious houses was of obvious interest to those in power.

In 1535 special commissioners made a valuation (the Valor Ecclesiasticus), as accurately as they could, of the endowed annual revenues of the Church in England and Wales; they omitted the friaries whose 'mendicant' status meant that their resources came solely from benefactions, by now for the most part much diminished. But the reports came in on nearly all the monasteries, nunneries, and secular colleges. Some religious houses seem to have had their incomes undervalued, but in general the commissioners' achievement was thorough and impressive. By the spring of 1536 the King had at his disposal a record of the income, gross and net, of all but a few monasteries.

Almost before this valuation had been finished another visitation of the monasteries was made, not by the bishops as in the past but under royal instructions and perhaps in the hope that its findings would give pretexts for suppression. Though many of the communities had fallen far below the fervour of their early days the visitors' reports, hastily made, had about them a strong flavour of what they must have thought that the King and Thomas Cromwell wanted to hear. Soon after this government visitation a few monasteries, none of any size or note, were dissolved. Then in 1536 an Act of Parliament officially opened the way for a great wave of suppressions which could be seen both as a measure of church reform and as a great act of financial 'resumption' by the Crown.

48 Newstead Priory, Nottinghamshire (Augustinian): scenic preservation

The opening phrases of the Act spoke of the poor state of the monasteries and nunneries which had fewer than a dozen inmates. As the Cistercians had seen in the great days of their new foundations there was substance in the point, and an analogy with Christ and the apostles had strengthened the case for an abbot and twelve monks as the initial minimum for a new abbey. Though communities as small as this, or even smaller, were able to live a pious and edifying life there were, by the sixteenth century, many small monasteries which were poorly endowed, down to single-figure membership and unable to live a well-ordered or fervent community life. Wolsey and others had already made away with a few dozen of these petty priories; their revenues had gone, not to the Crown, but to other ecclesiastical causes. Yet neither shortage of inmates nor lax observance were used to justify the numerous suppressions now authorised by Parliament. The criterion, laid down in the working clauses of the Act, was financial. Whatever the number of their monks, nuns, or canons all religious houses whose net income had been valued below £200 a year were due to be dissolved. Their property was not to go to other monasteries or to academic colleges but to the Crown. It remained to be seen how many of the hundreds covered by the Act's relevant clauses were in fact to go down.

There seems, at this stage of England's religious revolution, to have been some hesitation and confusion, if not in the mind of Thomas Cromwell the ruthless executant of royal policy, at all events in that of the King, whose instincts were more Catholic than Protestant. Whatever he may have intended in 1533, and however much he may have been enraged by the stand of some of the Observant Franciscans and Carthusians, Henry VIII did not, in 1536, mean to sweep away the whole of English monasticism. His religious settlement, under the sovereign as head of the Church in England and Wales, was not, in most matters of doctrine, liturgy, and church ornament of a fully Protestant character. Allowing for such features as the continuance of a Latin Mass, one could think of it as a kind of non-papal Catholicism. In such an 'Anglo-Catholic' state of affairs there was room, as Anglican communities have shown in the last hundred years, for the continued existence of monks and nuns, provided, of course, that the inmates of the monasteries and nunneries did not follow the example, over royal supremacy, of the martyred Observants and Carthusians. Of any such devoted heroism there

49   Cartmel Priory (Augustinian): view from south-east

seemed, in 1536, to be little chance, and whatever Cromwell and such advanced reformers as Bishop Latimer might say there seemed no reason to doubt the continuance, under Henry VIII and, given a new intake of novices, under later sovereigns, of the larger and better organised religious houses. Even in 1536 by no means all of those due for abolition under the £200 limit were then suppressed. The identity of the temporary survivors gives a clue, hard practicalities apart, to the King's ideas for better regulated religious houses in an English church of which he, and not the distant Pope, was to be the supreme head.

Few of the less wealthy Augustinian or Benedictine houses outlasted the first great instalment of suppression. Some, like the Augustinian priory of Ulverscroft in Leicestershire whose remains are still attractive, owed their survival to good reports by the commissioners; another Augustinian continuance was that of the Nottinghamshire priory of Newstead, romantically elevated, when its remains formed part of the Byron family's country mansion, to the status of an abbey. If any of the inmates of the houses now suppressed wished to continue the religious life they could transfer – for example from Cistercian Netley to Beaulieu within the same order – to some other monastery. But many of these monks and canons regular, particularly among the Augustinian canons and generally in East Anglia and the south-eastern counties, were ready for release from their vows. For such clerics it was easy to get other work as parish or chantry priests. In some other orders, and widely among the nuns, the desires of the religious were very different.

Of seventy to eighty religious houses which had, by the financial criterion, been due for suppression in 1536, and which continued beyond that year the majority were nunneries or houses of the better disciplined, more fervent groupings of the male religious. Their character, and good reports on many of them from the commissioners for the suppression, may have carried weight with the King who does not, at this stage, seem to have planned the total destruction of English conventual life. One also has to remember, with Cromwell and the government's financiers in mind, that some reprieved houses paid heavily for what actually proved to be a short-lived survival. But for whatever cause, some abbeys of the reasonably austere Cistercians (including Tintern), three Charterhouses, and several abbeys of the comparatively observant White canons were allowed to continue; of the last named all were in the North of England where the religious orders were more popu-

lar than in the South. More spectacular was the complete exemption, irrespective of their revenues, and alike of the priories which had canons only and the double communities of canons and nuns, of the Gilbertine houses. The continuance of these nuns came as a parallel to the exemption of many small nunneries of other orders.

The nuns stood apart from the monks and canons regular in the high proportion who wished to continue their life under vows. Many must have had genuine vocations, and no church livings were available for nuns as they were for monks or canons regular. Though some young nuns could and did marry after the suppression of their convents, for most nuns the secular world, in an age which offered little to middle-aged or elderly spinsters, must have seemed a bleak prospect. So many nuns now said that they wished to 'continue in religion'. Their rehousing in other nunneries, particularly in the North where no nunneries were of the size and wealth of Shaftesbury, Wilton, or Barking, would have been a major problem. Several of the smaller nunneries of Benedictines and Austin canonesses, the two houses of Franciscan nuns, or Poor Clares, and very notably some of the strict Cistercians, were therefore reprieved. Here again one hears of good repute in their surrounding country, particularly at Winchester where the Benedictine nuns of St. Mary's Abbey, or Nunnaminster, kept a boarding school for 26 of the daughters of the local gentry, the forerunner, one imagines, of many genteel convent schools in penal and modern times. The resources of this and some other convents, from fees, gifts, and the dowries of well-born novices, must have made them wealthier than their record of modest endowed incomes would suggest.

Two curious episodes involving the re-foundation, in one case twice over, of religious houses give colour to the idea that reform, not total abolition, was the King's initial policy in this crucial year of 1536. Though its income far exceeded £200 a year the Benedictine Abbey of Chertsey was dissolved. But its monks were then rehoused in the buildings, further up the Thames valley, which had been those of the dissolved Augustinian priory of Bisham. In Lincolnshire the Cistercian nunnery of Stixwould was dissolved, but its buildings were soon occupied by the Benedictine nuns of a small priory elsewhere in the county. The new occupants were only there for a year, being replaced, till Stixwould's final suppression in 1539, by a royal foundation of Premonstratensian canonesses. With such transfers, and with the continued existence both of the 'great and solemn' abbeys and of a fair number of the less wealthy communities the scene seemed set, under Henry VIII's new religious arrangements, for monasteries as a continuing element in the country's church life.

The Lincolnshire rising, and the northern rebellion known as the Pilgrimage of Grace, had political and economic causes as well as their strong element of protest against many aspects, monastic and otherwise, of the King's religious policy. Most of the North was, for a time, outside government control and the risings seemed a real threat to the régime. The insurgents, aware of the genuinely pious life of many monasteries which they knew, and of the charity dispensed by monastic almoners, were against the general trend of religious developments and against the numerous suppressions which had so far occurred. Robert Aske, the Yorkshire lawyer who was the best of their leaders, had praised the northern abbeys, declaring them to be 'one of the beauties of this realm'. So vehement, in some areas, was the reaction against the suppressions which had already occurred that a few monasteries, notably Cistercian Sawley and Augustinian Cartmel, even saw their inmates reinstated and monastic life resumed. On the collapse of the rising these restored houses were again suppressed, while some abbots and monks, in other parts of the country, who had compromised themselves were hanged for treason. There was no real risk that the remaining religious would renounce their acceptance of the King's ecclesiastical supremacy, but what had happened suggested that the monks, nuns, and canons might not, in future, be wholly reliable as supporters of religious change. A revised view of the political reliability of the monasteries still in existence may have been a factor, real if not decisive, in the policy of the government as this was soon unfolded.

From late in 1537, when the great Cluniac priory of Lewes surrendered, with the comforting innovation of pensions for the prior and the monks, many religious houses, voluntarily or under considerable pressure, surrendered and saw their goods taken over by the Crown. They included the briefly respited Bisham, wealthy Abingdon, Muchelney, Tavistock, Augustinian Darley just north of Derby, and William the Conqueror's foundation of Battle, along with its cells in Exeter and at Brecon. Most of these dissolutions came in 1538, before any further Act of Parliament. In the same year most of the friaries, many in a wretched state, were easily suppressed; the last few fell early in 1539. Even at so late a date there seems, in some of the great monasteries, a hope that

they would be allowed to continue. At Glastonbury, in that last year of the great abbey's existence, stone was still brought from its Mendip quarries at Doulting for repairs to the buildings. Then in May of 1539 the government's financial needs overrode any lingering intention to continue the monasteries on their existing estates. The final blow, given in an Act of Parliament, came when the property of all the monasteries, already surrendered or as yet unsuppressed, was made over to the Crown. A mitigating point, for the preservation of some monastery buildings and the keeping of some abbey revenues for church purposes, was the power given to Henry VIII to do as Wolsey had thought of doing, and to found some new bishoprics whose cathedrals would be dissolved monastic churches, and whose territory would diminish some unwieldy dioceses. The existing cathedral monasteries, as at Canterbury, Winchester, Durham and Worcester were to be dissolved like the rest, with deans and secular canons following the cathedral priors and their reliably resident monks.

The final process was easy and inevitable, with little opposition, even by the three Benedictine abbots of Colchester, Reading and Glastonbury who in various ways compromised themselves and were executed, to the actual mechanics of suppression. The commissioners could not finish their work in 1539. Suppressions went on in 1540, till in March of that year the great Augustinian abbey of Waltham in Essex, with its church among the country's largest monastic buildings, was the last to fall; its dissolution marked the end of England's endowed monasticism. Main points still at issue were the degree to which the religious life would somehow be continued, and the extent of re-use and survival in store for the churches and domestic buildings which had once been those of the monks, nuns, and canons regular.

Continuance and Survival

As nothing in the Suppression Acts condemned monasticism as such there was no overwhelming reason, before more actively Protestant policies came in Edward VI's reign, why some monks and nuns, with pensions to live on and perhaps on the 'mendicant' basis of private benefaction which had sustained the friars, should not continue the religious life in a modest way and in private houses. But hardly any made such efforts. Many monks and regular canons took church livings or, in the next few years, served chantries. A few monks from the Benedictine priory of

Monk Bretton in Yorkshire retired, with many books from their library, to a nearby house and there, for several years, continued their regulated life.* But most of those who continued in religion were from various communities of nuns.

The Bridgettines of Syon were a most devout and well-ordered community, with some nuns from families later prominent as Catholic Recusants. Most of the nuns continued their religious life, some of them not far away in Buckinghamshire, others, at Termonde in the reliably Catholic Habsburg Netherlands, the fore-runners of many communities

*See G.W.O. Woodward, *Dissolution of the Monasteries*, 1966, pp. 152–4.

50 Richmond, Yorkshire: early sixteenth-century stalls from Easby Abbey now in the parish church
51 Southwell Cathedral: lectern, *c*1500, from Newstead Priory

of English nuns on the Continent in penal times. Some nuns from the much admired Benedictine abbey of St. Mary's, Winchester kept together in the near neighbourhood of their devastated abbey. Other Benedictine nuns, whose abbesses were well pensioned, could and perhaps did manage some continuance of the same kind. At Fovant in Wiltshire, for example, the last abbess of Wilton lived on in retirement, with a fat pension of £100 a year, in a manor house which her abbey had owned. If some of her nuns, with their own pensions, joined her they

could have kept up a monastic routine, with plenty to live on and with a chapel fitted up somewhere in the house. But the most striking continuance was when Elizabeth Throckmorton, the last head of the flourishing and fervent Franciscan nunnery at Denny near Cambridge, took a few of her nuns across England to her family home, in due course a staunch recusant stronghold, of Coughton Court near Stratford-on-Avon. There, for some years and in quiet seclusion, these faithful 'votarists of St. Clare', whose observances may have been known to Shakespeare's immediate forbears, continued to hear Mass when they could and to say the offices they had recited in their Fenland convent. In the meantime, as at Denny itself, ruin or adaptation had affected most of the buildings once used by the religious.

The great work of physical destruction often started very soon after the dissolution of any particular religious house. Soo too its contents were quickly dispersed and scattered. A few parish churches, such as those of Lancaster, of Richmond in Yorkshire, and of Worle near Weston super Mare obtained choir stalls from neighbouring monastic churches. The fine lectern at Ramsey may well have come from the abbey church, while the late mediaeval brass eagle lectern now in the choir of Southwell Cathedral was originally at Newstead Priory. It was hidden in a nearby lake, was dredged up, and found its way to the shop of a dealer in Nottingham; from him, in 1805, one of the Southwell prebends, who was also Dean of Lincoln, bought it and gave it to the Minster. But most of the work, ornamental as well as structural, was soon chopped up, much of it to make fires to melt the lead from the roofs which was the most immediately valuable commodity to be realised from the monks' churches and domestic buildings. Squared stone of good quality was also valuable, and much of it soon disappeared, from such monasteries as Beaulieu, Faversham, and at Canterbury which were near the coast, to help build Henry VIII's important series of coastal forts and castles. Much of the destruction, and most of the dispersal of the estates of the religious houses, was done within a decade of their suppression. Surviving buildings are nonetheless fairly numerous; they vary greatly in the extent and causes of their preservation.

Four Benedictine abbey churches were soon wholly, or almost wholly preserved to become the cathedrals of Henry VIII's new dioceses of Westminster, Gloucester, Peterborough, and Chester. The Augustinian churches of Bristol and St. Frideswide's at Oxford were for the most part saved

for the same reason. The great abbey church of St. Alban's, and the eastern half of St. Mary Overie's Priory church in Southwark survived, as parish churches till modern times, to have the same episcopal good fortune.

A few monastic churches were saved, intact or nearly so, for use as parish churches. Lady chapels, as at Tewkesbury, Milton in Dorset, Great Malvern, and Romsey were apt, in such cases, to get destroyed, but a few churches, notably at Selby, Christchurch, Edington in Wiltshire, and the Oxfordshire Dorchester survived complete, though there was no need to keep many of their domestic buildings. Some nunnery churches, where the nuns' part and the parishioners' section were hard to subdivide, were similarly preserved, as one sees, in the sector of the City of London which escaped the fire of 1666, in St. Helen's, Bishopsgate. More frequently, however, if anything of a monastic church was kept for parochial worship it was the nave, in many cases used already by the parish which had built no separate church of its own. Elstow near Bedford is one such case, and Bridlington has a specially splendid Augustinian example. At Pershore, by contrast, the parishioners got the presbytery and transepts instead of the nave. A few churches, notably the eastern half of Cistercian Abbey Dore in Herefordshire, and the Benedictine nave of Thorney in the Fens, were restored for worship, with new roofs, after spells of disuse and partial ruin. More unusual, amid the remains of Cistercian houses, are the use as a parish church of the thirteenth-century refectory at Beaulieu, and of the chapter house at Forde, now in Dorset but originally in Devon, as the chapel of the fine private mansion which succeeded the abbey. The chapter house of the Carmelite Friary at Hulne in Northumberland also became the chapel of a mansion fitted out in many of the domestic buildings.

In a few cases churches remain, wholly or in part because they, and not the domestic buildings, were somewhat awkwardly converted into houses. The Dominican friary church at Gloucester was one, so too were the churches, both in Somerset, of the small Victorine priories of Woodspring and Stavordale. Best known, and with secular occupants even more illustrious than its founders and abbots, is the Cistercian church of Buckland not far from Plymouth. The main work of conversion was done by Sir Richard

52 Selby Abbey: part of choir limb, fourteenth century
53 Dorchester Abbey, Oxfordshire (Augustinian): Jesse window, fourteenth century

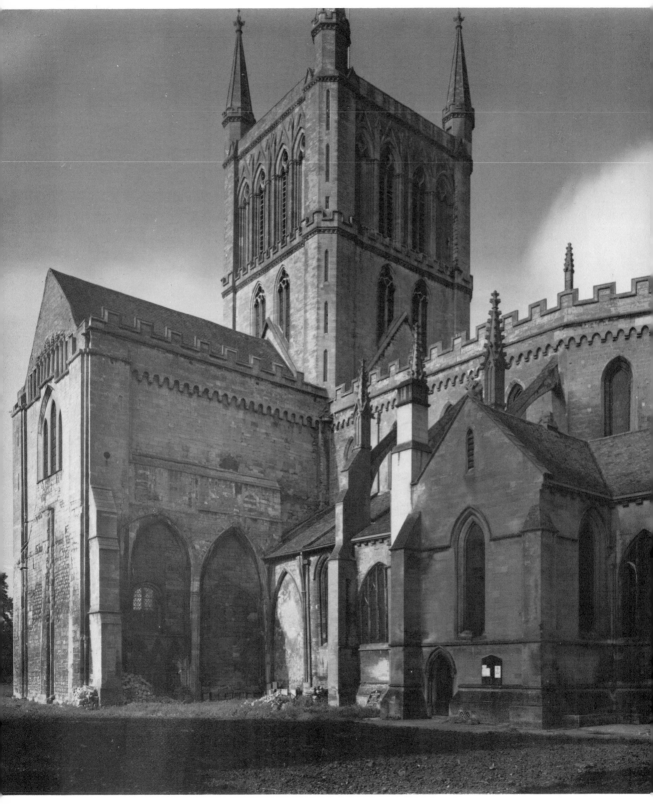

54 Pershore Abbey, Worcestershire (Benedictine): central tower, c1300

55 Abbey Dore, Herefordshire (Cistercian): the presbytery

56   Thorney Abbey, Isle of Ely (Benedictine): western façade, fifteenth century

57 Tintern Abbey (Cistercian): west doorway

Grenville, with Sir Francis Drake, by purchase, his successor in the estate. More unusually, at Ramsey in Huntingdonshire, it was the large lady chapel which became the nucleus of a mansion.

Most monastic churches were, however, deliberately destroyed or left, after the removal of the lead on their roofs, to fall into decay. In many cases, as at Cirencester where mediaeval England's richest Augustinian abbey was soon destroyed, their speedy and complete destruction was a condition of the grant of their sites to new owners. In towns, like Winchcombe, Reading, Faversham, Shaftesbury and on the site of Hyde Abbey in Winchester, demolition, to clear sites for new urban development, was apt to be specially thorough, but many abbeys in the countryside in due course disappeared almost as completely so that only excavation, in modern times, has revealed much of their plans. Such abbeys became quarries for the surrounding districts, so that the builders of farms and houses could take worked stone from their churches and living quarters. Yet in some remote

rural areas, particularly round the sites, still far from large settlements, of Cistercian abbeys the quarrying rate was slower and more modest, so that more extensive ruins, as at Fountains, Kirkstall, Tintern, and Augustinian Llanthony in its wild valley in the Black Mountains, lasted on till they could, like the ruins of many castles, be saved from further wastage by modern antiquarians and the expert endeavours of the Office of Works.

Where many of the domestic buildings of a monastery have lasted through to our own time they show variations in the amount that is preserved, and in the way in which they have been converted into farms or country mansions. Occasionally, as at Lacock in Wiltshire and in the Byrons' mansion at Newstead, the buildings round all three sides of the domestic enclosure were adapted and re-used, while at Cleeve in western Somerset the chapter house, dormitory, refectory, and other claustral buildings all lasted because they were used as a farm. Even at Wilton, where the nuns' church and domestic buildings were wholly razed, their quadrangular plan, with firm foundations in the alluvial soil of the Nadder valley, determined the plan of the great mansion soon built on the site.

58 Llanthony Priory, Monmouthshire (Augustinian): nave, late twelfth century

59 Cleeve Abbey: the refectory, fifteenth century

But many, perhaps most, of the country houses contrived by the conversion of monastic buildings used little but the western range of the cloister enclosure. This range, with its cellars, and with quarters and offices for the cellarer and other officials, was in any case the most domestic in character, and thus the easiest to convert, of the buildings used by the monks or canons. In many abbeys and priories, as at Castle Acre, Muchelney, and the small nunnery of Polsloe near Exeter, it contained the private apartments, readily re-usable, of the religious superior. To name but a few other abbeys or priories where this 'domestic' western range survived, one had Cistercian Flaxley in the Forest of Dean, Lanercost in Cumberland, Beaulieu, and Hayles and Bruton where the mansions so contrived have themselves now disappeared. At Malmesbury the refectory was, for a few years, the 'workshop' which held the numerous looms of weavers who worked for a rich local clothier, while the brass works for many years active in some of the domestic buildings at Tintern held an important place in the country's industrial history. Some great gatehouses, as at Thornton in Lincolnshire and at Cistercian Kingswood (see Fig. 25) in Gloucestershire,* survived, along with adjacent ranges of buildings, because they were easily used as houses. At Cerne and Montacute gate ranges of this type are now almost the only survivals, above ground, of buildings which made up the monasteries and their outer precincts.

Buildings which originally stood on the fringe of monastic precincts include gate chapels, or *capellae ad portas*, originally built for the use of guests and wayfarers and now, in the near neighbourhood of some ruined abbeys, used as parish churches. A notably fine example is at Merevale in Warwickshire, while another, likewise Cistercian, is now the parish church of Tilty in Essex. At Cambridge the aisleless church of St. Andrew the Less was the gate chapel of the Augustinian priory of Barnwell. Barns, such as those at Glastonbury, Cerne and Abbotsbury (see Fig. 40), survive from the farm buildings which worked the lands most immediately close to their abbeys, while at Bruton and Abbotsbury dovehouses, tactically sited on adjoining high ground, notably aided the economy of the religious who had them built.

Except for the cathedrals, St. George's at Windsor, and the academic colleges, nearly all the secular collegiate foundations were dissolved late in the reign of Henry VIII. Under Edward VI the chantries, to which there were, under a more Protestant régime, theological objections, followed the monasteries and colleges. The whole fabric of England's endowed religion had, by now, been deeply and drastically changed.

During Mary I's short reign there was, in or near London, a small-scale revival of the religious life. A few monks and friars, having retired to the Netherlands, were available to join others, still in England, to set the revived communities on their way. Had the Queen lived longer the process might have gone further, not so much by the restoration of old monasteries whose lay owners did not wish to give them up, but with new foundations on Counter-Reformation rather than mediaeval lines.

Observant Franciscans thus returned to the friary close by Greenwich Palace, and Dominicans were restored, not to the Blackfriars site in London which was no longer available, but to the partly preserved church and buildings once those of the Augustinian canons of St. Bartholomew's, Smithfield. Dominican nuns, before 1539 at Dartford, were also restored, first to what had once been their order's friary at King's Langley in Hertfordshire, but later, after the death of Anne of Cleves, who occupied the property, to their old home in Kent. Carthusians, from various priories existing before 1539, were established in the previously Carthusian buildings of Sheen near Richmond, while across the river the Bridgettine nuns, from exile abroad and a temporary English home, were reunited on their old site. No Cistercian abbey was revived, but a few one-time Cistercian monks had a hand, along with some Benedictines, in the most spectacular instance of monastic renewal. This was at Westminster which was revived, with no real continuity with the previous abbey, for a moderate-sized community whose numbers soon increased. Its abbot, John Feckenham, had originally been a monk at Evesham. These were the monks who, early in 1559, assisted, in the abbey church which they still served, at the coronation of Elizabeth I. But within six months Westminster and the other revived religious houses were again dissolved. Some of their members, most notably Carthusians from Sheen and some Bridgettines from Syon, went abroad to establish communities which were forerunners of a great upsurge, in various places abroad, of Recusant religious life.

*Till the 1840s a detached part of Wiltshire.

60 London, St. Bartholomew's, Smithfield (Augustinian): arches of apse

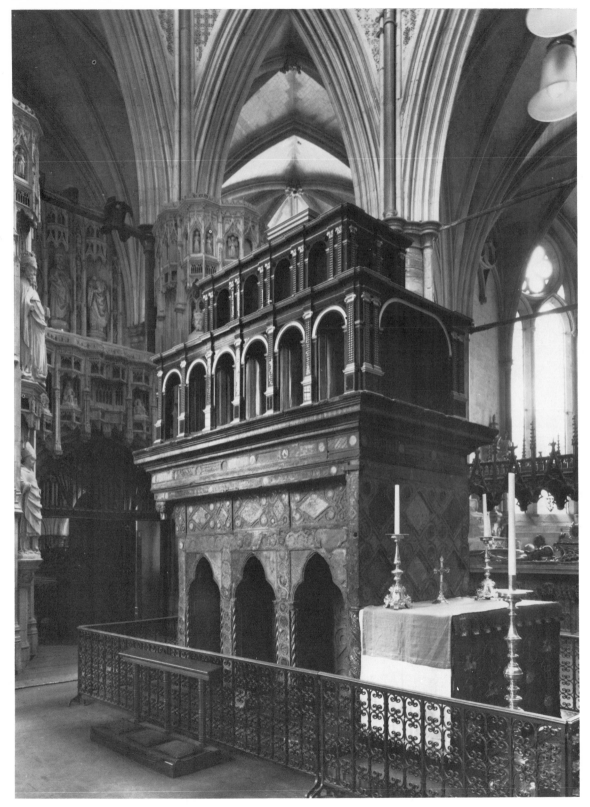

The Penal Interlude

The politics of post-Reformation England meant the almost complete extinction, for over two centuries after 1559, of its monastic life. Under Charles II a small convent was built in London for the Portuguese Franciscans who came as chaplains to Queen Catherine of Braganza. Then during James II's short reign there were further conventual chances. At York the teaching nuns of the Institute of the Blessed Virgin Mary established the Bar Convent in a private house just outside one of the city's gates, continuing their religious life, furtively and without habits, throughout the rest of penal times. In 1769 they started their present chapel, soon enlarged by the addition of a beautiful neo-classical sanctuary of circular shape. But the conventual life of English Catholics was, of necessity, nearly all lived in exile on the Continent. When one recalls the trials, through a long 'penal' spell (which at times included outright persecution) of the Catholics of England, the extent and religious depth of this continued life of monks, friars, and nuns was a notable phenomenon.

The Benedictines were the pioneers of this post-Reformation revival, and in 1604 a priory was founded at Douai in what was then the territory of the Spanish Netherlands. Some of these Benedictines then visited England and made contact with an old monk who was the last survivor of the Westminster Benedictines of Mary's restoration. This monk, Dom Sigebert Buckley, assisted in the clothing ceremony of two novices, and in a few more years the English Benedictines, now with four priories in various towns abroad, were formed into the English Benedictine Congregation which still exists. No 'penal' revival of English Cistercians or canons regular occurred, but the one priory of English Carthusians lingered on, at Nieuport, till the 1780s. The Benedictines remained the chief grouping of English monks, but with differences, as compared with the pre-Reformation centuries, in their way of life. The schools kept in their priories were more important than their mediaeval counterparts. The frequent departure of monks going, 'on the mission', to serve chaplaincies maintained, under difficulties and at times with danger, in some towns and by Catholic gentry in England marked a degree of pastoral work unknown on the eve of Henry VIII's dissolution.

The friars, of various orders, also figured in this revival, among Englishmen, of the religious life. They were based abroad but also worked on missions in England itself. The Franciscans, the Franciscan Capuchins who had not existed in England before

61 Westminster Abbey: shrine of St. Edward the Confessor
62 York, Bar Convent (I.B.V.M.): the chapel, by Thomas Atkinson 1768–69

Henry VIII's suppression, the Dominicans, and the Carmelites all had friaries on the Continent. There were, in addition, the non-monastic establishments of the English Jesuits and the English colleges, for training secular priests but run on the quasi-monastic lines of the Tridentine seminaries, at Douai, in Rome, and in Spain and Portugal.

More numerous, in convents and membership, were the English nuns of penal times; their flourishing state was a great tribute to the devotion of a dwindling number of Catholic families among the nobility and gentry. The Bridgettines at Lisbon maintained their continuity with Syon, but others, starting with a Benedictine nunnery founded at Brussels in 1598, and continuing with a remarkable spread of convents in the seventeenth century, were new ventures. The Franciscan nuns, or Poor Clares, were the first in the field, with the starting, in 1607, of their convent at Gravelines near Calais. Two years later English canonesses of St. Augustine started a house at Louvain. Several new foundations followed, many of them well filled with nuns and novices. The Franciscan and Dominican nuns, the Benedictines, and the Austin canonesses had their pre-Reformation equivalents. But the numerous convents of Carmelite nuns, as these had been reformed by St. Teresa, were a group never seen in England before the changes wrought by Henry VIII. The Institute of the Blessed Virgin Mary, founded by Mary Ward, an English Catholic, had several Continental houses before its brave venture, under James II, at York. Its vocation lay, to a large degree, in teaching, but other English nuns abroad, like the Blue Nuns in Paris, kept schools for the daughters of the Catholic gentry. But the enclosed, contemplative life predominated, and these English nunneries on the Continent were in some ways stricter and more devout than most of their mediaeval counterparts.

The buildings of these monasteries, friaries, and nunneries for English Catholics in exile were conventual in character. Some, like the Dominican priory at Bornhem near Antwerp and the Benedictine priory at Dieulouard in Lorraine, had earlier been used by other religious communities. Others, like some Carmelite and Poor Clare convents and the Benedictine nunnery at Dunkirk, were specially built. The priory of Benedictine monks in Paris was notable in that its church was the burying place of James II and others of the Stuarts.

English Revival

Early in the 1780s Englishmen could hardly foresee that the next ten years would, for political reasons unexpected before 1789, see the re-establishment in their country, on a scale well beyond that of the Bar Convent at York, of the conventual life of Catholic monks, nuns, and friars. Catholics were, indeed, now legally free to own property some of which was used for the fitting out of chapels more public than those to which their congregations had long been accustomed. Then in 1791 the Catholic Relief Act allowed the building, without steeples or bells, of public places of Catholic worship. These were, however, to be for only parochial use; the foundation of religious orders and convents was still forbidden. But in a few more years the Terror in France, the flight to England of many French secular clergy and religious communities, and the arrival in their native land of most of those who lived in the English Catholic convents in France made a dead letter of some of the Relief Act's restrictive clauses. The advance of the French Revolutionary armies into what is now Belgium, and into parts of western Germany, swelled the number of these conventual refugees. Some of these English communities had been able to save a few of their treasured possessions. But for all of them, now and for some years to come, there was an acute problem of accommodation. At first they were given homes in London town houses, or in country mansions, like those of the Arundells at Lanherne in Cornwall and of the Smythes at Acton Burnell in Shropshire, put at their disposal by families of the Catholic gentry from which many of the monks and nuns had come. In one instance, by a curious turn in historic fortune, buildings which had once been those of Benedictine nuns again housed nuns of the order which had possessed them before the Reformation. This was at Cannington in Somerset, where the domestic buildings of a small nunnery, considerably altered after the Dissolution, had become a property of the Catholic family of the Cliffords. The English Benedictine nuns of Paris first moved, on their arrival in England, to a mansion in Dorset, but in a few more years migrated to Cannington, where they adapted the quadrangular buildings to their new conventual purpose. Between 1829 and 1831, and a few years before their further migration to the community's present home at Colwich near Stafford, they filled the square space of a courtyard with a remarkable octagonal chapel, of classical style, with fine Corinthian pilasters, and surmounted by a cupola above a richly coffered dome.

Les Dames Angloises

63 Dunkirk, English Benedictine nuns (now at Teignmouth): the buildings, 1664, and later, by Dom Alexius Caryll

The Cannington situation was, however, unusual. Most of the Catholic religious communities found in late Georgian England gathered new resources and carried on the life of Masses, choir offices, spiritual exercises, and charitable work which they had long pursued on the Continent. The flow of postulants and novices, and of professions was resumed. Most of these activities were, for the time being, carried on in the houses which kind benefactors had put at the communities' disposal. Some nuns soon moved to other quarters, likewise of a domestic rather than of a conventual character. But at Lanherne, in its leafy, secluded valley in North Cornwall, the Carmelites, originally at Antwerp, have continuously occupied the historic manorial buildings to which they moved in 1794.

The first new buildings in post-Reformation England of a recognisably monastic type had been built, several years earlier than the new chapel at Cannington, at Lulworth in Dorset. The Catholic family of the Welds had there provided a home, and

land for a new monastery, for the reformed Cistercian monks of La Trappe who had come, as exiles, from their monastery in France. New claustral buildings, with cob walls and put up in what was said to be an 'Early English' style were built in 1795–96. The convent was a great novelty in late Georgian Dorset and aroused much comment and some controversy. But the monks stayed at Lulworth till, in 1817, they returned to what seemed to be the political safety of France under the Bourbon Restoration. The buildings have not survived. But in a few more years more durable work was done by English monks who decided to stay on in the country of their origin.

At Ampleforth, in Yorkshire, where the Benedictines originally at Dieulouard in Lorraine found a lasting home, the first additions to the Georgian house were domestic in character. Then in 1818–20 a more monumental refectory, with rooms above it and with its ceiling supported by two rows of Greek Doric columns, was run out at the back. Two years later the monks of the other English Benedictine priory, now at Downside in the Mendips, built a new block, in its planning un-monastic by mediaeval standards and with an upstairs, vaulted chapel whose Early English Gothic, by H.E. Goodridge of Bath who worked equally in Gothic and classical idioms, was correct enough for Augustus Pugin, a few years later, to praise it. Conventual buildings and chapels, a few of them classical but mostly Gothic as neo-mediaeval styles gripped Catholic and Anglican church architecture alike, followed in the coming years. For this was the time when old religious orders established themselves in more capacious quarters and when Gothic convents, by Augustus Pugin and others, were built for Sisters of Mercy, teaching nuns, and other communities which were of Counter-Reformation or later origin, and which had had no counterparts in mediaeval England. A renewed Cistercian contribution, though only found in two houses, was of some architectural note.

The late Georgian monastery at Lulworth had not lasted long, but in 1835 a Cistercian community from Ireland came to a site, in the Charnwood Forest country of Leicestershire, which duly became that of the still flourishing abbey of Mount St. Bernard. A Catholic squire was the monks' local patron, and in 1840 Augustus Pugin got out designs for a cruciform church, with a short presbytery in the mediaeval Cistercian manner. Its long structural nave, with lancets in a simple 'Early English' idiom, resembled what he was doing, about the same time, in the church in Nottingham which soon became a Catholic cathedral. A few years later England's one modern community of Cistercian nuns, during penal times in Paris and eventually in a house of the Arundells at Stapehill in Dorset, started conventual buildings, and a church with two parallel naves and sanctuaries in the manner of some mediaeval nunneries. Their architect, who also designed many monastic churches, conventual buildings, and parish churches for the English Benedictines, was Charles Hansom, a younger brother of Joseph Hansom, the prolific Catholic architect best known as the inventor of the cab which bore his name. The church of these Cistercian nuns was finished in 1851; by now the re-establishment, and the multiplication beyond some pre-Reformation bounds, of England's Roman Catholic monastic communities, friaries, and sisterhoods was well under way. Though there was no likelihood that the mediaeval orders would, in modern England where the Catholics were a minority denomination, reach the numbers of houses or religious they had boasted before the days of Henry VIII, there were some bodies of mediaeval religious, such as the Servite friars and Carmelite nuns, which had not existed in pre-Reformation England but whose members worked in the England of post-penal Catholicism.

64 Farnborough Abbey, Hampshire (Benedictine): aerial view

From about 1850, the adaptation and new building of Catholic convents, colleges, and community buildings continued apace as the intake of the various orders, whether or not they were monastic in the pre-Reformation sense, increased well beyond the numbers which had prevailed in penal times. Victorian Gothic, in its various aspects, was much the most favoured style. Such, for example, was the priory designed by Charles Hansom for the Dominicans of Woodchester in Gloucestershire, while Gothic of a heavier type was used, by Gilbert Blount in the 1860s, to house Dominican nuns at Carisbrooke in the Isle of Wight. Gothic conventual buildings, with an octagonal turret and spirelet above the sanctuary of the chapel, were also designed by Joseph Hansom for nuns who moved, early in the 1860s, to a fine hillside site near Newton Abbot in Devon. The buildings were for a community of Augustinian canonesses,

founded at Louvain in 1609 and with a distinguished history in penal times. To allow for their privileged devotion of the perpetual adoration of the Blessed Sacrament the sanctuary had a pillared octagon, of unusual design, as the setting for the altar and its high-pinnacled throne for exposition. Some of these buildings were for congregations and communities, such as the Jesuits, Passionists, and Redemptionists, which had arisen at or since the Counter Reformation, and which could not, in the traditional sense, be called monastic. Even the orders, like the Benedictines, of clearly mediaeval origins built churches whose internal arrangements were not as one had found them in mediaeval priories and abbeys, while their 'monasteries', as one saw them at Ampleforth, Belmont, Downside, Erdington, or the large Benedictine nunnery at Stanbrook, were blocks of study bedrooms quite unlike the cloister ranges and cubicled dormitories of earlier times. Here too the influence of post-mediaeval monasticism as this had developed in, say, France of the *ancien régime* or in southern Germany

and Austria, could readily be traced. So too when the Premonstratensian canons, many of them from Belgium, resumed work in England on a small scale the domestic block of their headquarters priory at Storrington in Sussex, Victorian Gothic of the 1880s, in red brick with cross crosslets picked out in yellow, was clearly a modern accommodation block of this kind.

Later in the nineteenth century, and more recently, some abbeys and priories embarked on the building of churches more ambitious in scale, and in their design reasonably close to monastic churches built before the Dissolution. Some are buildings, in the modern Gothic fashion, of size and architectural merit enough to justify their inclusion in this book's gazetteer section. Such are the Benedictine churches at Downside, Buckfast, and at Ampleforth. Here, the present church, constrained in its length by the shortness of its predecessor, and by the siting of the school and monastery blocks, has replaced Charles Hansom's modest church of the 1850s, which had, like

a parish church, no more than an unaisled nave and choir. Smaller in scale, and neither of them first built for Benedictines, are the Benedictine abbey churches at Belmont near Hereford and at Farnborough in Hampshire. More interesting, always Benedictine for its monks of the Solesmes Congregation, is the church of Quarr Abbey in the Isle of Wight which was started in 1911. Though its pointed arches are of Gothic inspiration the Gothic of this church by Dom Paul Bellot, a monk of the community who had trained as an architect in France and who had designed churches and monasteries on the Continent, does not display the somewhat backward-looking mediaevalism of the monastic churches whose underlying idea was that of 'back to the Middle Ages'. Its fine modern brickwork recalls Flemish or Baltic examples, but this church, pioneeringly at such a date in England, belongs in essence to the modern architectural movement. At Parkminster in Sussex England's one Carthusian monastery, with a tall tower and spire behind the altar end of a plainly rectangular church, shows a somewhat updated version, by a French architect for a community which was, at first, mainly French in its membership, of the traditional Carthusian plan.

Though the friars in England had a time of increased activity they had few chances to build churches or conventual buildings on anything like the mediaeval pattern. As many of them were, unlike their forbears before 1538, in charge of parishes their

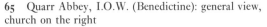

65 Quarr Abbey, I.O.W. (Benedictine): general view, church on the right

churches were laid out on parochial lines, with little by way of separate choirs for the recitation of the choir offices; these were, however, sometimes fitted out, unseen from the churches, within the friars' domestic quarters. Large friary churches of this modern type were built in such cities as London, Newcastle-on-Tyne, and in the Gorton district of Manchester. At Gorton, the great church of the Franciscan Friars Minor, by Edward Pugin and designed for a community most of whose first members were from Belgium, rises high above the streets where many of the original congregation must have lived. Its striking west front, with a central buttress rising to a sculptured crucifix beneath a gable which has, above it, a brick and stone turret and a leaded flèche, is a *tour de force* of mid-Victorian church architecture.

More conventional by the standards of Victorian Gothic is the great church of the Friars Minor at Forest Gate on London's eastern fringe. The friars came to the area in 1773, and in 1884 Cardinal Manning laid the foundation stone of the friary buildings which, to the north of the church, include a convincing four-sided cloister lit by a series of paired lancets and linking such apartments as a refectory and a common room. Behind the church's east end, and unseen by the worshippers, a choir has well-carved, late-Victorian stalls and other fittings both for choir offices and the community masses of a friary which now houses the headquarters of the English province of this particular Franciscan grouping. The slightly later church, by Peter Paul Pugin who worked much for the Friars Minor, is spectacular, with a nave larger than those of most of mediaeval England's friary churches. Its great clerestoried nave, early Decorated in style and with tall cylindrical pillars and octagonal capitals, is of nine bays. The chancel, 're-ordered' in recent years and simplified in its decoration, is of another three. As in many mediaeval monastic churches the windows in the aisle on the cloister side are smaller than those on the side which is unencumbered.

Some twenty years later the Franciscan Capuchins, in Iffley Road at Oxford, built a church whose simple Romanesque style, by Benedict Williamson who was both a priest and an architect, is anachronistic in that it looks back to a mediaeval period before friars existed. It has a concealed choir, and a gabled tower, with a copper spirelet, which is pleasingly typical of the 'Arts and Crafts' architectural phase.

At Newcastle the Dominicans' church is cruciform and contemporary with the Friars Minor's church in Manchester. It has some wheel windows, and a continuous row of lancets, round its French Gothic apse. The same order's London church at Haverstock Hill is of great size, with a Flemish flavour in its gaunt Gothic style.

A few friaries and their churches were of a more obviously conventual type. At Hawkesyard in Staffordshire the quadrangular buildings of the Dominicans were never finished, but the church, with its clear division between choir and antechapel, is a fine essay in the late Gothic of 'Oxbridge' colleges. At Chilworth in Surrey F.A. Walters, working for the Franciscan Friars Minor in a late Perpendicular style with some touches of 'Arts and Crafts' Gothic, built an attractive friary which has sleeping quarters above what would normally be the nave.

Anglican Communities

With a few exceptions such as that at Little Gidding, religious communities had long, by the middle of the 1840s, been almost unknown among Anglicans. But the continued existence, for a few years after Henry VIII's declaration of his own ecclesiastical supremacy, of many monasteries and nunneries had suggested that conventual life might be possible in an 'Anglo-Catholic' posture of religious affairs. The Tractarian or 'High Church' movement, gathering strength from the late 1830s, soon led, within the Anglo-Catholic wing of the Church of England, to the foundation, for the most part for women, of several religious communities. Though most of them, particularly the sisterhoods, started in an active, or missionary role, doing social work of a kind only slightly attempted by state and local authorities, and in some places anticipating similar work done by Roman Catholic communities, there later came a widespread move towards more contemplative disciplines. The life and work of these communities, occasionally marked by controversy and by a measure of eccentricity, became, and remains, an important element in the Anglican religious scene. Many of the buildings which housed it, and in particular some of the convents and chapels so founded, were the work of such leading designers as

66 Gorton, Manchester: Franciscan church, by E.W. Pugin, 1866–72

95

Butterfield, Street, Woodyer, Pearson, Bodley and Comper and became a considerable if comparatively little-known element in the country's Victorian and post-Victorian religious architecture.

A pioneering attempt to establish Anglican community life was that of Newman and his friends, with their 'monastery' contrived, at Littlemore near Oxford, out of a humble row of cottages; they had no chapel and held communion services in the local parish church. The venture, like that of Frederick Faber in his Huntingdonshire rectory, did not outlast Newman's conversion. The next phase in Anglican religious life also started in the 1840s, with female communities preceding those of men and attaining considerable strength before the first, impermanent effort to re-establish male monasticism.

Enclosed, contemplative community life like that of the Benedictine, Franciscan, or Carmelite nuns was, for many reasons, impossible for early Victorian Anglicans. Even among those of the High Church section of the Church of England the climate of opinion was still unfavourable for such ventures, while almost nothing was known of the rules by which such communities in the Roman Church were governed, or of the ethos and way of life of Roman

67 Hawkesyard Priory, Staffordshire (Dominicans): aerial view, Spode House beyond

Catholic contemplatives. 'Active' communities, for teaching and social work, like that of the teaching nuns or Sisters of Mercy in the Roman communion, seemed more promising. From about 1840 Newman, Pusey and others exchanged ideas on the commencement of such communities. Social conditions in the poor areas of many large towns, and the small scale of the social and educational work so far done by the state or local authorities, gave ample opportunities for social work, under community conditions, by dedicated, self-sacrificing churchwomen.

The first community of Anglican sisters, with Gladstone one of its sponsors, and with Pusey a spiritual adviser as he was to some other communities, was the Sisterhood of the Holy Cross. It started in 1844, in a house near Regent's Park in London and then, for the rest of its short separate career, was in Gothic conventual buildings by Butterfield. The sisters' charitable work, among the poor of a deprived area of London, included nursing, and theirs was one of the Anglican communities from which Florence Nightingale recruited some of her team for the Crimea and Scutari. Other communities, starting with single houses but growing into something like orders, with widespread activities and several convents (some of them overseas) were founded in the middle decades of last century. One, with more restrained ritual than one found in the chapels of some Anglo-Catholic convents, was at Wantage under a superior recommended, in his last Anglican years, by Manning who acted as the sisters' Father Director. The sisters did parish work, teaching and, like members of some other communities, the 'rescue' of penitent 'unfortunates'. Pusey devised rules for some of these early Anglican sisterhoods, while for others he was their spiritual Director.

Among the sisters themselves a striking character, fervent, energetic and a fine if at times domineering organiser was Priscilla Lydia Sellon, a naval officer's daughter whose Society of the Most Holy Trinity (locally known as the Sellonites) started work, very fittingly, in the less reputable parts of the naval town of Devonport. Mother Lydia had great energy and organising talent, and a strong sense of discipline; it has been said of her that she applied her father's quarterdeck methods to the running of a religious

68 Wantage, Berks, St. Mary's convent: chapel by J.L. Pearson

order. She had support and encouragement from Pusey, and the scale and extent of her activities in the West Country soon increased. Mother Lydia evolved a scheme for a nationwide network of religious houses, each one under her personal rule. She even envisaged herself as the 'Arch Abbess' of all Anglican sisterhoods. In her own Devonport community she evolved three 'Orders' – of Sisters of Mercy, of semi-conventual Sisters of Charity, and of enclosed and contemplative nuns, while a start was made, on a site near the Naval Hospital, on Gothic buildings, by Butterfield, of a strongly conventual type. Mother Lydia's community was another of those, Roman or Anglican, from which nursing recruits were sent to join Florence Nightingale. It was in keeping with Miss Sellon's somewhat aggressive tactics that soon after the Crimean War her sisterhood and that of the Holy Cross were merged, with Mother Lydia the Abbess of the group whose rule, largely Benedictine in its inspiration, also contained Poor Clare features and other elements.

Mother Lydia's plan of conventual imperialism got no further than the one amalgamation of 1856. Several other communities of women had by now got well established, mostly combining their life of private and liturgical prayer with such 'social' work as teaching, visiting the poor, and the rescue of more or less penitent prostitutes. The Clewer sisterhood, near Windsor, became particularly well known, while the founder of the East Grinstead Sisterhood was the High Church hymn writer and liturgical scholar John Mason Neale; his sister founded another community, at first in London's East End, which also ran an industrial school and did heroic work in cholera epidemics. The expansion of these Anglican communities continued in the mid-Victorian decades. Most of them were 'active', on works of charity, and as their chapels often had a private status, and lay outside episcopal control their liturgical practices were often more 'advanced' than those of parish churches in these early Anglo-Catholic, or ritualist days. Less extensive, in some cases more controversial, and often more difficult in their relationship with Victorian bishops, were the first efforts to start religious communities for men. The first, though not the most durable endeavour was, moreover, as much marked by picturesque eccentricity as by sincere devotion.

It was, perhaps, predictable that the first Anglican effort towards revived monasticism was not by way of a community of a new type but lay in a somewhat erratic attempt to re-create one of the great mediaeval groupings. Joseph Leycester Lyne, fired by High

Church enthusiasm and a deacon, but never a priest, in Anglican orders was for a time a curate in the Plymouth parish which contained Mother Lydia Sellon's Gothic convent. From her, as well as from his own monastic longings, he got the idea that his leadership was to be the driving force behind the rebirth of monastic, and particularly of Benedictine life within the Church of England. But however Benedictine his eventual community might be, 'Father' Ignatius confused the impression he gave by taking his name in religion from the founder of the non-monastic Jesuits, and by including Franciscan elements with the mainly Benedictine appearance of his habit.

After short sojourns in East Anglia and near London the brethren, who had little experience of monastic life, and who evolved their régime as they went along, moved in 1869 to the remote place which was to gain fame, or notoriety, as the main scene of 'Father' Ignatius' conventual activity. Theirs was, moreover, the first attempt to revive monastic life in what had, before the Reformation, been a conventual house. This was at Llanthony, in a deep valley of the Black Mountains where there stood the fine ruins of a priory of Augustinian canons founded in the twelfth century (see page 195). The first idea was to restore, for this neo-Benedictine community, the old conventual buildings. But the owner would not sell, so 'Father' Ignatius bought land, higher up the valley, on which he proposed to build new conventual quarters, and a church whose style was to bear a close resemblance to that of the original Llanthony. The domestic quadrangle was built, but the church was never finished. It was here, with liturgical and penitential extravagancies going far beyond mediaeval precedents or nineteenth-century monastic practices, that the small band of monks contrived, amid many hardships and difficulties, to create a passable semblance of monastic life. Their founder, handsome, eloquent, sincere and autocratic, took complete control, but was often away on preaching tours to raise money for his priory. A small community of nuns, who had broken away from another quasi-Benedictine community when 'Father' Ignatius had 'excommunicated' most of them, also came to Llanthony, living in separate buildings contiguous to those of the male religious. The whole story was admirably recorded, with suitable references to the more lurid press accounts, by the late Mr. Peter Anson.* The experiment lasted till Lyne's death in 1908, and for a few years more.

*See *The Call of the Cloister*, 2nd revised edn. 1964, pp. 51–71.

69 Capel y Ffyn, Breconshire: new Llanthony priory, 'Father' Ignatius' grave

Other Anglican communities of men were more soundly and thoughtfully based than that of the Llanthony Benedictines. The Society of St. John the Evangelist, better known as the Cowley Fathers, seemed, when Fr. Richard Benson founded it in 1865, to be more collegiate (and 'active') than monastic in character; it was hence more acceptable to Bishop Samuel Wilberforce who sympathised, more than most of his fellow bishops, with the revival in community life. The Cowley Fathers, in due course with a fine, friary-like church by Bodley, did a wide variety of mission work in England and overseas. The Community of the Resurrection, unlike others in the Church of England in that it placed its headquarters in the North, at Mirfield near Leeds, combined the training of ordinands with the pastoral and missionary work of a mainly learned community. One of its most

70 West Malling, Kent (Benedictine nuns): original cloister arcade, thirteenth century

scholarly members, Walter Howard Frere, ended his career as Bishop of Truro. The Society of the Sacred Mission, eventually based on a large Victorian Gothic mansion at Kelham near Newark, also trained ordinands. All these communities, though indebted to the traditional orders of western Christendom, had a character more distinctive than one found among pseudo-Benedictines or assimilated Franciscans.

The Anglican Benedictine story did not end with the death of the founder of Llanthony. A brotherhood, Benedictine in character, had been founded in 1896 by Benjamin (later Abbot Aelred) Carlyle. After a start in London's dockland, and some other moves the community, 'advanced' in its Anglo-Catholicism and saying its offices and masses in Latin, settled, for the second time, on Caldey Island off Tenby. Here, with the church and other buildings of a small mediaeval priory already there, was another instance of modern monks hoping, in this case successfully, to re-occupy an old monastic site. But their new abbey

buildings, with their pretentious abbot's house and a strange, minaret-like tower, were of a character anything but mediaeval. The religious life of these monks, blending Cistercian and Benedictine customs, was of a type very much its own. Remote as they were, and isolated even from the mainland of Wales, the Caldey monks found it easy to become what was styled an *ecclesiola in ecclesia*, with many differences, in doctrine, liturgy, and discipline, dividing them from the mainstream of Anglicanism. Like members of a few other communities, some of the Caldey monks lived, so Ronald Knox found, in 'an air of make-believe'; the same visitor discerned a 'vaguely electric atmosphere' in a community whose position was clearly somewhat false. It was no surprise, and was indeed logical, when most of the community, with which the few survivors of Llanthony had merged, in

99

1913 joined the Roman Church. Some, however, continued as Benedictines within the Church of England, first in a house at Pershore and then, at Nashdom in southern Buckinghamshire where, in the unmediaeval setting of a great classical mansion by Lutyens, the community still flourishes.

Anglican sisterhoods, existing or newly founded, continued to grow in the second half of last century. Most of them were 'active', but the contemplative aspects of conventual life, and the running of retreat houses, became increasingly important. Some communities often moved before settling down in permanent mother houses. Among them were the Benedictine nuns who stayed away from Llanthony. They were the first modern nuns to occupy, for a time, the property which contained the remains of a mediaeval Benedictine nunnery, at West Malling in Kent. They later moved, with a régime of increasingly Roman character, to Milford Haven. Already affiliated to Caldey, they joined the Roman communion in the same year as most of the Caldey monks. Other nuns, who followed the rule of St. Benedict and at first used the Latin breviary, remained within the Anglican community and they are the present occupants of the site at Malling.

Some communities, with patrons who seem to have had more money to give than the benefactors of most Roman Catholic convents, had buildings and chapels, by nationally important Victorian church architects, of considerable splendour. One of them, the Community of All Saints which had early been associated with the well-known London church of All Saints, Margaret Street, moved in 1901 to London Colney in Hertfordshire. There they settled in domestic buildings of great architectural excellence by the Roman Catholic architect Leonard Stokes*; a fine chapel by Comper followed in the 1920s. One sisterhood, the Society of the Precious Blood, at first on parish and visiting work in a tough area of Birmingham, eventually followed the Malling example and settled, at Burnham in southern Buckinghamshire, within the site and in some surviving buildings, of a mediaeval abbey of Austin canonesses. Their choice was fitting, as they too had a rule based on that of St. Augustine.

The whole position of the Anglican communities had eventually to be considered by the bishops to whom, to quote Mr. Anson, formal obedience had in some cases been 'more . . . a doubtful counsel of

perfection than that of a precept'. As far back as 1897 the Lambeth Conference had first discussed this somewhat wayward element in the Anglican church, but the communities' position was not finally regularised till well into this century.

The Modern Scene

For the first third of this century, and till the coming of the Second World War, the Roman Catholic and Anglican religious communities continued on well-established lines. Many of them, particularly sisterhoods on nursing, teaching, and social work, were in the main of an unenclosed, comparatively unconventual type. The Benedictines of the English congregation continued their monastic life; this was combined, in the monasteries of this congregation, with the running of boarding schools and the serving of parish churches, close to the abbeys or further afield. Other monks still followed their more traditonal régime of prayer life and choir worship; so too did the communities of contemplative nuns, still at this time on the increase with a specially vigorous growth, aided by the recent example of Ste. Thérèse, the 'Little Flower' of Lisieux, of Carmelite houses. Some important monastic churches were finished or nearly so. At Buckfast the French and German Benedictines continued work on their new church, in the transitional Norman style and mostly a faithful reproduction of the mediaeval ground plan. At Mount St. Bernard the Cistercians built a simple central tower, and a long eastern limb (actually used as the nave) in the manner of Pugin's earlier work. The English Benedictines employed Sir Giles Scott for the first part, within the restricted length of the earlier church, of the new church at Ampleforth, while at Downside the same architect designed for them the tall southern tower and the nave whose western end remains unfinished. At Douai Abbey in Berkshire they started an ambitious church, revivalist Perpendicular in brick and stone; only the lady chapel and the eastern end of the choir were actually put up. At Oxford the Dominican friars built their well-known, much frequented church, somewhat oddly proportioned with its broad nave and a set of small chapels leading off it on one side. Among Anglican communities the best-known new building was the small but striking domed church at Kelham.

For the post-war period one may, architectural moves apart, speak of three main phases; these affect all kinds of Catholic religious communities, monastic

---

*By a historic irony these buildings are now used by Roman Catholic nuns.

71 Mount St. Bernard Abbey, Leicestershire (Cistercian): monks in choir, a modern scene
72 Ampleforth Abbey, Yorkshire (Benedictine): the church by Sir Giles Gilbert Scott

or those working largely outside their conventual buildings. First there came a time when many Catholics felt that things could continue much as they had done before 1939; such developments as vernacular liturgy and the varied manifestations of *aggiornamento* were not foreseen. Religious communities, non-monastic congregations, and the secular clergy replenished their numbers and, so far as building restrictions allowed, work continued, mostly in previously accepted styles and plans, on the building and completion of monastic churches. At Buckfast the church, as designed by F.A. Walters, was completed, but an eastern chapel of a much more 'contemporary' type was later added. At Ampleforth the central tower and nave limb of Sir Giles Scott's church were finished, but on simpler lines and with a more economical lack of moulded and carved decoration than in the earlier part. The Ealing Benedictines and the Carmelites in Kensington both had severe war damage. In the latter case a totally destroyed church was replaced, in a Gothic idiom characteristic of its architect, by Sir Giles Scott. The chapels of many convents and convent schools were newly built or extended; as one came to the 1960s a much more 'contemporary' idiom was used for many buildings of this kind.

Then a veritable typhoon of rethinking and change in the Roman Catholic Church was unleashed by the second Vatican Council, though this was not the only factor. In the Catholic Church and in the Anglican communion new situations, in religious outlook, in liturgy, and in other matters came when the religious bodies of England had to think of themselves as beleaguered, or missionary churches in a largely post-Christian country. Changes and new ideas have had their effect on the basic way of life, and on many details such as dress and the making known of personal names, both on 'active' and 'contemplative' religious communities. There is still, moreover, a social situation in which much work which was, in the early Victorian period, carried on by religious orders is now within the scope of national or local government. Changes and unsettlement within the Church itself have, however, had the main bearing on the purpose and strength of the religious orders.

At the time when there was much unsettlement, if not about the basic teaching of the Catholic Church, at all events in matters of liturgy, social teaching, and priestly discipline it was no surprise that both the secular clergy and the religious orders should be affected. The abandonment of their ministry, with or without their superiors' consent, by secular or 'religious' priests is no new thing, but it has recently been more frequent, and certainly more widely publicised. So too, uncertainty in the Church as an institution, by no means all of it over such matters as priestly celibacy, led, in England and Wales as in other European countries, to a sharp fall in vocations both to the secular priesthood and to the religious orders and congregations. Though it seems that the downward trend has now, in some sectors at least, been reversed in a third phase it appears that, for some years to come, the religious orders of men and women will, numerically speaking, play a smaller part in the activities of the Church; the same, one gathers, applies to some Anglican communities. For a more detailed assessment one must look at the situation group by group. In architecture, moreover, there have still been some remarkable achievements.

THE MONKS AND CANONS

The Benedictines of England and Wales are fewer, in monasteries and in monks, than they were before the Reformation. Yet they now present a more varied and complex picture than they did at that earlier time.

They are, for instance, divided between four 'congregations' – English, of Subiaco, of Solesmes and Olivetan. Their activities are no longer almost wholly claustral and contemplative. With the English Benedictines the running of boys' boarding schools* is a most important part of their work. Many Catholic parishes are served, as a continuance of the mission work forced on the English Benedictines in penal times, by monks from the monasteries now in England. Many parishes so served are far from the abbeys whence their priests come, so that these monks live, away from their monasteries, in houses like the presbyteries of the secular clergy. The parishes so staffed are widely scattered. Several are in strongly Catholic Lancashire, while others, as at Cardiff and Abergavenny, are in South Wales. Warwickshire and Worcestershire have a fair number of these parishes, with one at Cheltenham an important outlier of this South West Midland group. A strong concentration, strung out along the coast, is in Western Cumbria, with its origins lying in the eighteenth century when Irish immigration started, increasing as more workers were needed in the coal mines of that coastal belt. Other parishes, much closer to such abbeys as Downside, Belmont, Ampleforth, or Worth, are served by monks who live in their abbeys but who journey by car to the churches under their care. At Ealing in West London a very large Catholic parish is centred on the abbey itself; here, and elsewhere, several convents of nuns have monks as their non-resident chaplains. A more distant external activity stems from Worth whence a small community is building up the life of a Benedictine priory at Lima in Peru.

Within the abbeys, along with such activities as school and parish work, the vital monastic routine of choir offices is kept up, along with prayer and study and, in a few abbeys, the editing of reviews and periodicals. The English Benedictines, like other religious orders, have had their recent difficulties, with such problems as defections and diminishing vocations, in the recent years of ecclesiastical uncertainty and change. As they, like the other congregations, have no common pool of novices and juniors, their young aspirants being reckoned abbey by abbey (with Ampleforth ahead of the others and a recent inflow at Downside) it is on an abbey by abbey basis that one must try to assess future strength.

The three English abbeys of the Subiaco congregation, in its name recalling the monastic colony of St.

*Including one at the Scottish abbey of Fort Augustus.

Benedict's early career but in its present form a little over a century old, vary considerably in their activities. At Ramsgate, whose church was designed by Augustus Pugin, the service of nearby churches, with monks living away from the abbey, is noticeable; so too is the saying of Mass, by monks of the abbey itself, in several convent chapels in the Isle of Thanet. At Prinknash on its Cotswold slope, as also at Farnborough with its curiously domed church, in late French Gothic by Gabriel Destailleur, a French architect employed by the Empress Eugénie to build it as a family mausoleum, the emphasis is more on contemplative enclosure. But Prinknash, with many visitors, and the work of its lay brothers on modern glass for church windows, on metalwork, and on their widely sold pottery, is better known than most English monasteries. At Quarr in the Isle of Wight the one English abbey of the Solesmes congregation is now, after the return to France of the monks who came as exiles from anti-clerical laws, mostly English in its membership. As at Solesmes itself study and liturgical scholarship are prominent.

The smallest of England's Benedictine groups is that of the Olivetan congregation. Its origin, in the fourteenth century, was as a movement of reform and of more rigorous observance, among the Italian Benedictines. Its founder, Bernardo Tolomei, retired to the monastery of Monte Oliveto near Siena, and the abbot of Monte Oliveto remains the General of a Benedictine grouping which has now spread widely, to include abbeys in France, Belgium, and Brazil. Its one English house, with its parish at Cockfosters in northern London, goes back to the 1930s, and its community was, on its arrival under Abbot Bosschaerts from Belgium, decidedly 'progressive' both in its liturgical life and in its contacts with other Christian denominations; these contacts, along with friendly relations with the local Jews, have been easier in these ecumenical days. The church, well known from the frequent relay of its services on radio and television, was originally built as a social or parish hall. It is of white brick, and has the monks' living quarters above it; with its low windows it is not unlike many factories and commercial buildings of its time. Abbot Bosschaerts' scheme for a much more ambitious church, to lie on the other side of a quadrangle, near the adjacent, and now prospering, Olivetan nunnery, was never carried out.

The reformed, or Trappist Cistercians still have their two abbeys of Mount St. Bernard and on Caldey Island off the coast of South West Wales. Both have many visitors, with Caldey selling perfumes and other goods at the abbey and in Tenby. These activities, important for the abbeys' finances, do not impinge on their life of seclusion, contemplation, prayer, and liturgical worship which is the essence of Cistercian life and which is carried on, irrespective of numbers, by communities which may in future be smaller than in recent years. With the Cistercians as with other contemplative communities, the future cannot be forecast, or organised in advance, in the way in which one can plan ahead for the expansion or reduction of some outside business or professional activity. Vocations can be prayed for, but they cannot be planned; they depend on spiritual dispositions which can, as some religious orders now find, bring expansion as well as the diminution which occurred, fairly widely, in the years after 1960. In the meantime one notes that at Mount St. Bernard retreats are given in a guest house now mainly used for that purpose. At Caldey there are monks from several countries; one member of the community is the first Norwegian, since the Reformation, to work as a Catholic bishop in his native country. Important ecumenical work, more than in most places in Wales, is carried on at this abbey.

Self-denial, seclusion, and the pursuit of spiritual perfection, with no external activity but with prayer whose scope reaches well beyond the confines of the monastery, are still the mark of England's one Carthusian priory, with its separate cells and with a church and some other sections for corporate use, at Parkminster in Sussex.

Augustinian canons regular, of a character akin to that of the Black canons before the Reformation, and White canons regular of Prémontré, still work in England, on a small scale and with no real continuity with the Augustinian and Norbertine communities suppressed under Henry VIII. The work of these small groups of canons regular lies more in the serving of parishes than in formal conventual life. The 'Black' canons are mainly represented by the Canons Regular of the Lateran who serve some parishes in and near London. But their main work, with a conventual headquarters, and a recently built church, is at Bodmin in Cornwall. In that county a high proportion of the Roman Catholic churches are staffed, residentially or by canons who travel from Bodmin, by this section of the Augustinian family. The White canons still have their headquarters priory at Storrington in Sussex, with parishes in Lincolnshire, round a large church in Manchester, and elsewhere. A significant work, organised from Storrington, is that which helps the Catholic Church where it is threatened with persecution or, as in countries of eastern Europe, suffers actual restriction and difficulty.

THE FRIARS

The five orders of friars who have worked, since the end of penal times, in England and Wales are still important in this country's modern Catholic life, though in some cases with smaller numbers in the last two decades. They now include a small body of Servites, an order of mediaeval Italian origin but unknown in pre-Reformation England. The first Servites to work in England came, in 1864, from Italy; for some more years the Servites in this country were all of Italian birth. But English recruits in time transformed the membership of a province which now has a fair-sized priory in Kensington, a few parishes out of London, and at Begbroke near Oxford (where the small and attractive church is by the distinguished architect Leonard Stokes) a Servite centre with a wide range of activity. As in some other orders there is, among the Servites, an emphasis on smaller, less rigidly organised communities, while the selection of novices is more carefully made than in some previous periods. There are also a few convents of Servite nuns, contemplative or on the more 'active' work of teaching in schools.

The Franciscans, all told a considerable body of over three hundred friars, are in the three groupings of the Friars Minor, the Conventuals, and the Capuchins whose origins, on the Continent, lie in the Counter Reformation period so that they had no friaries in pre-Reformation England. The Friars Minor and the Conventuals (who came to England in 1905) most closely continue the pre-Reformation Franciscan tradition; the Conventuals' habit, grey as distinct from the brown of the Friars Minor, may come close to that of the 'Grey Friars' who worked here from the thirteenth to the sixteenth century. All three Franciscan groups work, more than in the Middle Ages, on the running of parishes. The Friars Minor have some two hundred friars in an Anglo-Scottish province, and their recruitment is now more promising than in recent years. With their provincial headquarters at Forest Gate (see page 94) they also serve parishes in Bristol, Manchester, and other towns. Their novices go first to the friary at Chilworth near Guildford, and in a more pioneering move the Friars Minor and the Conventuals share a purpose-built study centre, of modern design, within the precincts, close to Canterbury, of the University of Kent. The Capuchins, with their headquarters church in North Wales, and with parishes in Chester,

Crawley and elsewhere, are active on a smaller scale. At Oxford their house in Iffley Road, now known as Greyfriars, has the status of a Permanent Private Hall. It accommodates undergraduate residents, and is also a hall of residence for student members of all three Franciscan branches.

The Dominicans are, as always, a largely intellectual order. They have long been associated with 'progressive' Catholicism and they have, in the last two decades, been affected both by problems of innovation in the Church and by the falling away of some of their members. But they still serve several parishes, and though they have given up their schools they run three University Catholic chaplaincies and carry on other pastoral and literary activities. They reckon that they can, with their new entrants, maintain their existing commitments, but in the meantime the Victorian friary at Woodchester (in any case inconvenient and hard to maintain) has been pulled down, and the training of novices occurs at Oxford.

The Augustinian friars, again at work in this country though a much smaller body than they were before the Reformation, serve some parishes and run a large grammar school at Carlisle. One of their parishes, at Clare in Suffolk, is unusual in that the friars occupy the considerable remains of a mediaeval friary of their order.

Another act of reoccupation, with the important remains of a mediaeval friary re-used, and much developed, by the same order which was there before Henry VIII's time, has been achieved, at Aylesford near Maidstone, by the Calced Carmelites. The English Carmelite friars are now in the two groupings of the Calced (of the 'old observance') and of the Discalced, who are more under the influence of sixteenth-century reforms and are more austere and traditional in their régime. The Discalced Carmelites came back to England in the 1860s. Their best-known church, rebuilt, since its wartime bombing, is in Kensington, but they also have parishes elsewhere and, at Wincanton in Somerset, a twin-towered friary church of a marked conventual appearance. The Calced Carmelites, with their house at Aylesford widely known to many thousands of visitors for pilgrimages, conferences, retreats, and ecumenical activities, and with another centre of Carmelite work, a few miles away, in the ancient buildings of Allington Castle, seem to be in a phase of renewed and promising activity. In the half-century which has passed since their coming to England the Calced

73 Aylesford: the sanctuary

Carmelites have come to staff some parishes in England and Wales and, like the Franciscan Friars Minor, they now have a better flow of novices than some religious orders and congregations of Counter-Reformation origin. The importance of such centres as Aylesford and Allington, and of their northern counterpart at Hazlewood Castle near Tadcaster, with its mediaeval chapel and historic associations with 'penal' Catholicism, has made for a temporary concentration, as a prelude to later expansion, of Calced Carmelite activities.

NUNS AND CANONESSES

Carmelite nuns, of the order reformed in the sixteenth century under the dominant inspiration of St. Teresa of Avila, are prominent among England's enclosed and contemplative nuns. These communities, over sixty all told and including the one Cistercian nunnery still at Stapehill in Dorset and the Dominicans in their Victorian convent in the Isle of Wight, are still numerous, though some closures and amalgamations have of late slightly lessened their number. The position in modern English Catholicism of these enclosed communities, many of them with origins going back to 'penal' convents established in the seventeenth century on the Continent, is of varied interest and importance. Though their relative position may be somewhat less than it was when far fewer 'active' communities existed, the flow of entries to these contemplative convents seems now to have improved after a difficult spell when the membership of many convents was much weighted in favour of those past middle age. A lack of numbers seems to have caused less pulling in of activity than it has in some orders whose work mainly lies in such spheres as teaching, nursing, and social work. Yet the position varies, in the larger groupings, from convent to convent. The spiritual repute of some superiors has attracted recruits to a few communities, though nothing in recent years has been as spectacular as the achievement, earlier this century, of the Carmelite prioress of Notting Hill in London who sent out more new foundations than the great St. Teresa herself. There has also been a tendency for more vocations in convents which are in well-populated areas, and which thus find it easier to become well known among the laity.

Several of England's convents of enclosed nuns are Benedictine. Four are affiliated to the English Benedictine congregation, while the abbey at Ryde is linked to the Solesmes congregation whose monks at Quarr Abbey are not far away and act as chaplains to the nuns. The other Benedictine abbeys and priories have different origins and links; some, as at Oulton in Staffordshire and the abbey at Teignmouth whose life as a community started at Dunkirk, had Continental origins in penal times. The nunnery at Stanbrook near Worcester is much the largest of these Benedictine communities; both there and at Ryde the numbers equal those of some large English abbeys of nuns not long before the final dissolution year of 1539.

Of the other small groupings the most historic, uniquely linked to a community which existed before Henry VIII's reign (see page 55), is the Bridgettine Abbey of Syon. It is now, after its long stay in Lisbon and short spells in various parts of England, in a largely Georgian mansion set, in generous parkland, at Marley in South Devon. A moderate-sized community uses a chapel, of Romanesque character, which was built soon after the Bridgettines' arrival in the 1920s.

Some of the other small contemplative groupings have no more than one or two convents apiece. The Augustinian Canonesses Regular still inhabit their strikingly Victorian Gothic priory on its fine hillside site near Newton Abbot in Devon; they are, at the moment, linked to a convent in Ireland which also maintains the practice of Perpetual Adoration. Other communities, like the Visitation nuns with their modern chapel and refectory added to a Victorian mansion at Waldron in Sussex, belong to orders of post-Reformation origins.

Easily the most numerous convents of enclosed nuns in England and Wales are those of the Franciscan nuns (Poor Clares) and of the Carmelites. Some of the Poor Clare communities go back over three hundred years to foundations made on the Continent for novices from England's 'penal' families. They include some of fair size, the community at Arundel being the largest. Some, as at Sclerder near Polperro in Cornwall, near Hereford, at Darlington, and at Woodchester (not far from the site once occupied by the Dominican friary) where Charles Hansom, in 1869, completed an ambitious, wood-vaulted chapel, are in Victorian Gothic buildings of clearly conventual character. More numerous still are the convents of the Carmelites. In the tradition of an order which has, since St. Teresa's time, kept its communities of moderate size, few of them have more than two dozen sisters. Some are in buildings which were once private houses, and which have had few 'conventual' alterations or enlargements. One in central Wales attracted some attention when disused railway carriages were ingeniously and successfully

74 Darlington: Poor Clares' Abbey, by Joseph Hansom, finished 1857

converted into cells. All told, the Carmelite nuns of England and Wales number over five hundred, fewer than they were some years back, but with prospects of future increase.

The numerous communities of sisters, outside enclosure, who do teaching, nursing, and a wide range of social work are many of them of comparatively recent origin. Though some follow modified versions of the Rule of St. Augustine their life and work stands apart from that of the more strictly claustral Austin Canonesses at work in pre-Reformation England. Augustinian Canonesses, other than the enclosed and contemplative community near Newton Abbot, are still, however, active in other directions. An important group, originating in Lorraine before 1600, was on teaching work in France till some of its members moved to England, as a result of anti-clerical measures in 1904. Known as the Congregation of Our Lady, its members were in the main on teaching work. The house at St. Leonard's on Sea was given a chapel of clearly conventual type. Though teaching is still an

important part of these Canonesses' activity they have recently, in addition, turned to social and parish work, with an emphasis, in London and Cambridge, on work among University students. Established, by now, in England for over seventy years the Congregation is now English in its membership.

SOME ANGLICAN DEVELOPMENTS

The religious life continues, with some changes, as a well-recognised element in the life of the Anglican church in England. The priory of St. Paul, near Alton in Hampshire, has become Benedictine in its devotional and liturgical life. The Anglican Benedictines at Nashdom continue, in the essentially domestic surroundings of their Lutyens mansion, as a community of nearly thirty, including some novices. One also has the continued work of the men's communities of a more distinctively Anglican type. The

75 East Grinstead, Sussex (Society of St. Margaret): the new church and upper chapel, 1975

Community of the Resurrection still runs its theological college at Mirfield near Leeds; also a retreat house in the beautiful riverside village of Hemingford Grey near Huntingdon. In London's East End, an interesting new development is the joint care, by members of the Community and some Anglican sisters, of the ancient almshouse foundation (originally, near the Tower, on the site of St. Katherine's Dock) known as the Royal Hospital of St. Katherine; the Community is also active in the 'high' setting of the Anglican Church in South Africa. The Cowley fathers, whose prospects have improved with the coming of some young new entrants, still have their mother house at Oxford, with work among undergraduates and other students in addition to the giving of missions and retreats. Their Westminster house maintains a varied ministry in the capital, while a new venture, in Sussex, is on what the Fathers call 'exploratory' work, finding common ground between the western and eastern Christian traditions. In the Society of the Sacred Mission changes have been more dramatic. As the Society no longer trains ordinands it has left its spacious original mother house at Kelham near Newark. Its headquarters is now a small priory, with new domestic buildings, in the new town of Milton Keynes, with Willen church, a delightful building, mainly of about 1680, by Robert Hooke who was a

close associate of Wren, its main worshipping centre. At Willen, and in its two other houses at Lancaster and Sheffield, its members carry on a variety of community work, the running (at Lancaster) of a study and conference centre, and Christian witness in a large industrial area. The Society also has provinces in South Africa, and in Australia with an outlying establishment in Japan.

Among the numerous Anglican sisterhoods one change has meant the abandonment, for new and more up-to-date buildings, of an important set of Victorian conventual buildings. At East Grinstead in Sussex, where the Society of St. Margaret has a resident community of between thirty and forty, the domestic buildings and the fine chapel by Street have been given up, the domestic buildings being converted for housing; as the chapel is a 'listed' building it is being preserved. A new convent, with a modern chapel, was opened early in 1975, the architect being Mr. Kenneth Smith of London. In an upper chapel, behind the altar, windows of abstract designs, by Mr. Alfred Fisher, add colour and character to the chapel as a whole.

Apart from the many 'active' sisterhoods on teaching and social work, one can briefly notice some groups of Anglican nuns whose life is claustral and contemplative, and which thus come closer to the mediaeval conventual pattern. Several such communities live an enclosed Benedictine life. The largest, with between forty and fifty nuns and occupying buildings once those of mediaeval Benedictine nuns, is that at West Malling; like some other communities which once took an 'advanced' stand in liturgical and devotional matters they have largely exchanged Latin for English in the services in their chapel. At the far end of their grounds a small community of Anglican monks, living by Cistercian rules, was founded in the 1960s. They use a mediaeval barn as their chapel, and among other duties they help the nuns as chaplains in their new church.

A more contemplative way of life, based on the Rule of St. Augustine, is that of the fair-sized Anglican community of the Precious Blood at Burnham near Maidenhead. Ecumenical contacts with the religious orders and laity of other denominations also feature in the nuns' life, so too do the giving of retreats and the holding of quiet days. For chaplains they rely on the Anglican Benedictines at Nashdom a few miles away; in this respect they resemble several convents of Roman Catholic nuns. For just as Anglican Benedictines and Cistercians serve as chaplains for convents of nuns near at hand so also, among many examples, the Discalced Carmelites of Wincanton say

Mass and hear confessions for the handicapped Sisters of Jesus Crucified at Castle Cary, and the Downside Benedictines drive over, for the same reason, to the small community of the Sisters of Mount Sion who run the domestic side of the new Renewal and Conference Centre at Ammerdown. How far any corresponding arrangements, with male religious acting as chaplains for nuns and canonesses, were possible in the mediaeval period, outside such 'double' houses as those of the Gilbertines and the Bridgettines it is hard to tell. Geography would, however, have made it impossible in many areas, in the western counties, for instance where such leading nunneries as Shaftesbury, Amesbury, Wilton, Wherwell, and Lacock were awkwardly far from the nearest monasteries and are known to have had resident secular priests as their chaplains. But nowadays, with cars or trucks as important in the monastic economy as horses were for the efficiency of mediaeval communities, and with secular clergy fewer than they were before the Reformation, the position has changed. If a convent of nuns cannot have a male religious as a resident chaplain it is easy for such a priest to drive over if the distance is reasonable. Such arrangements well fit the notion that matter-of-fact practicality, such as St. Teresa approved, is more typical of the religious life than the roseate romanticism with which some of its uninformed admirers have tended to surround it.

A Gazetteer of Sites

This section gives short sketches on the basic history and architecture of conventual sites, for the most part of pre-Reformation origin, but a few of them of existing abbeys and priories, which are worth visiting at the present time. They are arranged, from the North southwards and down to Cornwall, according to the county boundaries as they were before 1974; there are separate sections, with a similar North–South geographical arrangement, for Wales and the modern convents. Of the ancient foundations, in each county, Benedictine and Cistercian houses come first, e.g. Blyth in Nottinghamshire, then other strictly 'monastic' establishments. Houses of Augustinian canons come next, with nunneries and friaries to follow.

My main basis of selection has been to choose monastic sites where there are substantial remains, or where churches, or portions of them, are still used for worship. A few seriously ruined monasteries, such as Bury St. Edmunds and Glastonbury, are included because of the sheer importance of those particular abbeys. But others, like Jervaulx, or Byland despite the imposing fragment of its west front, have been excluded. All monastic sites, however, are of *some* interest and importance, even though there may now be little to see.

On three counties, as they were before the local government upheaval of 1974, there are no separate sections as their monastic remains are few, with none of the sites calling for individual description. These are Westmorland, where little but the late Perpendicular tower remains of the Premonstratensian abbey of Shap, Rutland, and Huntingdonshire. In the last-named county the great Benedictine abbey of Ramsey was overwhelmingly dominant, with an imposing church and revenues, in 1535, more than those of any other Fenland monastery. Its remains are scanty, though its thirteenth-century lady chapel, which projected from the north transept was, unusually, preserved in the fabric of a later mansion. Better preserved evidence of this abbey's building activity is the beautiful fifteenth-century bridge, with a chapel on its central pier, over the Ouse at St. Ives where Ramsey had a small dependent priory.

Though the monastic cathedrals and abbey churches which, since the Dissolution under Henry VIII, have gained the status of Anglican cathedrals, are often mentioned in my initial text they do not feature in this section. So, in Gloucestershire, Tewkesbury is in but St. Peter's at Gloucester is out, while in London, Southwark Cathedral is excluded while St. Bartholomew's Priory is covered. The somewhat special case of Bath 'Abbey' is briefly mentioned in the section on Somerset.

I have personally visited nearly all the abbeys, priories, and friaries mentioned in this section. Where, as at Brinkburn, Bayham, and Ramsgate I have been unable to get to the sites I have indicated the point with an asterisk, but have used what information I have available.

Guidebooks, and other booklets, of varying quality, can be had at many of these sites. Where the churches are still in use they are often brought out by the church authorities. Where ruined monasteries are cared for by the Department of the Environment they are described either in full-scale, highly authoritative guides or in much shorter works known as abridged or display-card guides. Where no suitable literature is available on the spot visitors can, for England, find passages in the appropriate volumes of the Penguin Books 'Buildings of England' series, in the Victoria County History of England, and often in the transactions of County Historical or Archaeological Societies. There are few sites for which visitors must wholly rely on their own knowledge of such matters. What I have here done is to give those interested a basic indication of what is worth noticing.

76 St. Ives, Huntingdonshire: bridge and chapel,
*c*1415, by Ramsey Abbey

England

NORTHUMBERLAND

The monastic establishments here were mostly small and modestly endowed, and in a turbulent county they suffered much from attacks and ravaging from both sides of the Scottish border. A few, however, survive in a reasonable state of preservation, and there are considerable remains of the Premonstratensian abbey at Blanchland.

Lindisfarne Priory* Of the Anglo-Saxon monastery, where St. Cuthbert ruled both as bishop and abbot, nothing now remains; the achievement of this religious house survives in the illuminated splendour of the Lindisfarne Gospels. After the Norman Conquest the monastery on Holy Island became a small 'cell', or dependency, of the great Benedictine cathedral monastery at Durham, and most of what can still be seen dates from this architectural period of Norman Romanesque. The exposed and precarious position of such a monastery, off the Northumbrian coast and close to the border, caused it to become a coastal fort as well as a religious house.

The original plan of the church contained a nave of six bays, transepts with an apsidal chapel off each one, and a short apsidal presbytery. This presbytery was lengthened, late in the Norman period, and given a square east end. This extension, and the fourteenth-century insertion of a large east window, were the only important architectural changes made to the monastic part of the church. Large parts of the crossing piers and of the transept walling still stand, also the eastern part of the northern nave arcade whose incised decoration, like the surviving portions of the church's vaulting, resemble work in the priory's mother church at Durham. The west wall of the nave, with its combination of simple arches with cushion capitals, and the more elaborate zig-zag ornament of the fine western doorway, is still an imposing survival, with alterations made in the fourteenth century to improve the fortification of this part of the church.

The domestic buildings, most of whose remains are of the thirteenth and fourteenth centuries, were on the southern side of the church. The prior's lodging was not in the western range but in the eastern section; here too alterations were made in the interests of stronger fortification.

Tynemouth Priory*   The ruins of this priory are sited inside the fortifications of a castle which occupied the whole of the northern sector of a promontory on the Northumberland side of the mouth of the Tyne; even in their ruined state the buildings are an imposing sight as one comes in or out of the Tyne by ship. The priory, successor to a destroyed Anglo-Saxon monastery, was the largest Benedictine house in Northumberland, but its status was only that of a large 'cell', or dependency, of the great abbey of St. Alban's; some of its priors went on to become important abbots of the mother house. To their great inconvenience the priors were responsible for the upkeep of the fortifications, the main survival of which is the massive gate-tower which, with its barbican, was built in the last years of the fourteenth century.

Of the original Norman church, which had an apsidal presbytery with radiating chapels, the main remaining portions are the crossing piers and one bay of the northern arcade. The nave was lengthened westwards in the thirteenth century; much of its west wall survives, with a richly moulded doorway and remains of a large perpendicular west window built to let in more light. The Norman presbytery was replaced, early in the Gothic period, by a much longer, square-ended presbytery with a lady chapel in a somewhat unusual north-eastern position. The unaisled eastern bays of this presbytery, with wall

arcading, fine lancets of an early type, remains of vaulting, and a vesica-shaped window, remain almost to their full height and are the priory's most spectacular relics. Beyond it, the attractive Percy Chantry, of the fifteenth century, is almost intact and retains its lierne vault with over thirty vigorously carved bosses.

The remains of the domestic buildings, of various dates and adapted to meet the demands of the frequent entertainment of important lay visitors, were south of the church and within the fortifications.

Hexham Priory   The church which now dominates the town was that of a priory of Augustinian canons regular, founded early in the twelfth century. But there are some remains of its predecessor, the Anglo-Saxon cathedral built, about 674, by St. Wilfrid. This was an important apsidal and basilican church, and its small reliquary crypt is intact beneath the nave of the later priory. Another important feature is the low-backed stone chair which was, when sited in the eastern apse of St. Wilfrid's cathedral, the throne of the early bishops.

The Augustinian priory church was built, in its present form, in the early Gothic period of the late twelfth and early thirteenth centuries. Its nave, which had only a northern aisle, was destroyed at the Dissolution, and was replaced, in a style similar to that of the Early English transepts, about 1908. The priory was never of more than moderate wealth, and like other religious houses in the border counties it suffered much destruction and ravaging from the Scots. For these reasons it saw little architectural change after its completion in the thirteenth century. Its choir limb (whose lancetted eastern wall is now modern) and transepts are still used for worship and show a rich variety of early Gothic work, from the transitional period between Romanesque and Gothic to the mature Early English of the transepts. There are variations between the two sides of the choir limb, and between the architectural treatment of the two transepts; in both of these there is, apart from the clustered columns of the arcades, some curiously 'stilted' window arcading in the clerestorey stage. In the south transept the long night stairway from the level of the dormitory is specially well known, while the rood screen which leads into the choir is a rich piece of early sixteenth-century woodwork. In the actual choir, which always had a timber roof, a late mediaeval chantry chapel is partly of stone and partly of delicately carved woodwork.

77   Tynemouth Priory, Northumberland (Benedictine): the Percy chantry, c1450

79 Brinkburn Priory, Northumberland (Augustinian): exterior from south-east

Brinkburn Priory*   In the valley of the Coquet this was a small priory of Augustinian canons regular, founded late in Henry I's reign. It was never wealthy and the church saw few architectural changes after its completion about 1200. The domestic buildings, south of the church, were merged in the structure of a post-suppression mansion, but the church, though partly ruinous in the eighteenth century, substantially survived, though without a roof, till 1858 when it was re-roofed and brought back into use as a fine survival of monastic architecture.

The church has an aisleless presbytery, a crossing with a squat central tower, transepts each with two projecting chapels, and a nave, as at Hexham, with only a north aisle. The church displays a mixture of round-arched Romanesque features, and fine lancets, particularly in the east and west walls, more typical of Early English Gothic. The nave arcade has octagonal columns, moulded capitals, and chamfered arches, while pairs of round-headed arches are in its triforium stage. Some trefoil-headed arcading, of a later thirteenth-century type, occurs in the north porch and along the cloister side of the church's south wall.

78 Hexham Priory (Augustinian): in the north transept

Newcastle, Dominican Friary*   This friary was founded by 1239 and lasted a little over three hundred years. There are considerable remains which, like those of the Dominican friary at Bristol, owe their preservation to their being made over, soon after the suppression, to some of the local tradesmen's guilds who long used them as meeting rooms or let the lower rooms as homes for their retired members. The church has gone, but part of the eastern range still stands, also some of the refectory, and much of the western range. Most of the surviving features, including the chapter house's entrance, are Early English, but there is also a large part of a fine traceried window of the fourteenth century.

Hulne, Carmelite Friary*   Near Alnwick, this has some of the country's best preserved remains of a mediaeval friary; the rural setting, and the conversion of the buildings into a mansion, made for better preservation than one finds in most urban friary sites. Hulne was founded, about 1240–42, as a Carmelite friary. The remains include the south and west walls of an unaisled rectangular church, with fine sedilia and other details of the thirteenth century, and single or two-light windows. Some of the cloister alleys projected, while others were 'inbuilt' into the domestic ranges, while the chapter house, with a later east window, survived because it became the chapel of the mansion.

CO. DURHAM

The religious houses of this county were few, and the monastic scene was dominated by the great cathedral monastery of Durham to which Jarrow and Monkwearmouth, with their historic associations and pre-Conquest remains, became cells in the post-Conquest period.

Another cell of Durham was the priory of *Finchale*, founded late in the twelfth century on the site once occupied by the cell and chapel of the hermit St. Godric. The church and the domestic buildings were laid out in the thirteenth century, originally for a medium-sized priory. But Finchale never had more than a few resident monks, and was later used as a place of holiday and recreation for monks from Durham. The thirteenth-century church, of which there are some attractive remains, was reduced in size by the demolition of its aisles, with some late decorated windows put into the walls which blocked the arcades. There are considerable remains of the domestic buildings, in which a large prior's house lay well to the east of the dormitory range.

CUMBERLAND and FURNESS

Only three of the religious houses in this region were of major pre-Reformation importance, one being the Augustinian cathedral priory at Carlisle. But Cumberland and Furness are notably rich in monastic survivals, with remains at Wetherall (Benedictine) and Calder (Cistercian) as well as those mentioned in more detail.

St. Bees Priory   A small priory of Benedictine monks was founded here about 1120, and though the domestic buildings have gone, nearly all the church survives; like Brinkburn it has been re-roofed, and brought back into use, in the post-Dissolution period. Three of the crossing arches and much of the structure of the transepts form part of the Norman church; so too does the west wall of the nave with its rich doorway of one plain and three zig-zag orders, with foliate and animal capitals. Close to it is an unusual Romanesque carving of St. George and the dragon on a triangular-headed stone. The heavily restored central tower is Early English, as also are the arcades of the nave with their moulded arches and mostly octagonal pillars. The clerestorey, in 'survival-ist' Perpendicular, dates from the re-roofing of the nave in 1611.

Most of the presbytery, a fine piece of early Gothic building, with lancets in its east wall parted by tabernacled work and fine northern lancets whose shafts have 'waterleaf' capitals, became roofless but was re-roofed, about 1817, when it became a lecture room for a theological college which was then founded at St. Bees, and which continued till 1894; the building is now the music room of St. Bees School. Its large southern chapel, of about 1300, has been destroyed, but the arches are embedded in the presbytery wall.

Holmcultram (at Abbeytown)   This was the leading Cistercian abbey in Cumberland and was founded, about 1150, as a daughter house of Melrose. It is most important as the only Cistercian abbey in England part of whose nave is still used for worship. It had a turbulent history, with several raids by the Scots, particularly in 1319 when Robert Bruce plundered it although his father was buried there.

The eastern part of the church, and the domestic buildings, have disappeared. Much of the nave had, by the sixteenth century, become the local parish church, and the fine western porch of 1507 was added to serve parish needs. After the Dissolution the parishioners first tried to keep the whole church, but after the tower fell in 1600 heavy repairs were needed. The present condition of the nave is due to alterations of 1724–30, when it was reduced to six bays, with the roof lowered almost to the top of the arcades and with the aisles destroyed. To allow for galleries, two tiers of windows were pierced in the new side walls. The east window, 'debased' Perpendicular of about 1600, seems to have been reset in a new east wall.

The arcades survive from the late twelfth-century nave. They have clustered columns, scalloped or plain trumpet-shaped capitals, and pointed arches. The roof was put up in the eighteenth century, re-using some mediaeval timbers. The fine west doorway combines a rounded arch of Romanesque shape with early Gothic moulded orders.

In recent years some buildings south of the church have been made into an attractive arts and tourist centre, with a library, a gift shop, and a café.

Furness Abbey   Originally founded in 1123, on a site near Preston, for monks of the Savigniac Order which later joined the Cistercians. In 1127 the abbey moved to the more remote site of Furness where, despite Scottish raids, it became important and

80   Brinkburn Priory: interior view

81 Furness Abbey (Cistercian): transept and eastern
range

82 Furness Abbey: presbytery sedilia, c1500

prosperous, with large agricultural and iron-mining interests and property in Ireland and the Isle of Man. By 1535 it was the second richest Cistercian abbey in England.

Its site, narrow and set between two streams which converge lower down the valley, was in many ways awkward and made for some unusual arrangements in the abbey's layout. The main stream runs north and south very close to the domestic buildings, so that the monk's latrine block was built parallel to the dormitory, with the original infirmary (later the abbot's house) on a north–south alignment.

Little remains of the original work on the church, or of the buildings on the south and west of the site. But the red sandstone ruins of the eastern part of the church, and of the eastern domestic range, are most impressive. So too is most of the structure of a late Perpendicular western tower, built in this position after the monks had failed to build a central tower and, because of the restricted site, jutting some way into the nave.

The choir and the transepts are for the most part fine transitional Norman work of the late twelfth century, but the presbytery was remodelled, without elongation, in the Perpendicular period, with a large east window and canopied quadruple sedilia, with an elaborate piscina, which comprise one of the finest groups of this kind in England. The eastern domestic range is also of great splendour; the thirteenth-century chapter house, originally vaulted and with its slim pillars still partly standing, is approached by three arches which are rounded though wholly Gothic in their decorative character. Higher up, a large part of the long dormitory, with its rows of simple lancets, can still be seen.

Though the refectory range has almost disappeared, there are important remains, south of it, of the spacious second infirmary, mostly of about 1300. The best remains are in the vaulted chapel, with a 'stilted' east window, and in the pantry, still with its chamfered vault, which led towards an interesting octagonal kitchen built above the easternmost watercourse.

Lanercost Priory Beautifully situated, in the valley of the Irthing and amid unspoilt countryside near Naworth Castle this is, to my mind, one of the five or six most satisfying monastic sites in the country. It is unusual in that the ruined crossing and presbytery are cared for by the Department of the Environment, while the nave is used as the parish church.

This priory of Augustinian canons regular was founded about 1166. Like other border religious houses it suffered much from devastation by the Scots, and in 1306 Edward I stayed there while on the last of his Scottish campaigns. Its revenues, diminished by disasters, remained modest and the church saw little architectural change after its completion in the thirteenth century; much stone from the nearby Roman Wall was used in its construction. The north aisle of the nave continued in use, and the rest of the nave was roofed and made usable in the eighteenth century, the present wooden roof being still more recent.

The presbytery and transepts, with a squat tower over the crossing, are excellent work of the earliest Gothic period, with most of the windows lancets; two tiers, of three lancets each, are in the east wall. The arcades on the north side are much lower than those to the south, and the chamfered vault of the northern chapel survives; there is no triforium stage, but the clerestorey is arcaded to provide a walkway. The fine tomb of Sir Thomas Dacre (d. 1525) is well preserved below a modern canopy.

As at Hexham and Brinkburn the nave has only one aisle. Its eastern section originally contained the canons' choir and rood screen; the arcade has three simple arches, on octagonal columns and beneath a fine arcaded clerestorey. The west front, the last part of the church to be finished, has a finely moulded Early English doorway, a trefoiled arcade above it, and three beautifully arcaded lancets.

Most of the domestic buildings south of the church have disappeared, but the western range was turned into a mansion by the Dacres. The best domestic relic, with plain octagonal pillars, no capitals, and a simple vault, is the undercroft of the refectory.

Cartmel Priory A rare and splendid example of a complete monastic church used for worship. It was that of a priory of Augustinian canons regular, founded late in the twelfth century and never of more than moderate wealth. A unique event in its history, perhaps due to the more convenient drainage facilities provided by a stream to the north-west of the church, occurred when the domestic buildings were moved from the southern to the northern side. A re-sited cloister doorway and night stairway, and the blockage of some lancets to allow for new buildings, give evidence for the change. The domestic buildings have almost disappeared except for a fine vaulted gateway, of the fourteenth century, which led from the outer courtyard to the town.

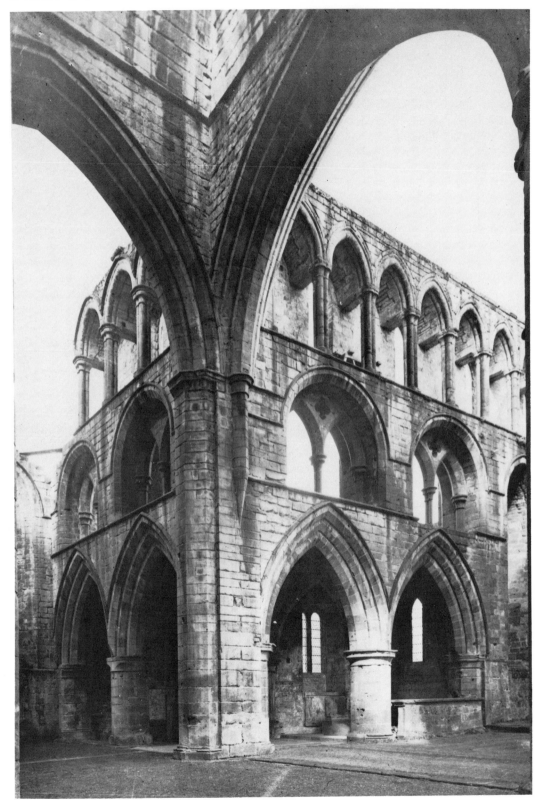

The church is cruciform, with a low central tower, and, above it, the rare feature of a fifteenth-century lantern set diamond-wise to the tower below it. The crossing and the presbytery have some excellent work of the Transitional Norman period, with richly ornamented round arches in the presbytery, and in the triforium a row of small pointed arches. The north aisle of the presbytery has its simple vaulting of that period, but the southern aisle, which was used by the parishioners, was enlarged and rebuilt in the fourteenth century, with excellent curvilinear windows. Like York Minster and other great churches in the North, the priory has a vast Perpendicular east window, of nine lights and still keeping some early fifteenth-century glass. The nave, short and somewhat undistinguished, of three bays and with octagonal pillars, was built at about the same time.

After the Dissolution in 1537 most of the church became ruinous and disused. But early in the seventeenth century Cartmel Priory, like Bath Abbey, Abbey Dore and some other one-time monastic churches, was restored and refitted for worship, the benefactor being George Preston of Holker Hall. The fifteenth-century choir stalls and misericords survived, and above them Preston placed the magnificent Flemish Renaissance screens whose pierced carving, and arabesque work on composite classical columns, places them among the finest post-Reformation church woodwork in England. Other furnishings of the seventeenth century are also of good quality and the church has some fine Georgian mural monuments.

YORKSHIRE

As the largest county in England, Yorkshire had, not unnaturally, particularly many monasteries and other religious houses. Though the Benedictine monks were somewhat under-represented, Cistercian houses were specially numerous and important. There were several houses of canons regular, and many nunneries, most of them small. The county's monastic remains are of great importance. Apart from those listed in detail, one has such relics as the Cistercian ruins at Jervaulx and Roche, the lofty east end of Guisborough and the west end, likewise tall and impressive with the empty half circle of its western rose window, at Byland. At Egglestone in Teesdale there are Premonstratensian remains in fair quantity, while one

83 Lanercost Priory, Cumbria (Augustinian): interior view

84 Watton Priory, Yorkshire (Gilbertine): the prior's house, two-storeyed oriel

has the beautiful Augustinian outer gateway at Kirkham and the house, with its brick-built hall and an imposing oriel window, of the Gilbertine prior at Watton.

York, St. Mary's Abbey Founded in 1089 St. Mary's became the largest and wealthiest Benedictine abbey in the North of England. The Norman church was wholly replaced, from about 1270, by a Gothic building which had a long eastern limb and a sacristy projecting from the southern choir aisle of the new extension. The whole church, completed in a comparatively short time, was of an architectural quality fitting the importance and standing of the abbey. Pathetically little now remains. The best survivals, geometrical Gothic and early Decorated in style and of great beauty, are parts of the west end and the northern aisle wall of the nave, a crossing pier and part of the north transept. The ground plan of the Norman presbytery, with parallel apses, is outlined in the grass. Some remains of the domestic buildings lie under the Yorkshire Museum, while large stretches of the abbey's outer precinct wall still stand, as also does a part of the Great Gatehouse.

York, Holy Trinity, Micklegate The remains of this small Benedictine priory, at first an 'alien' priory of Norman foundation, but 'denizen' from 1426, are in many ways more cheering than those of St. Mary's Abbey. Two Norman crossing piers remain, but the east end has been replaced by the Victorian chancel of a church still in use. The thirteenth-century nave and its southern arcade of five arches remain from the old church. The north-western tower is of the fifteenth century, but has remains of the Early English triforium on its south side, while the attractive Early English west front is mostly a modern reconstruction.

Whitby Abbey* This Benedictine abbey was the successor to the religious house, of Celtic origin but continuing till its destruction by the Danes, over which the famous St. Hilda ruled at the time of the important Synod of 664. When the Norman monastery was founded its monks took over the upland site (somewhat inconvenient by mediaeval monastic standards) of the earlier foundation; it still contained ruins of the numerous separate cells and oratories of a monastery of the Celtic type.

The peak period of Whitby Abbey's history was in the thirteenth century, when a start was made on the complete replacement of the Norman church. It is from this rebuilding, with the long square-ended eastern limb common among the more important monasteries of the North, that the impressive ruins of

85 Whitby Abbey, Yorkshire (Benedictine): choir limb looking east
86 Selby Abbey, Yorkshire: in the Norman nave, twelfth century

Whitby Abbey still remain. Most of the work, with fine lancets in the presbytery and north transept, with dogtooth moulding, a charming little rose window and the unusual feature of thirteenth-century ballflower ornament, is in the Early English style, and much more survives of the northern than of the southern side of the church. The ruins of the nave have, however, some Decorated windows and other features.

Most of the domestic buildings have gone, and till the 1760s the ruins of the church were much more extensive than they are now. Samuel Buck's engraving of 1711 shows the nave and the south transept still standing, while the central tower did not collapse till 1830.

Selby Abbey Perhaps the most important monastic survival in Yorkshire and one of the few mediaeval Benedictine churches in England which survives almost complete, at all events at ground level, for present-day worshipping use. The abbey church, whose domestic buildings have disappeared, has experienced many misfortunes, but is still of first-rate architectural importance.

The abbey was founded in 1069, and the Norman church, like some other northern abbeys with a set of parallel apses, was started about 1100. Important work of this first building period remains in the transepts, in the lower part of the tower, and in the eastern half of the double-bayed nave. One pillar has decoration akin to Durham work, and the vault shafts in the nave show that a vault, perhaps like that at Durham, was also intended at Selby. The nave, like some others in monastic churches, was built piecemeal, so that the arcades and the triforium are partly in the transitional style, while the whole of the clerestorey is early Gothic. The west doorway is particularly splendid late Norman work, while the north porch shows the transition from Romanesque to Gothic, and most of the west front is excellent Early English. The intended western towers were never built before the Dissolution; the present towers were finished in 1935. For some time after the Dissolution the church was disused, but in the reign of James I it was, like the nave of Bath Abbey, brought back into use.

The top of the central tower collapsed in 1690, destroying most of the south transept which was not replaced till 1912. In 1906 a serious fire destroyed the wooden roofs over the whole of the abbey, so that the present wooden ceilings, the top stage of the central tower, and most of the furnishings are later than that time. The most beautiful part of the church is the long choir limb, built at various dates in the fourteenth century, with a sacristy (see page 25) off its south aisle, and without a triforium stage but with a walkway just below the Decorated clerestorey windows; the general effect is akin to that of the elongated choir limb at Lichfield Cathedral. The great east window, of seven lights with curvilinear tracery, is specially splendid and must, with the large gable window above it, have been finished about 1340. The Perpendicular period is best represented by the great window in the northern transept.

Fountains Abbey Considered by many to be England's greatest monastic ruin, Fountains, like Rievaulx, owes much of its massive preservation to its becoming the romantic *pièce-de-résistance* in a Georgian landowner's landscaped park. Its purchaser, who added the Fountains site to the existing part of Studley Royal, was William Aislabie, whose father had been Chancellor of the Exchequer at the time of the South Sea Bubble scandal, and who was then obliged to leave public life and retire to his Yorkshire estates.

The monastery, not far from Ripon in the remote and uncultivated valley of the Skell, was started in 1132 by some Benedictine monks from St. Mary's at York who wished to lead a more austere life than that prevalent in their abbey. Their convent was soon integrated into the Cistercian order, and Fountains later became the richest and most extensive Cistercian abbey in England. Its buildings were notable not only for the splendour of the church but for the great extent of the domestic quarters and for the way in which the little river was split into several channels and 'managed' to serve the purposes of the community. The church shows how the increasing numbers of monks soon made it necessary to extend their worshipping space, while the domestic quarters show how an important and flourishing Cistercian abbey had to provide for a large community of lay brothers. The western part of the church is better preserved than most of its eastern limb; so too the best domestic remains are seen in the western half of the precincts.

The oldest and most completely Romanesque work in the church is seen in the simple transepts. The nave, inspired by early Burgundian Gothic with its cylindrical pillars, simple pointed arches, and in the aisles with the cross arches which parted a series of transverse tunnel vaults, stands almost entire and is of great architectural importance. The western, or 'Galilee' porch has disappeared and the west window, like the east window of the presbytery, ended as a large Perpendicular one of several lights. Except for the aisle walls not much is left of the fine Early English presbytery till, beyond the site of the high altar, one has the very fine Early English ruins, with lancets and trefoiled arcading, of the church's eastern feature which projected, in the manner of transepts, to make of this great chapel, with its nine altars for the saying of private masses, a T-shaped east end for the much-lengthened church; it probably inspired the similar, but slightly later feature at Durham Cathedral.

In the fifteenth century an attempt was made to heighten the low central tower of the original church. As the piers of the crossing could not take the extra strain Abbot Huby (1495–1526) then built the imposing tower, adjacent to the north transept, which was the last part of the church to be built.

The ruins of the domestic buildings (mostly of the twelfth and early thirteenth centuries) include much of the eastern range, which had a beautiful aisled and vaulted chapter house built not long before 1200, and considerable remains of the refectory, the infirmary,

87　Fountains Abbey: eastern transept, thirteenth century

88 Rievaulx Abbey: the choir

and the abbot's house. But the most imposing domestic remains at Fountains are in the western range which housed the lay brothers. The cellarium or undercroft of this range, whose southern end was the lay brothers' refectory, retains the whole of its simple vault, with a central row of pillars without capitals, for an unimpeded length of about three hundred feet; one has to remember that this was, in monastic times, subdivided by walls into several compartments. Other remains are of the guest houses and, across the river, of the bakery, the brewhouse, and other buildings needed by a large and self-supporting community. A two-arched bridge of the thirteenth century remains intact near the café, and gave separate access to these buildings. All the abbey remains, particularly the church as one sees it from the east, gain greatly from the beautifully landscaped setting created in the Georgian era.

Rievaulx Abbey As at Fountains the ruins profit greatly from their landscaped setting of Georgian parkland. The north–south flow of the river Rye, in a comparatively narrow valley and at one time closer to the abbey than it is now, meant that the abbey buildings are aligned north to south and not in the normal way.

Founded in 1131 Rievaulx was the first Cistercian abbey in Yorkshire, and it soon became a large and flourishing community. Though the remains of the lay brothers' quarters do not suggest that they were ever as many as the six hundred said to have been at Rievaulx in St. Aelred's time, the professed monks became numerous enough to justify great expansion of the church in the thirteenth century.

89 Kirkstall Abbey, Yorkshire (Cistercian): north transept arcade

Though much simple Romanesque work survives in the transepts, the long nave, Burgundian in its inspiration with its early pointed arches and transverse tunnel vaults in the aisles, has mostly disappeared, though some altars in its side chapels remain almost entire. The spectacular part of Rievaulx is seen in the Early-English remodelling of the eastern side of its transepts and in the seven-bay choir and presbytery limb which is also Early English, with clustered columns, moulded capitals, lancet windows, and also, as in Salisbury Cathedral, an important anticipation of Geometrical Gothic in its clerestorey openings. The vaults, unfortunately, have all collapsed.

A good deal, mostly of twelfth-century date, remains of the eastern domestic range. The chapter house, reduced in size when monastic numbers were smaller after 1400, was apsidal like that at Durham Cathedral. The finest domestic survival at Rievaulx is the refectory, a noble room of the thirteenth century which, in the normal Cistercian manner, runs at right angles to the adjacent cloister walk to allow for a warming house on one side and on the other for a kitchen to serve monks and lay brothers alike. The sloping site allowed for a large vaulted undercroft.

Kirkstall Abbey After a start elsewhere this Cistercian community settled, in 1152, on its site in the valley of the Aire. Originally, and till the time of the Industrial Revolution, its position was rural and remote; only in the nineteenth century was it engulfed in the outskirts of the growing city of Leeds. The buildings, with no changes in the dimensions of the church before the Dissolution, are still remarkably convincing, in some ways even more so than at Fountains and Rievaulx, in their display of Cistercian planning. The ruins are well preserved by the Leeds Corporation, a small museum being fitted out in the vaulted gatehouse on the other side of the main road.

The church still has the short presbytery of the twelfth-century plan. The quadripartite vault of this presbytery still stands, but the original windows were replaced, as in other abbeys, by a large window, transomed and of nine lights, in the Perpendicular style. The other Perpendicular addition, built early in the sixteenth century and perhaps by the designer of the great tower at Fountains, was the upper part of the central tower, two sides of which somewhat precariously survive. The transept chapels (three off each one) retain their barrel vaults. The nave, comparable with that at Fountains but in a slightly later style and still with groined vaults over its aisles, is remarkably intact, and its western doorway, of five orders under a shallow projecting gable, is a masterpiece of its period.

The domestic buildings which remain are mainly of the twelfth century. The chapter house, with two rounded entrance arches instead of the usual three, still has its ribbed vaulting over the original room and over the extension of the thirteenth century. Other rooms in the eastern range also have their vaults but the dormitory range is roofless. The abbot's house largely survives to the east of the dormitory and there are considerable remains of the lay brothers' range and of the projecting refectory and its adjacent kitchen. The *lavatorium*, or trough for the washing of hands, before and after meals, has some of its attractive trefoil-headed arcading of the middle years of the thirteenth century.

Mount Grace Priory Sited, near Northallerton, close beneath the western escarpment of the Cleveland Hills, Mount Grace is the only one of England's mediaeval Carthusian priories to leave substantial and convincing remains. The ruins, with their church and 'communal' buildings on a restricted scale, well show the difference between the Carthusian way of life and that of the other orders. As the priory was founded in 1398 its buildings were in the Perpendicular style, though with a few glances back at the earlier, or Decorated idiom.

The church was originally a plain rectangle, but late in the fifteenth century it got a westward extension, with two transeptal chapels and a short nave. These later portions, along with the earlier tower placed like the tower of a friary church, are the church's chief remains. The chapter house, the small refectory built for use on feast days, and other communal buildings lie along the southern range of the great cloister. So too did the prior's cell, with the ornamental feature of an upstairs oriel window. Most of the other cells were spaced out, at intervals, round the other three sides of the cloister. One of them has been re-roofed and reconstructed. Each 'cell' was in fact a cottage, with four ground-floor rooms, a garden, and a privy at the bottom of that garden.

Bridlington Priory The Augustinian priory here was founded in 1113 and became a large and important establishment. The fourteenth-century great gateway is the only domestic building still standing, but some richly ornamented arches from the Norman cloister arcade have been reconstructed and re-erected in the nave. Most fortunately the ten-bay nave was parochial before the Dissolution and remains as a parish church. It is the finest Augustinian nave still standing in England. As the destroyed choir limb was of eight bays the complete church must have been of great splendour, and the surviving nave is of great architectural importance.

Paired lancets in the north aisle show that the nave was started in the thirteenth century, but building was slow and was not complete till the fifteenth century. The eastern arches of the arcades, the glazed triforium, and some clerestorey windows of a triangular shape with curved sides, are early Decorated and show some affinity to work in York Minster. The western bays on the southern side were rebuilt in the Perpendicular period. Here again, and in the great

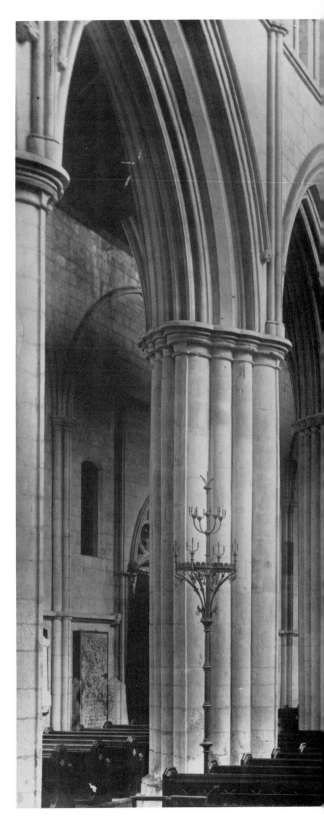

90 Bridlington Priory, Yorkshire (Augustinian): the nave

transomed west windows of nine lights, there are likenesses to what one sees at York. The west towers intended for the mediaeval priory were never built, and both of those now seen are, in their different ways, fine modern achievements.

An important internal feature is the tomb slab, with Romanesque designs and bird and animal carvings, of the black Tournai marble best known in Hampshire churches.

Bolton Priory   Notably attractive, and in a remote and picturesque setting, by the river Wharfe, like those of many Cistercian abbeys, this was in fact a priory of Augustinian canons. Its nave, being parochial before the Dissolution, remained in use, while the transepts and choir were, as at Fountains and Rievaulx, preserved as a romantic feature in a landscaped estate; one of the Georgian owners was that arch-Palladian the third Earl of Burlington.

Like many other mediaeval religious communities this one started elsewhere, but moved to Bolton in 1154. Transitional Norman work still exists in the north transept. But the original short presbytery was replaced, in the fourteenth century, by a fine presbytery, longer than its predecessor and still with fine Decorated features in its sequence of curvilinear panelling and in the tracery of windows here and in the transept. The effect of the changes must have been very much that of the unaisled but transeptal college chapels soon built at Oxford. The nave, with a north aisle, is Early English, the arcade and clerestorey being of no special distinction, but the south wall, with a set of paired lancets, has the rare feature of an alleyway cut in the thickness of the wall. In this it resembles the nave, surviving because it was parochial before the Dissolution, of the Benedictine nunnery church of Nun Monkton. The excellent Early English west front, with lancets, arcading, and panelling, survives just behind the eastern side of the imposing west tower which was started in 1520 but never finished; had the tower been completed the façade would have been pulled down to make way for a large tower arch.

The domestic buildings of the priory have almost disappeared, but the much altered great gateway still stands as the central part of the mansion owned by the Duke of Devonshire.

Easby Abbey*   Attractively sited in the valley of the Swale near Richmond this Premonstratensian abbey was founded about 1155, and the earliest parts are Transitional Norman. The river, and the drainage watercourse lie west of the abbey, so that the dormitory and its associated latrine block lay, as in Durham and Worcester cathedral priories, on this side of the cloister. Not much is left of the church bar some fourteenth-century remains of the south transept; the best ecclesiastical relic of the abbey is in the church at Richmond where the splendid early sixteenth-century choir stalls, being new and admired at the time of the Dissolution, were set up for preservation.

The finest relic of the abbey is the refectory, with remains of an undercroft of the thirteenth century and beautiful upper windows still with much of their early Decorated tracery. Much also remains of the western range, divided between the canons' quarters and the guest house, and ingeniously planned so that the canons and guests could use different storeys of the sanitary block while keeping all their quarters separate.

Malton Priory (at Old Malton)   This is the only place in England where part of a Gilbertine priory church is still used for worship. Founded in the middle of the twelfth century the priory was one for canons only and was not a double community of canons and nuns. What remains is most of the western part of the nave which was parochial before the Dissolution. The aisles were destroyed in the eighteenth century and, as at Holm Cultram about the same time, the clerestorey was eliminated. But there is a fine triforium stage, of the late twelfth century with pairs of pointed arches under round containing arches. Between the triforium bays the vault shafts have scalloped or early foliate capitals while the pillars which support the rounded arches of the arcades are round on the south side and octagonal (with one of them panelled in the late Perpendicular period) on the north. Most of the fine west front is Early English, but its fine doorway is rounded and has some Romanesque decoration. The north-west tower has almost wholly disappeared and, as in many other monastic churches, the original fenestration of the west wall has been replaced by a large transomed Perpendicular window whose upper part is now unglazed.

Nun Monkton Priory   A small Benedictine nunnery, founded in the twelfth century. The eastern part of the church was used by the nuns and has mostly been destroyed, along with the domestic buildings. But the unaisled nave, most of which was parochial, has survived, with much reconstruction at its eastern

91   Malton Priory, Yorkshire (Gilbertine): west front

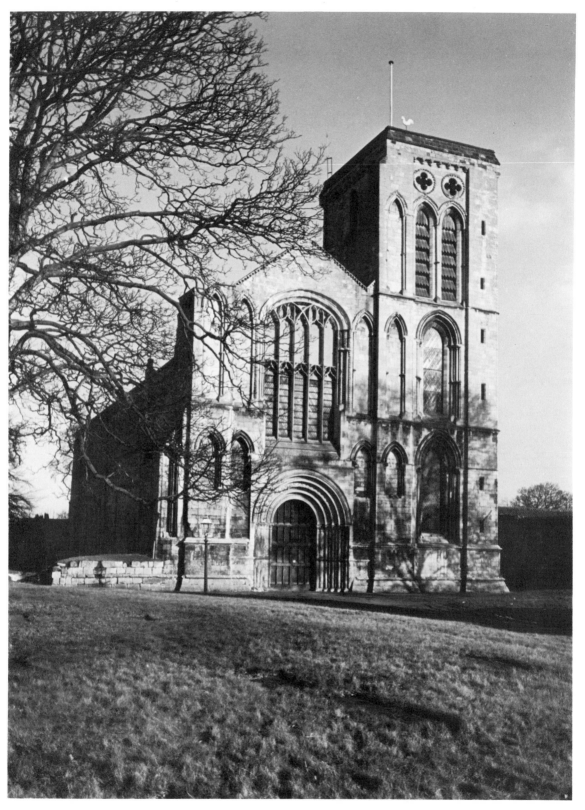

end in the 1870s. It is of great architectural rarity and interest, the design of its side walls being like that once seen in the unaisled nave of Ripon Minster.

The low western tower is of about 1200, and is narrower than the nave, so that the fabric comes down into the nave with its south-east and north-east corners upheld by sturdy internal piers. It has a fine western doorway; the five orders are moulded or have chevron moulding. The side windows of the nave are early lancets, simple from the outside but inside forming part of an unusual arrangement. A built-in alleyway runs, like a triforium passage, in the thickness of the wall. Each lancet has a plain rear arch and then a moulded inner arch whose shafts have annulets and moulded bases. Between each of these arches there is a pair of narrow arches whose shafts have annulets and which have, above each pair, a trefoil-headed blank arch. Each of these pairs of arches has a vertical edging strip, with dogtooth decoration for the more westerly groups but with more elaborate treatment in the eastern bays which may have been part of the nuns' section of the church.

LANCASHIRE (not including Furness)

Unlike Yorkshire, Lancashire outside Furness had few mediaeval religious houses, and has correspondingly few monastic remains. Only one abbey has here to be given detailed treatment. Of the other monasteries one need note only the thirteenth-century octagonal chapter house of the Premonstratensian abbey of Cockersand, vaulted with a central pillar and at least one trefoil-headed archway. It survived because the Georgian owners of the property turned it into a mausoleum.

Whalley Abbey* Founded in 1178 at Stanlaw in Cheshire this Cistercian community moved to Whalley in 1296, so that all the buildings were later than that date. The church, which had a ten-bay nave, has left few remains except for some portions of its south transept. Some of the eastern range survives, but the chief remains of the claustral buildings are in the western range, still roofed and with buttresses and windows of the Perpendicular period. There are two fine vaulted gateways, one of the fourteenth century, the other of the fifteenth.

CHESHIRE

Except for the church and splendid domestic buildings of St. Werburgh's Abbey at Chester, now Chester Cathedral and thus outside the scope of this section, little remains of Cheshire's none too numerous old monastic establishments. The particularly splendid Cistercian abbey of Vale Royal, whose church was over four hundred feet long, has almost wholly disappeared.

Birkenhead Priory This small Benedictine priory was founded about 1150, and from the fourteenth century the monks controlled the famous ferry crossing over the Mersey. The Transitional Norman north arcade of the nave still stood in the 1720s, but nowadays the best relic of the priory is the vaulted chapter house, also Transitional Norman. This was preserved because it long served the worshipping needs of a small hamlet whose great commercial and industrial expansion came much later than that of Liverpool across the Mersey. The fourteenth-century vaulted undercroft of the refectory stands beneath a modern structure. Much of the west range, with vault shafts of the cloister alleyway and mostly of the fourteenth century, also remains from the domestic buildings north of the church.

STAFFORDSHIRE

This is not a rich county for monastic remains, though there are some ruins of the Cistercian abbey of Croxden. At Burton-on-Trent the choir of the Benedictine abbey church, made collegiate for a few years after its dissolution in 1539, still stood till the eighteenth century when it was replaced by the present church.

Tutbury Priory A small priory of Benedictine monks, founded in the Norman period as a dependency of a Norman abbey, but 'denizen' from the fifteenth century. The nave was parochial and most of it, including some Norman Romanesque work of the highest quality, remained as the parish church to which Street added an apse in the 1860s. It is of six bays, and after the Dissolution the north aisle, on the cloister side of the church, was pulled down, being replaced in 1829. The clerestorey was also dismantled, and a new one was created by glazing the triforium openings. Apart from the eastern part of the south aisle, rebuilt in the Decorated period, the old portions of the church are nearly all Norman Romanesque.

92　Birkenhead Priory, Cheshire (Benedictine): the chapter house

The six-bay arcades have round or quatrefoil pillars, and the west wall has two tiers of fine arcading and an ornate frame to the main west window. More spectacular, and proving that even a small priory could boast architecture of outstanding quality, is the west front. This has interlaced arcading, rich window decoration, and ornamented roundels, while the great west doorway, of five orders with beakheads and foliate, human, and animal carvings as well as the more usual zig-zag decoration, is among the most splendid in the country. The southern doorway, of three orders and with a boar-hunting scene on the lintel below a plain tympanum, is also outstanding.

DERBYSHIRE

This county had few monastic houses, with only the Augustinian abbey of Darley, near Derby, of even moderate importance. The site of the small Premonstratensian abbey of Beauchief is now within the city of Sheffield; the western end of its nave, with a fine doorway of the thirteenth century, is now the tower of a post-Reformation church. At Repton a fair amount of the small Augustinian priory is incorporated in the buildings of Repton School. Professor Pevsner has pointed out the importance, as an early example of brick architecture in an area away from England's more pioneering districts in the architectural use of brick, of the tower which was added, not long after 1437, to the prior's lodgings.

NOTTINGHAMSHIRE

The county had a moderate number of religious houses, including Welbeck which was reckoned as the chief Premonstratensian abbey in England. Monastic relics there are scanty, but there are some remains of the Carthusian priory of Beauvale, and at Newstead, one of the priories which was upgraded to an abbey by later romanticists, the fine Geometrical Gothic west front stands as an adjunct to the 'Gothick' mansion of the Byrons.

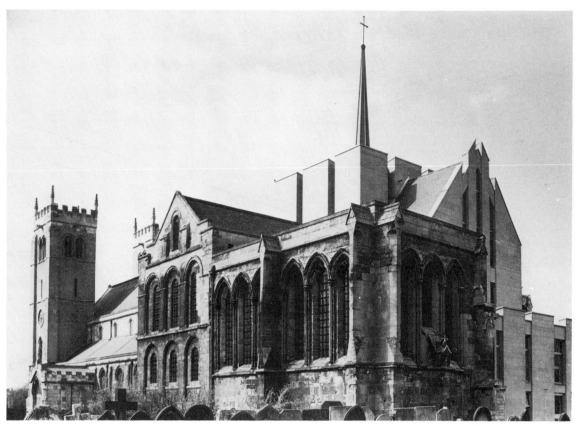

94 Worksop Priory, Nottinghamshire (Augustinian) as recently extended

Blyth Priory Though it represents only about half of the original building this is a notably important church in a beautiful village. Founded in 1088 as a 'cell' of a Benedictine abbey in Rouen it became independent in the fifteenth century. Five bays of a six-bay nave were parochial, being wholly shut off from the monks' part of the church. They thus remained, with the addition of a fine Perpendicular tower whose battlements are conjoined, in a rare manner, by ogee-shaped pinnacles.

The main fabric of the nave is most impressive in an early Norman manner, with shafted piers whose capitals have primitive volutes. The northern triforium arches now have Perpendicular windows, but the open gallery is still on the southern side. The simple Norman clerestorey has been little altered, but the nave, in the manner of that now at Gloucester

93 Tutbury Priory, Staffordshire (Benedictine): west doorway, twelfth century

Cathedral, has a simple thirteenth-century vault. The southern aisle was widened for parish use, and given new windows, with 'basket' tracery, about 1300.

Worksop Priory This was an important house of Augustinian canons, probably founded soon after 1119 and eventually with a church nearly three hundred feet long. The nave was preserved thanks to its parochial use, and the church is also of great interest for extensions finished as recently as 1974. Little now remains of the domestic buildings which lay north of the church, but the great gatehouse, mostly of the fourteenth century and with an attractive little chapel projecting on its southern side, is of notable splendour.

The crossing and transepts are neo-Norman of the 1920s, but the Early English lady chapel, which ran out east from the original south transept, has been re-roofed and restored from its former dereliction. The main glory of the church is the splendid late Romanesque nave of about 1180, of nine bays plus another between the two western towers which are also, with later battlements and pinnacles, of the late twelfth century. The aisles are vaulted, and the detail of the arcades, with their alternating round or octagonal columns, and of the triforium arches above them, is of great beauty and in some ways unusual. The small arches fitted in between the main triforium arches are a rare feature. So too is the placing, above those arches and not above those of the arcades or the main triforium openings, of the clerestorey windows. The result is that the nave is of a somewhat modest height, not really enough for its imposing length.

In recent years a short eastern limb, and a low tower with a delicate flèche, have been added to the church from distinctively modern designs by Mr. Laurence King. As the new altar, square in shape, is under the tower the new 'chancel' is imposingly filled by the organ, while spacious vestries lie further to the east on part of the site of the destroyed choir limb of the Austin canons.

LEICESTERSHIRE

This county is not well-off for monastic remains, and there is hardly anything to see of the large and important Augustinian abbey at Leicester which was the county's chief religious house. Part of the nave of the small Augustinian abbey church at Owston remains, in a much altered state, as the parish church.

Ulverscroft Priory   Leicestershire's best old monastic remains are here, charmingly set on a picturesque site in the Charnwood Forest country. The priory was a small house of Augustinian canons. Founded in the 1130s it was dissolved in 1534, but its good repute was such that it was, most unusually, refounded for another five years. A fair amount is left both of the church and of the domestic buildings. The plan of the church was that of a plain rectangle, without transepts but with a fourteenth-century western tower of which much still stands. In the sanctuary some good Decorated windows have the rare feature, also seen in the choir of Lichfield Cathedral, of quatrefoil panelling round their inner jambs.

LINCOLNSHIRE

This large county had many mediaeval monastic foundations, but is poorly off for extensive monastic remains. At Thornton, in the north, the great gateway of the Augustinian abbey is among the most impress-

95   Croyland Abbey, Lincolnshire (Benedictine): the west front

ive in the country, and considerable remains have been excavated, and then covered over, at the Benedictine site of Bardney.

Croyland Abbey This was a great Benedictine house, of Anglo-Saxon origin, on an 'island' in the fen country not far from Peterborough and Thorney. Its church was replaced, twice over, by Norman Romanesque buildings; a crossing arch and some arcading at the west end remain from the second of these churches. The west front also has a fine doorway of the thirteenth century, also panelling and statues which flank, and surmount, the frame of a large west window from the Perpendicular rebuilding of the nave and its western towers. The whole of this nave survived the Dissolution as the local parish church, but the central roof fell in 1720, and the north aisle alone now remains in parochial use. It is a fine, simply vaulted building of the fifteenth century, while the sturdy north-western tower has a curiously stumpy and unimpressive spire. The fifteenth-century screen originally parted the lady chapel, at this Abbey in the north transept, from the rest of the crossing.

NORTHAMPTONSHIRE

This is not a good county for monastic remains, for very little remains of the several pre-Reformation religious houses once within its borders. The Cluniac and Augustinian houses in Northampton itself have left virtually no remains, but just outside the town the mansion of De La Pré Abbey (now the County Record Office) preserves, in its quadrangular plan but without surviving mediaeval features or details, the layout of an abbey of Cluniac nuns. At Canons' Ashby the western part of the nave of a small priory of Augustinian canons is still, with some good Early English features, in use as the parish church.

SHROPSHIRE

Shrewsbury Abbey Founded by Roger de Montgomery not long after the Norman Conquest, this became one of the most important Benedictine monasteries in the Welsh Marches. The transepts and the original east end have gone, but as the nave was used before the Dissolution as a parish church, it survived, though mutilated by the loss of its clerestorey, as the parish church of this part of the town. The western range of the domestic buildings still stood about 1830, but was soon destroyed, along with

other remains to the south of the church, when Telford drove a new road through the site. The one good fragment of the domestic buildings is the refectory pulpit of the fourteenth century.

The eastern three bays of the nave are simple Norman work with squat cylindrical pillars of a typically West Midland type. The triforium arches of these bays were glazed to replace the old clerestorey, but the triforium stage is lacking in the nave's two western bays which are early Perpendicular work, as also is the western tower with its excellent west window of seven lights. The whole of the nave clerestorey is Victorian work by Pearson, who also designed the dignified crossing, chancel, and sanctuary which were added to the church in the 1880s.

Much Wenlock Priory Another foundation of Roger de Montgomery, this was an important Cluniac priory, and one of the two in England of which there are still important remains. The Norman church was replaced by a large and splendid building, most of which can be dated from the thirteenth century. Much of its south transept still stands, along with a fair amount of the southern side of the nave, where three bays of the aisle retain their vaulting, built low enough for a room to be sited above it. The best Norman relic is the ruined chapter house, with interlaced wall arcading of high quality. A building to the east of the dormitory site was part of the infirmary, while the prior's house, a building of about 1500 of purely domestic character, has panelled walling between two continuous tiers of late Perpendicular windows.

Buildwas Abbey Pleasantly set in the Severn Valley near the early industrial sites of Ironbridge and Coalbrookdale, Buildwas is one of the best Cistercian ruins in England. Originally Savignac, it was founded in 1135, and almost all its buildings were finished in the twelfth century and remained unaltered till the Dissolution. The abbey, whose domestic buildings were on the northern side, had a typically Cistercian plan. Most of the church remains except for the aisle walls of the nave which has seven bays, Transitional Norman work with no triforium and early pointed arches. A good deal also survives of the crossing arches, of the low central tower, of the transepts, and of the presbytery with its large eastern lancets. The fine vaulted chapter house and the parlour, likewise vaulted, are the best remains of the domestic buildings.

96 Much Wenlock Priory, Shropshire (Cluniac): chapter house, Norman arcading

97 Buildwas Abbey, Shropshire (Cistercian): view looking east

Haughmond Abbey This important, attractively sited Augustinian house not far from Shrewsbury was founded about 1135 and attained moderate wealth and importance. A sloping site meant that the high altar was approached up several steps, while the domestic buildings were more irregularly planned than in most mediaeval monasteries. Very little of the church survives, and the best remains of the main cloister are the *lavatorium* and the chapter house. The *lavatorium*, near the refectory which had round-headed windows and small-scale arcading, has two good round-headed recesses. The chapter house was lengthened eastwards, and given an apse, not long before the Dissolution, but the finest feature of the whole abbey ruins is its entrance arch with its two flanking windows, all excellent round-arched Transitional Norman work, with side shafts but with canopied statues inserted, in the fourteenth century, between those shafts.

More spectacular remains are those of the outer courtyard, lying south of the main cloisters, and with the infirmary, an excellent building with Decorated

98 Haughmond Abbey, Shropshire (Augustinian): chapter house entrance

windows, in that position because the hill slope to the east prevented the canons from building their infirmary on the normal eastward site. The abbot's house, with an attractive oriel window of about 1500, adjoins its eastern end.

Lilleshall Abbey Not far from Newport in a remote site more like that of many Cistercian monasteries, this was an abbey, originally Arrouaisian (see page 20), but soon fully Augustinian, which got established on its present site about the middle of the twelfth century. As in some other religious houses of small or modest size the church and the other buildings changed little after their main completion about 1200. The long nave was always unaisled, and the presbytery was never lengthened, though it got a large Decorated east window. The best remains are those of the church. The ruins of the presbytery, crossing, and transepts are late Norman or Transitional, with a notably splendid late Norman doorway which led from the cloisters into the church. The nave had a western tower, and the west doorway is of great splendour, round-headed yet 'Early English' in its shafts, mouldings, stiff-leaf capitals, and dogtooth ornament. There are some remains of the domestic buildings, particularly of the refectory and of the northern half of the eastern range.

HEREFORDSHIRE

Leominster Priory   Early religious houses in this town had a somewhat chequered history, and the priory, whose important nave still stands was found-ed, in 1123, as a 'cell' of Henry I's great Benedictine abbey at Reading. It retained its dependent status till the Dissolution, and was the richest monastery in the country still holding that subordinate position. The monastic part of the church, and the domestic buildings on the northern side, have disappeared, but as the nave was used, before the Dissolution, as the parish church it remains and is, on several counts, of great interest. As an outer south aisle was added in the fourteenth century the present church is almost as wide as it is long. The tower, Norman in its lower part but with two upper stages of the Perpendicular period, is at the west end of the original nave.

The oldest part of the church is the Norman nave, still with its narrow north aisle and with short cylindrical columns of a West Midland type. The triforium and clerestorey are comparatively plain, but the west doorway, whose shafts have richly carved capitals of a sculptural type akin to other work in Herefordshire, is slightly pointed. Two of the nave bays have their arches unusually stiffened by the insertion of masonry which leaves room for only very narrow arches between squared masonry surfaces. This was to allow for the extra weight of a vault, perhaps a tunnel vault intended to be like one at Reading of which no traces remain. In such a case the Leominster vault would have recalled that over the third church of the great Burgundian abbey at Cluny to which, in its early days, Reading Abbey was subject.

In the thirteenth century the south aisle of the nave was widened to make a new parish nave; this was later given a large Perpendicular west window, with two of its mullions widened to make buttresses in the manner of similar windows at Gloucester. The outer south aisle is fine Decorated work, with particularly rich ballflower ornament round its windows and on the mullions and tracery.

Abbey Dore   This is one of the most satisfying monastic sites in the country, largely because it is the only example in England of a Cistercian choir limb still used for worship. Never a large or wealthy abbey before the Dissolution it is more famous for the restoration of its eastern part in the Laudian period of the seventeenth century, and for its continued preservation.

The abbey was founded about the middle of the twelfth century, but the transepts, the chapels leading off them, the first bay of the presbytery, and the remains of the nave are from the late twelfth-century transition from Romanesque to early Gothic. The eastern bays of the presbytery, with a most attractive ambulatory, square-ended and vaulted and with five chapels leading off it, are Early English work not much later than 1200. Little building work seems to have been done after this eastward elongation.

After the Dissolution the nave was destroyed and the eastern limb, though kept for parochial use, seems to have become almost ruinous. Then in the 1630s it was re-roofed, re-furnished, and put back into use by Viscount Scudamore, a high churchman of the Laudian persuasion who was influenced by advice from Archbishop Laud himself; the restored church was reconsecrated in 1635. The ceiling, the screen, the seating in the choir, the western gallery, and other items are all important Renaissance woodwork of that period, and the fine glass in the eastern lancets is dated 1633. The rescue of Abbey Dore is a parallel to what happened, in the same century, at Cartmel, Bath Abbey, and Thorney.

Craswall Priory   Sited in a deep valley in the Black Mountains country this site, of more than Cistercian remoteness, has England's only substantial remains of one of the country's few priories of the Grandmontines – an order whose austere self-denial exceeded even that of the Carthusians. The priory was founded in the thirteenth century and the remains are of that period, with some features derived from the order's mother house of Grandmont near Limoges. Such are the rounded apse in the French manner, the chapter house running north and south in a narrow eastern range and, on the north of the sanctuary, the chapel recalling the reliquary chapel of St. Stephen of Muret, the founder of the Grandmontines. Although the ruins are much overgrown and partially masked by their own debris it has recently been noted that the surviving walls have been little disturbed.

Herefordshire also has, at Aconbury, the nave of a small priory of Austin canonesses, at Garway the

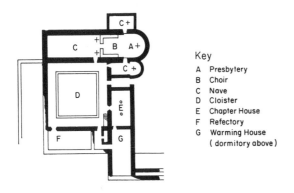

99 Craswall Priory (Grandmontine): plan

Key
A Presbytery
B Choir
C Nave
D Cloister
E Chapter House
F Refectory
G Warming House
(dormitory above)

eastern limb of a Templars' church and the partially exposed foundations of its circular nave, and near Goodrich, among farm buildings, the refectory of the small Augustinian priory of Flanesford which was founded as late as 1346.

WARWICKSHIRE

Though the county had several pre-Reformation religious houses it is not well-off for impressive monastic remains. The large gate chapel of the Cistercian abbey of Merevale is now the parish church, while the Cistercian main gateway of Stoneleigh, an attractive work of the fourteenth century, still stands and was used by Augustus Pugin as a model for some gateways of his own. At Kenilworth a gateway and some fairly important excavated remains of the Augustinian abbey can be seen, while in two places one has the towers and spires of friary churches. At Atherstone the chancel and late fourteenth-century tower and spire of the parish church are the choir and steeple of an Augustinian friary, while at Coventry the beautiful octagonal tower and tall spire of the Franciscan church is one of the three steeples which give the centre of the city its famous silhouette.

Temple Balsall   Here one has the unusually interesting church of a Templars' preceptory, rebuilt about 1290 only a few years before the suppression of the Knights Templar. The church, of four bays, is rectangular and resembles a college chapel. It has an east window of five lights and side windows of three or four, all fine work of the 'geometrical' Gothic period. Till the Dissolution the church was owned by the Knights Hospitaller. It then fell into decay but in 1662

was re-roofed and restored as an almshouse chapel. It became a parish church about 1850, with restoration, and another new roof, by George Gilbert Scott.

WORCESTERSHIRE

The county was part of the strongly Benedictine area in the lower Severn basin, and its most important religious houses were Benedictine. Worcester Cathedral was served by Benedictine monks, and another Benedictine abbey of great importance was at Evesham, where the remains are scanty except for the detached bell tower, richly panelled but never given its intended fan vault, which was built a few years before the Dissolution. Of the county's other religious houses the most notable remaining examples are as follows:

Pershore Abbey   A religious house of some kind was established here late in the seventh century, and the abbey was fully Benedictine from about 983. As in other abbeys the Anglo-Saxon church was wholly replaced by a large Romanesque building; the remains of the nave arcade and various details in the south transept show that it much resembled the abbey church at Tewkesbury and was probably designed by the same master mason.

By the time of the Dissolution most of the parishioners used the abbey nave, so that part of the church would in any case have been saved. But they arranged to exchange the nave for the transepts and choir limb. The north transept fell down in 1686, but most of the rest of the abbey church still stands as an extremely beautiful monastic relic.

The south transept and the crossing arches remain from the comparatively early Norman church. The east wall of the transept may have had a 'four-tier' elevation with a two-storeyed triforium; the present rib vault is of the fifteenth century. The presbytery, with its clustered columns and deeply moulded arches, is an extremely fine eastward extension in the Early English style, of architectural note in that its triforium passage and clerestorey are run into a single stage. Its eastern bay cants inwards to connect with the arch into the lady chapel which was pulled down at the Dissolution. The aisles retain their simple vaults, but the central space had to be re-roofed after a bad fire in 1288 and the present vault is an extremely fine lierne vault, with rich foliate bosses, of the early Decorated period. The beautiful lantern tower, a work of high architectural quality, is of about the same period.

Great Malvern Priory One of the best monastic churches of medium size which is still in use, the priory church shows a remarkable contrast between the simple Norman architecture of its earliest parts and the more ornate Perpendicular of its massive rebuilding in the fifteenth century. It also has some of the finest late mediaeval glass in the country, and, thanks to the priory's ownership of a tile kiln which supplied tiles all over the Midlands and western counties, it has England's largest accumulation of mediaeval tiles, some of them dating to the 1450s.

Founded in 1085 the priory was at first a dependency of Westminster Abbey but later became independent. The nave has a simple Norman arcade with stocky cylindrical pillars of a West Midland type; there is no triforium and the clerestorey stage was rebuilt with large Perpendicular windows. The south transept has disappeared and the north transept, curiously lower than the nave and presbytery, is part of the great rebuilding of the fifteenth century. The tower has an attractive lierne vault, and a vault was also planned for the admirable Perpendicular presbytery, which actually has an almost flat timber ceiling. The best exterior feature is the central tower, clearly akin, with its panelling and traceried battlements and pinnacles, to that at Gloucester Cathedral.

Little Malvern Priory An interesting example of a small Benedictine house whose rebuilding was due to a reforming bishop late in the fifteenth century. Of Norman foundation the priory had, by 1480, fallen into great decay and indiscipline. Bishop Alcock of Worcester (for whose later activities see page 58) visited the priory, sent the monks to Gloucester Abbey for two years to re-learn the principles of the monastic life, rebuilt the eastern part of the church and in 1482 allowed most of the monks to return. The priory continued, so far as one knows satisfactorily despite its small numbers, till 1536. The transepts and south chapels have been destroyed; what remains is the presbytery along with the crossing and the central tower. All this is Perpendicular work of the fifteenth century, mostly simple but with a panelled tower and a large east window. The church has some fine glass of Alcock's time.

GLOUCESTERSHIRE and BRISTOL

Gloucestershire was particularly well filled with religious houses, and the expression 'as sure as God's in Gloucestershire' is said to have arisen from this monastic abundance. The great Benedictine abbey church of St. Peter's at Gloucester became Gloucester Cathedral under Henry VIII, and the same change to cathedral status came to the eastern half of St. Augustine's abbey at Bristol. Of the remaining abbeys some, like Winchcombe, Hayles, and Cirencester have massively disappeared, but a few others have left important remains.

Tewkesbury Abbey Apart from Westminster Abbey, and some of the monastic churches which are now cathedrals, this is the most splendid mediaeval monastic church remaining in England, remarkable not only for its architecture, but for the finest and most historic group of mediaeval tombs and chantries erected, by members of great aristocratic families, in any church apart from Westminster Abbey. This Benedictine abbey had been re-founded and augmented, late in the eleventh century, by Robert Fitzhamon, one of whose daughters married Robert Fitzroy, Earl of Gloucester. The abbey then became the chief burial place of the Earls of Gloucester, or of those who succeeded to the Earldom's great estates. It was also, after the battle of Tewkesbury in 1471, the resting place of Edward, Prince of Wales, and of many Lancastrians who died in the battle, while the Duke of Clarence, Edward IV's brother, is also buried there. The parishioners had the use of the nave, but after the Dissolution they bought the rest of the church, bar the splendid eastern lady chapel, with its apsidal termination, for parochial use. Some late Perpendicular panelling, which once adorned the inner side of the northern cloister walk, remains along the outer side of the wall of the nave's south aisle, but otherwise hardly anything, except for the abbot's house and the main gateway which led in from the town, remains of the domestic buildings.

The church, architecturally akin to the older parts of Pershore Abbey, is mainly a great Norman Romanesque building. Even in the apsidal presbytery, where the arcade and the upper stages were reconstructed in the fourteenth century, the moulded arches rise from cut-down cylindrical columns (once as high as those in the nave) of the Norman period. The nave has simple Norman arches on tall round pillars like those once standing at Pershore, while its pairs of triforium arches have in part been masked by a fourteenth-century vault. The most striking Norman features are the west front with its great retaining arch and twin turrets, and the central tower whose arcaded upper stages, of about 1140, make it the finest Norman tower in England.

The earliest important addition to the abbey was a

100 Tewkesbury Abbey (Benedictine): Norman west front, window now of 1686

101 Tewkesbury Abbey: presbytery and tombs

large chapel, with a 'nave' of four bays and a sanctuary of two, which was added, somewhat awkwardly, onto the end of the north transept. It was built in the thirteenth century, in an early Gothic style, with some details, particularly its stiff-leaf foliage and some decoration on the arch which parted the sanctuary from the rest of the chapel, which suggest a date not long after 1200. A fine doorway, deeply moulded and with five shafts on each side, leads through to the north transept. The 'nave' of this chapel was destroyed at the Dissolution, and its sanctuary was much altered, with Decorated windows and fairly simple vaulting, on a 'Union Jack' pattern and with bosses displaying the Clare and Despenser arms, in the fourteenth century. But much of its fine trefoil-headed arcading, with spandrel carvings not unlike those in the 'elder' lady chapel at Bristol Cathedral, remains, though some of it was harshly interrupted by an arch of the fourteenth century which was cut through to link this chapel of St. Nicholas with the larger one of St. James (now without its vault) which in the fourteenth century replaced the apsidal Norman chapel of the north transept. All this part of the abbey, though it gets less attention than the choir and its radiating chapels, is important for the somewhat piecemeal growth and development of a great monastic church.

The most spectacular part of the abbey is its presbytery limb. The Norman aisles and ambulatory were simply vaulted late in the thirteenth century or soon after 1300, while the main transformation of the eastern part of the church came in the first third of the fourteenth century. The radiating chapels were soon replaced by a splendid group, apsidal like those of a French chevet and elaborately vaulted. In these, and under the new arches of the presbytery, there is the abbey's superb group of canopied tombs and chantries, particularly those of the Despensers, their heiresses, and the ladies' husbands, and the chantry chapel, erected early in the fifteenth century, of Robert Fitzhamon. The transformation of the presbytery, and the building of its rich and complex vault, was probably carried out by the Despensers, shortly before their fall in 1326, in the peak period of their wealth and political influence; it has been suggested that masons of the 'Court' school may have been involved in the design work. The splendid glass in the presbytery windows must have been put in about 1340, and completes the decoration of this great

102 Tewkesbury Abbey: tomb of Hugh Despenser, d 1359

burial place of the feudal aristocracy. The building of the large lady chapel, with a low entrance arch but a fairly high vault, was part of this same process of expansion. The vault of the nave, comparatively simple and less beautiful than that over the presbytery but with fine bosses showing the life of Christ, is another work of the fourteenth century, as also are the curvilinear windows of the nave aisles.

Under the tower some fourteenth-century stalls and misericords remain from the monastic fittings. On the northern side their ornamented backing survives, but opposite to them this work has gone to make way for the organ, in its Jacobean case, which was originally at Magdalen College, Oxford. By Cromwell's orders it was moved to the chapel at Hampton Court where Milton probably played on it. Later returned to Magdalen it was sold to Tewkesbury in the eighteenth century.

Deerhurst priory The church here is particularly well known for its Anglo-Saxon architectural features, most notably the triangular-headed openings on the east side of the tower, for the ruins of its apsidal choir, and for the remains of the chapels built on each side of the eighth-century nave. As a monastery Deerhurst was of more importance in the Anglo-Saxon period than it was after its gift, before the Norman Conquest by King Edward the Confessor, to the abbey of St. Denis near Paris. As an 'alien' priory it was taken over by the Crown in the fifteenth century, and after a spell of ownership by Eton College it became a cell of Tewkesbury a few miles away. The few monks in residence presumably used the apsidal Saxon choir, while the nave, with its attractive Early English arcades and fourteenth-century clerestorey windows was, and has remained, the parish church. The eastern range of the domestic buildings, late Gothic with early Tudor alterations, still stands south of the church.

St. James' Priory, Bristol Founded about 1129 by Robert Fitzroy, Earl of Gloucester, this small Benedictine priory was always a cell of the abbey at Tewkesbury. It was closely associated with Bristol Castle and it was here, not in the more imposing church at Tewkesbury, that Earl Robert was buried after his death in 1148. Most of the nave seems soon to have been used by the laity, and in 1374 it became a full parish church. The much-restored tower dates from about this time.

The monastic half of the church and the domestic buildings were largely standing about 1630, but have now disappeared. What now remains, and is still used for worship, is the western part (five bays out of six) of the Norman nave, comparatively simple Norman work with a clerestorey but no triforium, and with a south aisle widened about 1698 and a Victorian outer north aisle. The western façade, perhaps finished about 1150, has interlaced arcading and a much-worn wheel window whose design looks forward to wheel windows of the early Gothic period.

Leonard Stanley Priory An attractive and complete small priory church, most of it Norman and with an unusual history. Founded in the 1120s for Augustinian canons it was soon abandoned by the Augustinians and became a Benedictine cell of St. Peter's Abbey at Gloucester; some of its admirable Norman work may date from after the transfer. Unaisled and cruciform, with a tower on a rectangular rather than a square plan, the church is mainly an excellent late Norman building, with some elaborate shafted doorways adorned with zig-zag moulding and, round the north doorway, a hood mould with dragon's head finials like those at Malmesbury. The top stages of the tower and several windows are of the fourteenth century, but the south transept, which seems once to have had a projecting chapel, has its Norman fenestration, and on the south side of the nave three Norman windows are set high, with very deep splays, to allow for the northern cloister walk. The tower arches are simple, with paired wall shafts. The presbytery has shafts for a vault which may never have been built; the main shafts have sculptured capitals of outstanding Romanesque sculptured quality. The western part of the nave was parochial before the suppression; the lower arch of its rood loft stair brutally intrudes on a fine cusped tomb of the fourteenth century.

Flaxley Abbey The remains of this attractively sited abbey in the Forest of Dean are the most substantial of any of Gloucestershire's Cistercian houses, there being more to see than there is of the larger monasteries of Kingswood and Hayles. The abbey was founded in the middle years of the twelfth century, and its economic resources included an important iron forge. The monastic remains form part of a country mansion not normally open to the public. Of the church some of the wall of the southern nave aisle still stands as the backing of a Georgian orangery. But the best surviving portion is the western range, with its fine, simply vaulted lay brothers' cellarium of the second half of the twelfth century. Upstairs there

103 Leonard Stanley Priory, Gloucestershire (Benedictine cell): general view

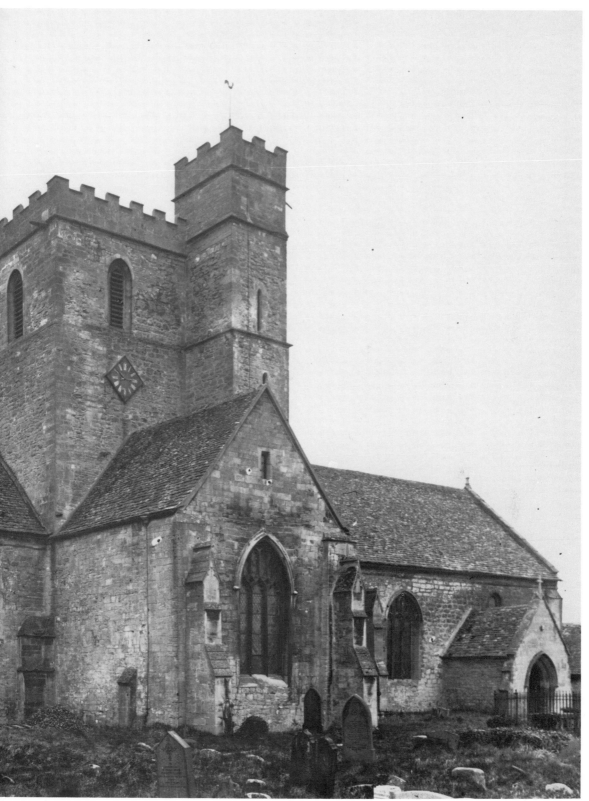

have been many alterations, but the southern end of this range was well remodelled, in the fourteenth century, as the abbot's residence.

Gloucester, St. Oswald's Priory The comparatively scanty remains of this priory are among the few monastic ruins in England to display above-ground Anglo-Saxon work. The monastery here, in the Saxon period of more consequence than St. Peter's Abbey, had an important history before the Norman Conquest. It may have been the burial place of the sainted King Oswald of Northumbria, and may also have contained the graves of Ethelfleda, the redoubtable 'Lady of the Mercians' and of her husband Ethelred. Most of the present ruins come from the northern arcade and north transept of a later priory of Augustinian canons, but in the eastern bay the upper arch above an arch of the Norman period is probably Anglo-Saxon work of the tenth century, while recent excavations have shown that the church had side chapels of the type misleadingly known as 'porticus' and, from the tenth century, the important Carolingian feature of a western apse.

Gloucester, Dominican Friary Gloucester is one of England's best towns for friary remains, having substantial survivals of both its Dominican and its Franciscan friaries.

Of the Dominican friary one has most of the eastern half of the cruciform church, partly of the thirteenth century but with a later north transept. After the suppression the building was turned into a house by a rich clothier, Sir Thomas Bell, and the various Tudor windows are of his time. The church is now being slowly restored, with the removal of floors, fireplaces, and other domestic insertions, by the Department of the Environment. Sir Thomas Bell used the domestic buildings as a cloth manufactory. Some of the west range still stands, but the most important survival is the southern range, whose upper floor has small square-headed windows and study recesses contrived in the thickness of the side walls; this room could have been used as a library by the members of this learned and studious order.

Gloucester, Franciscan Friary The thirteenth-century buildings of this friary have disappeared, and nothing remains of its choir or central tower. But most of the nave, rebuilt in the late Perpendicular style of the early sixteenth century, still stands and is preserved as a historic ruin. Its western end is masked by the façade of a dignified Georgian house, but one still has much of the arcade, with its slender pillars and

arches still fairly acute, which parted the nave from its single, northern aisle. The aisle, probably fitted out as a chantry chapel for the Berkeleys who had founded the friary and who rebuilt its church, had a splendid east window and, on its outer side, large windows with panelling below and between them.

Bristol, Dominican Friary These important remains exist because the buildings were, as in the Dominican friary at Newcastle on Tyne, used after the suppression by some of Bristol's trade guilds or companies. Some of the buildings were later bought, for various social uses, by the Quakers whose Bristol Meeting House already stood within the friary site – hence the present name of Quakers' Friars for the buildings which now, in an excellent act of re-use of historic buildings vacated by their previous occupants, serve jointly as the Bristol Register Office and as the permanent planning exhibition of the Bristol Planning Department.

The friary was founded in the thirteenth century, but the nave seems to have been rebuilt two centuries later, as part of a large Perpendicular window remained, till recent years, *in situ* in a garage wall and has been reinstated elsewhere in the buildings. The main survivals of the mediaeval friary are two parallel buildings. The larger, of the thirteenth century but much restored in the Victorian period, lay along the southern side of the cloisters and may have been the friars' dormitory or a library-cum-work room. It has a fine triplet of trefoil-headed lancets moved from the smaller hall, a timber roof largely of the fourteenth century, and a two-light Decorated window whose tracery resembles some in the contemporary choir of Bristol Cathedral. The original purpose of the other room, long the Bakers' Hall, is uncertain; it has a fine timber roof, about seven hundred years old, which was very well restored in 1974.

OXFORDSHIRE

In Oxford itself the chief monastic remains, apart from the cathedral which was the main part of St. Frideswide's Augustinian priory, are those of some of the monastic colleges. In Worcester College a picturesque late mediaeval feature is the row of varied *camerae*, or separate residences for the student monks of different Benedictine abbeys which were part of Gloucester Hall. The Marian foundation of Trinity College has a fifteenth-century range, with later dormer windows, of the Benedictine Durham College, while the most imposing buildings with a monastic collegiate background are the fine fifteenth-century gatehouse, the western range, and part of the southern range of the Cistercian St. Bernard's College where buildings put up for student monks were found a new use, in Mary I's reign, as the college of St. John the Baptist.

Dorchester Abbey   This small town near the confluence of the Thames and Thame held an important place in the early ecclesiastical history of Wessex and by the end of the Anglo-Saxon period was the headquarters of the large, unwieldy diocese which stretched right across England from Oxfordshire to the Humber, and whose cathedral, from 1092, was at Lincoln. Secular canons continued to serve the church for some decades, but in 1140 Bishop Alexander of Lincoln replaced them with a community of Augustinian canons, replacing the older church by a Norman one whose nave partly remains, but whose cruciform plan was obliterated, bar the western wall of the south transept, by the reconstruction of the eastern half of the church in the thirteenth and fourteenth centuries. The whole of the church was happily preserved, for parish use, after the suppression, and much of its architecture is of great interest and rarity. The south aisle divides, at its east end, into a double chapel, while in the sanctuary the three Decorated windows are remarkable in that they are completely traceried, without the usual vertical mullions. The east window has, in the middle, a strange pier, projecting inwards in a triangular shape and acting as a central buttress, while all the windows have small figures and other carved decoration on their tracery, one of them being a 'Jesse' window with some of the relevant figures on the stonework. Other Decorated work in the abbey is excellent in a more usual way, and the church has some important tombs and good glass.

BUCKINGHAMSHIRE

A poor county for monastic remains, only two sites calling for separate notice.

Chetwode Priory, a few miles from Buckingham, was a small foundation, of the thirteenth century, for Augustinian canons. Its poverty brought about its closure in the fifteenth century, and it became a cell of the much larger Augustinian abbey of Notley. Its cruciform church then became the parish church, but the nave, crossing, and transepts have since disappeared, the present low tower being seventeenth-

century Gothic work. What remains is the presbytery, with a northern chapel largely of the fourteenth century; there is enough to prove that even a small monastic church could, in its initial building, have architecture of high quality. The Early English work at Chetwode is remarkably good, with a splendid set of five eastern lancets and fine side lancets in sets of three. The church also has the rarity of some excellent thirteenth-century glass.

Burnham Abbey   This was a comparatively late foundation of Augustinian canonesses, made in 1266 by Richard, Earl of Cornwall, the brother of Henry III. The remaining buildings are now (see pages 100 and 109) occupied by the Anglican sisters of the Precious Blood.

Not much remains of the unaisled church of the original nunnery, and although the refectory range outlasted the Dissolution to become the main element in the mansion of the Wentworth family most of it was pulled down after about 1830; a fine late mediaeval fireplace and a brick doorway and fireplace of the Elizabethan period can still, however, be seen. The best remains of the mediaeval nunnery are in its infirmary block, and in the eastern range of the cloister buildings, where the Early English chapter house, with a single doorway and three eastern lancets, is the chapel of the present community. Additional modern buildings have also been put up to serve their needs.

HERTFORDSHIRE

The great Benedictine abbey of St. Alban's was overwhelmingly dominant in this county, and the remains of its other religious houses are not impressive. At Royston the nave of the present church, with a modern chancel, is the choir and presbytery of the Augustinian priory. The work is all of the thirteenth century, with the fine lancets in the walls of an unaisled presbytery soon blocked by the eastward extension of the aisles before the end of the thirteenth century.

BEDFORDSHIRE

Dunstable Priory   This was an important house of Augustinian canons, founded by Henry I in the 1130s. As most of its nave was parochial by the time of the Dissolution it remains in use, but with its clerestorey removed, its triforium stage glazed, and its south aisle rebuilt in modern times. The present seven-bay nave is a fine late Norman work, with a rich though much worn west doorway, of the same period, with interlaced arcading. The west front was much altered, after the fall of the original western towers, in the Early English style. The north-west tower, somewhat low for the general dimensions of what must have been a large and splendid church, was built, in the fifteenth century, to hold the parish bells.

Elstow Abbey Another example, near Bedford, of the continued parochial use of the nave of a conventual church, in this case that of an abbey of Benedictine nuns. As in some other conventual naves, the building pace was slow enough for the western bays to be Early English rather than in the Norman Romanesque style of the earlier portion. The eastern three bays are of comparatively early Norman work, with squared pillars and simple arches, while the Early English western bays are more elaborate, the capitals being foliate and the arches above them well moulded. The division of styles is repeated in the clerestorey, but good Early English work appears in the western façade. At the Dissolution the pulpitum wall was heightened to complete the parish church's eastern termination.

The abbey has the rare feature of a detached belfry in the Perpendicular style, while the brasses include one of an early sixteenth-century abbess. Part of the vaulted cellarium range is now a vestry, while a seventeenth-century Holy Table is contemporary with John Bunyan who came from Elstow.

CAMBRIDGESHIRE and the ISLE OF ELY

Thorney Abbey Smaller and less wealthy than some of the other Fenland Benedictine abbeys, Thorney is none the less of great importance for its remains, and for the way in which most of its nave was brought back into use about a century after the Dissolution. This was done, between 1638 and 1640, by the Earl of Bedford who had large estates in the district. The renovated church was for the use of the people who had come to Thorney to work on the drainage of the neighbouring fens.

The abbey was an Anglo-Saxon foundation, but was replaced in the Norman period. The eastern part of the church has disappeared, as also have the domestic buildings. The present church includes the five western bays of the structural nave, but nearly all of the clerestorey has been destroyed, also the aisles,

so that the arches of the arcade have been filled in, with windows at that level and in the blocked triforium arches. The arcades are excellent Norman Romanesque, with alternating round and clustered pillars and bold shafts which suggest that the nave may have been vaulted from the start and not only in the late Gothic period. The plaster ceiling is of the Earl of Bedford's time, and although the re-use of this part of the church makes a parallel with Abbey Dore, Thorney has no Carolean church fittings. The present transepts and chancel are neo-Norman of the 1840s, but the most imposing part of the church is its lofty west front. The western doorway and its flanking panelling are fine Decorated work, with the date 1638 above them. The Norman western turrets are attractively capped by small octagonal turrets of the early Perpendicular period, while those turrets are joined by a cross piece, with nine canopied niches containing their statues of about 1400, which recalls what one sees between the western towers of some churches in north-western Germany.

Cambridge Of the two monastic colleges run by the Gilbertines and Benedictines, the Benedictine Buckingham College has left important remains which now form three sides of the old court of Magdalene College. Established in the fifteenth century, mainly under the auspices of Croyland Abbey but also for student monks from other abbeys in the eastern counties, the college later received benefactions, including the money to build its early Tudor hall, from the Dukes of Buckingham from whom it got its new name. The mediaeval buildings, of clunch faced with brick, include a staircase whose first-floor rooms preserve the old arrangement of a central living room with small individual studies off each corner.

Some of the Dominican friary buildings still stood over forty years after the suppression, and were available for other uses when in 1583 the site was bought by Sir Walter Mildmay for the foundation of Emmanuel College. The friars' church, whose nave may have been unaisled, became the hall and kitchen range of the new college. It has been much altered and refurnished, but mediaeval buttresses still support the northern side of the hall. Loggan's print of 1688 shows that the friary's western range, with its fifteenth-century buttresses but re-windowed for college purposes, still stood at that time.

104 Cambridge, St. Radegund's Priory (Benedictine nuns), now Jesus College: in the chapel, Norman and early thirteenth century

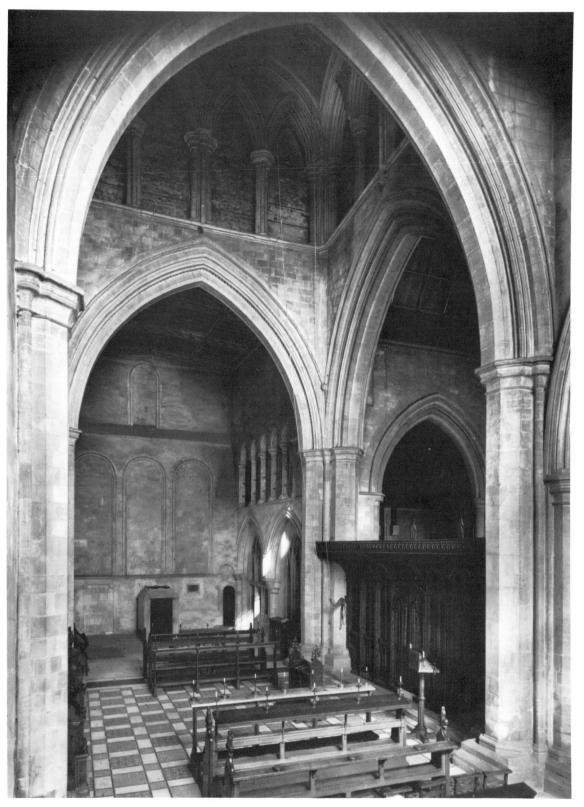

The most notable conventual remains in Cambridge are those of St. Radegund's priory of Benedictine nuns. Founded in the twelfth century, and soon augmented by gifts from King Malcolm IV of Scotland, the nunnery was never large or well endowed and by the last decade of the fifteenth century it was in a hopeless state of both poverty and indiscipline. In 1496 (see page 58) John Alcock, Bishop of Ely, arranged for its suppression and then founded Jesus College whose members were to use the buildings of the priory which were skilfully adapted for their new academic purpose. The church and the domestic quarters of the nunnery are still the central element in the much extended buildings of Jesus College.

The eastern part of the nuns' church was adapted for use as a college chapel, the chapels on each side of the presbytery being pulled down. The north transept has important late Norman work, but the crossing arches, the fine arcading in the tower, and the presbytery are Early English. In the presbytery the shafted side lancets are original work, but the eastern triplet was restored by Augustus Pugin who was responsible for some of the important glazing, refurnishing, and redecoration carried out in the chapel during the nineteenth century. The early Gothic nave was shorn of its aisles in Alcock's time; some of it remains as part of the ante-chapel, but most of it was converted into the master's lodge. The domestic buildings, which were in a bad state by 1496, were raised by one storey, refaced with brick, rewindowed, and internally gutted and refitted as college rooms. The refectory, with a new roof and an attractive oriel window added on one side, became the college hall. The main elements of the priory plan remained, however, and in the nineteenth century the entrance arches to the chapter house, a good composition of the early thirteenth century, were rediscovered behind later plaster. The top stage of the tower, simple battlemented work of the fifteenth century, remains from the time of the Benedictine nuns.

Denny Abbey Out in the fen country between Cambridge and Ely, the monastic buildings of Denny had an unusual history of occupation by three successive religious orders. Denny was first a cell of the Benedictine cathedral priory at Ely. It soon became a possession of the Templars and then, some years after the suppression of the Templars it became a large and observant house (see page 77) of the

105 Norwich, Dominican friary: the choir, now refurnished

Franciscan nuns, or minoresses; the foundress, the widowed Countess of Pembroke, was also the foundress of Pembroke College, Cambridge.

The monastic buildings are now included in a farm. Inside the farmhouse one finds the crossing arches, some of the nave, and part of the transepts of an excellent late Norman priory church. The presbytery was replaced by the choir of the Franciscan nuns. The main relic of their new buildings, now a barn, is the large refectory, with Decorated windows of the Countess of Pembroke's time.

NORFOLK

Outside Norwich, where the cathedral was the church of a Benedictine cathedral priory, the monastic sites of an important county have been much ruined. At Thetford the remains of the Cluniac priory are more eloquent of its ground plan than they are of its above-ground structure, while at Walsingham, where the Augustinian priory was a leading place of pilgrimage, there is little but the eastern wall of a large and imposing church. The best preserved remains are the naves of two Benedictine monasteries which were founded as cells of the great abbey of St. Alban's.

Binham Priory This was founded in 1091 and remained a cell of St. Alban's till the Dissolution; excavations have shown that its presbytery had parallel apses as in the parent abbey. Considerable remains of the domestic buildings, including the chapter house, have also been excavated, but the main survival is in the seven western bays of the structural nave which was parochial before the Dissolution and has so remained. The eastern bays are excellent early Norman work, with clustered columns, cushion capitals, and an inner clerestorey arcade with a large arch and two small flanking ones in each bay. The western part of the nave was not finished till the thirteenth century, most of its architecture being excellent Early English, with lancets in the clerestorey, but with the west wall ornamented with particularly fine panelling of a Geometrical type. The west windows of the aisles have early plate tracery, and the great west window, mostly blocked, is an early and splendid example, from before 1244, of fully developed Geometrical Gothic.

The somewhat mutilated fifteenth-century font is one of the 'Seven Sacrament' fonts for which Norfolk is well known.

Wymondham Abbey Founded in 1107 as a cell of St. Alban's, Wymondham Priory became an independent abbey in 1448. The structural nave was divided between the monks and the parishioners. The church's history was marked, and its fabric was conditioned, by frequent disputes between the two parties. The original crossing of the church, and its eastern limb, have mostly disappeared, as also have the domestic buildings, but the nave which remains is a splendid survival, with the rare feature of a tower at its eastern end and another at the west. The eastern tower, replacing an original central tower, has two attractive octagonal stages above a square base. It is early Perpendicular and was not built over the original crossing, but, much more unusually, over the three eastern bays of the structural nave. To take the extra weight some Norman arches below it were filled in, along with some in the part of the nave used by the parishioners, while many of the Norman pillars in the nine western bays of the nave were cased with extra stonework to give them extra strength. The least altered Norman work is in the fine triforium arches of the parochial nave, but above that level the clerestorey, and the splendid hammerbeam roof with its angel figures, are of the fifteenth century. The widened north aisle, with its own hammerbeam roof, is of the same period. The great western tower, started in 1445 to hold the parishioners' bells, is massive and splendid despite the fact that its intended pinnacles were never built.

The blank eastern wall of the nave is largely covered by a fine altarpiece by Comper, with a tester and a rood beam above it.

Castle Acre Priory One here finds the most impressive remains in England of a Cluniac monastery. Of Norman foundation, it originally had a church with parallel apses, but this was elongated eastwards, and given a square east end, in the Gothic period. Most of the church ruins are Norman, and as in many monastic sites in the eastern and southern counties, the worked stone was mostly removed after the Dissolution, leaving little of many pillars but the flint rubble core. But at Castle Acre one bay of the late Norman south nave arcade remains, with a round pillar having diagonal ornamentation as at Durham Cathedral, while most of the west front is still standing, along with much of one western tower and part of the other; together these features make up one of the finest Norman western façades in the country, with three west doorways, rich interlaced arcading and blind windows filled with scale-pattern

106 Norwich, Dominican friary: the nave (St. Andrew's Hall)

decoration. Like many other Norman west fronts this one was later pierced by a large Perpendicular window.

Of the domestic buildings much of the eastern range still stands, with many Norman dormitory windows; to the south a long, narrow latrine block is well preserved over the watercourse which ran lengthways below it. The best domestic remains, well preserved as they were easy to use as a house after the Dissolution, are those of the western range, with a late Norman vaulted vestibule, a projecting porch of the fifteenth century, and the fine prior's house with work of various periods, including a Decorated chapel and private apartments which have two oriel windows from a date not long before the Dissolution.

Norwich, Dominican Friary   The finest remains of any mediaeval friary church in England are those of the Dominican priory at Norwich. Their preservation is due to their acquisition, soon after the suppression, by the City Corporation, while the unaisled choir was long used, like the now destroyed nave of the Augustinian friars in London, by a Dutch congregation. The nave is now, as St. Andrew's Hall, the city's chief concert hall, whose organ fills much of the space between the nave and choir; the hexagonal tower above this space collapsed in 1712.

The eastern wall and some side windows of the one-time choir are of the fourteenth century, but the rest of the building is of the Perpendicular period, having been rebuilt after a bad fire in 1413. The aisled nave has seven bays with slim pillars, an unusually wide central space and a clerestorey above it. The domestic buildings lay on the northern side. The vaulted southern alleyway of the cloisters remains from the fourteenth century, and there are considerable portions of the eastern and western ranges. The site was originally that of the friary of the Friars of the Sack, but the Dominicans moved there, in 1307, after the Friars of the Sack had become extinct. A crypt, with important brickwork of the thirteenth century, which was part of the original friary buildings, has recently been fitted out as a coffee bar for those who come to the St. Andrew's and Blackfriars Halls.

SUFFOLK

Though there were many religious houses in mediaeval Suffolk the county is not outstandingly well-off for monastic remains. At Butley the main gateway of the Augustinian priory is excellent work of the fourteenth century, with a remarkable display of East Anglian flushwork decoration, while a fair amount remains of the Premonstratensian abbey at Leiston.

Bury St. Edmund's Abbey Overwhelmingly dominant in its own county, with the largest church in East Anglia, the great Benedictine abbey at Bury St. Edmund's was among the most important in England. It is now sadly ruined, and except for its two gateways the site is worth visiting more for the sheer importance of the abbey in the days of its glory than for the impressiveness of what is still there. The two most spectacular relics of the mediaeval abbey are the two gate towers. One of them is a magnificent Norman building with several tiers of windows and wall arcading above its gabled archway; it led directly to the west front of the abbey church and was also the belfry of the neighbouring church of St. James. The other gateway, leading from the town to the abbey's outer courtyard, is a magnificently ornamented structure of the first half of the fourteenth century; its upper storey was arranged as two separate halls, the outer one having cross-shaped arrow slits for defensive use. The church, one of the greatest Romanesque buildings in Europe, remained for the most part a Norman structure, with no eastward elongation (it was anyhow over 500 feet long) but with a north-eastern lady chapel of about 1275. The outer walls of its re-excavated crypt are in reasonable condition, but otherwise one has little but foundations and the rubble core of walls and pillars. The best remains are those of the great *Westwerk* which was even more imposing than that at Ely Cathedral; this building survived, without its outer facing of worked stone, because houses were built into its massive structure; their back gardens cover the western end of the nave. More convincing survivals are the abbot's bridge over the river Lark, some fine buttressed walling from one side of the Hall of Pleas, and some stretches of the outer wall of the precincts.

Clare Priory The remains here are those of the first Augustinian friary founded in England; the buildings, like those of the Carmelite friary at Aylesford in Kent, are now used again by the same order of friars that was there before the suppression. The founder, in 1248, was Richard de Clare, the fifth Earl of Gloucester and a member of the eminent feudal family which took its name from its possessions in Suffolk. The priory remained under the patronage of the de Clares, and among many people of great distinction buried there were Joan of Acre, a daughter of Edward I who married the sixth Earl of Gloucester, and Lionel Duke of Clarence, Edward III's third son whose first wife was a de Clare heiress.

As this Augustinian friary was in a rural area it never needed the large preaching nave of an urban friary. Excavation has shown that its nave was comparatively short, with a north arcade of five bays and a chapel flanking the narrow tower which, as in many friary churches, stood between the nave and the choir which was of six bays, unaisled but with a southern chapel. The southern wall of the nave partly outlasted the suppression to serve as one wall of an enclosed garden. A wall of the eastern range, with chapter house arches of the fourteenth century, remains for the same reason, also an attractive vaulted room of the fourteenth century, at the southern end of the western range whose lower rooms now house a community centre. The main survival of the friary is this western range, with a doorway and buttresses of the fourteenth century and, in the cellarium hall, a ceiling with particularly fine moulded and carved beams from a date shortly before the suppression. This building, like the western ranges of many monastic houses, was re-windowed and re-furnished as a mansion.

South-east of the main buildings a block which was probably the infirmary is now the chapel of the present friary.

ESSEX

Monastic remains in this county are fairly extensive, but only one site, at Waltham, is of outstanding importance. The gate chapels of the Cistercian abbeys of Little Coggeshall and Tilty are now parish churches, while particularly fine gateways remain from the Benedictine abbey at Colchester, and at St. Osyth's where an adjoining building was the Augustinian abbot's house.

Prittlewell Priory A Cluniac foundation, inland from Southend which was once no more than the southern end of Prittlewell parish. A little of the

107 Bury St. Edmund's: great gate, fourteenth century

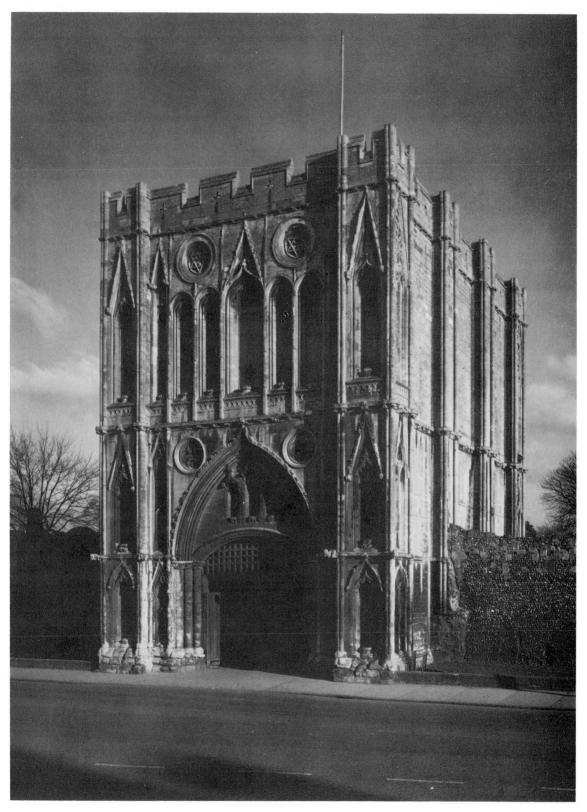

church remains, chiefly of the southern wall of the nave which must have served as a garden wall for the mansion fitted out in other monastic buildings. The whole of the refectory range still stands, with lancets, wall arcading, and other thirteenth-century work. In the western range, which contained the prior's house, there is thirteenth-century vaulting, and half-timbered work of later dates. The buildings are now used as a museum run by the local authority.

Colchester, St. Botolph's Priory* Of great historic importance as the first house of Augustinian canons in England (see page 19). It never became a large or wealthy priory, but has fairly considerable remains of its nave and western façade; the latter, with late Norman decoration and the remains of a round window, must date from some half a century after the arrival of the Augustinians in 1100. In the nave the arcade with its cylindrical columns and the triforium arches are back to their unfaced or unplastered rubble core; as at St. Alban's Abbey the Norman builders, with the ruins of Roman Camalodunum close at hand, used a large admixture of Roman brick.

Little Dunmow Priory This was another early foundation of Augustinian canons. The only important relic is the southern aisle of the presbytery which may have been the lady chapel and is now the parish church. Its arcade of five arches is early Gothic of about 1200, with moulded arches and early foliate capitals. The aisle was splendidly widened and re-modelled late in the fourteenth century, some tracery being late Decorated, the rest early Perpendicular. A tomb of Walter Fitzwalter, who died in 1432, has notably fine effigies of him and his wife, while the chair used in the Dunmow Flitch contest is made up of thirteenth-century stallwork.

Waltham Abbey Founded in the eleventh century and rebuilt, before his accession, by King Harold as a college of secular canons, the establishment was reorganised in 1177 as one of England's most important abbeys of Augustinian canons regular. Waltham Abbey also had the distinction, in 1540, of being the last religious house to be dissolved. Its church was also, as a result of extensions in and soon after 1177, the largest Augustinian church in England, with a complete cruciform church, over 300 feet long, added to the east of the nave and transepts of the collegiate building. The earlier nave, with its eastern double bay

somewhat later in character than the other Norman work, was used by the parish and so continued after the Dissolution. It has important and interesting work in three and a half double bays; some of the pillars of the arcade have incised decoration of the kind also seen in Durham Cathedral. Some important re-construction was done in the fourteenth century, the west front being remodelled at the same time, while a fine Decorated chapel was built off the south aisle of this western nave. The western bell tower, whose fabric harshly masks much of the arcading of the early Decorated west front, was built, in the 1550s, probably by the re-use of material from the ruined canons' church.

Beeleigh Abbey* A Premonstratensian Abbey, originally founded near the coast but moved, about 1180, to a site near Maldon. A little of the refectory still stands, but the chief remains are those of the eastern range, and date from the thirteenth century. The vaulted chapter house has a central row of columns and the unusual feature of double rather than triple entrance arches. The undercroft of the dormitory is also vaulted, and the dormitory also survives, with the typically Essex feature of late mediaeval brick buttresses.

LONDON

Many London religious houses, including two nunneries in the City and all the friaries, were destroyed at the Dissolution or in later years. Some, however, remain wholly or in part; among the remains is that of the London Charterhouse, whose chapter house is now a chapel. South of the river the only important survival is the eastern part of the Augustinian priory of St. Mary Overy. But as this church, the best one in London in which one can see English Gothic of the thirteenth century, is now Southwark Cathedral it lies outside the scope of this book.

Westminster Abbey The richest, and among the largest of England's Benedictine abbeys, with a special historic position as the coronation church, and as the burial place of several sovereigns and many other members of the royal family. The abbey's close links with the Crown caused its preservation, after its second suppression (see page 86), as a collegiate church. Its cathedral status, after only one bishop of Westminster to occupy the see created by Henry VIII, had lasted only ten years. Apart from a large sacristy north of the nave, its northern 'Galilee' porch,

108 Prittlewell Priory, Essex (Cluniac): cloister doorway, Transitional Norman, restored

and a detached belfry of the thirteenth century, the abbey's church remains entire, though with much restoration and the renovation of nearly all its exterior stonework.

Earlier churches had stood on the site, but the abbey's real foundation was by Edward the Confessor, with its sanctity enhanced, after the King's burial in the church whose consecration had occurred only a few days before his death early in 1066, by his canonisation. The abbey is the only English church which has continuously housed the body of a saint. Its architectural interest matches its historic renown. Twice over, in English terms, an architectural exotic, the church was never finished before the Dissolution. After schemes, by Wren and others, for some sort of a central tower and spire, no central feature was ever built, and the two western towers were put up in the eighteenth century to designs by Hawksmoor, mainly Gothic but with some Baroque design.

Westminster Abbey has here to be considered less as a national Valhalla than in mediaeval and monastic terms. Its position as a place of burial and commemoration for a somewhat odd assortment of eminent people, and as a great showplace of post-Reformation English sculpture, was to some extent foreshadowed by the burial in its church of many kings, queens, and other royal personages. But almost all its pre-Reformation tombs are of abbots or monks, of a few other high ecclesiastics, of members of the royal family, or of important court officials and associates of royalty.

The Confessor's church, with three parallel apses, was of great significance in that it was designed and finished, before the Norman Conquest, in the Norman Romanesque style, closely resembling such Norman abbeys of the eleventh century as Jumièges and Bernay. Nothing of it now stands, and the chief remains of the abbey's Norman buildings are in the undercroft of the dormitory range, whose siting explains the lack of a western aisle in the south transept of the Gothic church which slowly replaced that of the Confessor.

An eastern lady chapel was built about 1220, and in 1245 Henry III started the new church, basically French Gothic, with special derivations from the new cathedral at Amiens, but with many details, particularly in the triforium arches, of an English Gothic type. The short apsidal presbytery, with its radiating chapels and the chapel of St. Edward beyond the high

altar, the crossing, the transepts, and the first five bays of the structural nave, were built during Henry III's reign. Though the present choir stalls and the western side of the screen are of the nineteenth century, they are backed by the original walls, so that the church still keeps its proper monastic subdivision. When, under Richard II, the building of the nave was resumed the work was a remarkable instance of stylistic assimilation to the basically French Gothic of the earlier church. Some points of detail, particularly the Perpendicular character of the column bases, do, however, distinguish this work of the early Perpendicular period from the architecture of the abbey's eastern and central sections. The west wall was, however, designed from the first in the Perpendicular style.

Off the south transept the chapel of St. Faith, now among the most secluded and devotional parts of the abbey, was at first the monks' sacristy. As the eastern aisle of the south transept (now Poets' Corner) had the private entrance from Westminster Palace it was never fitted up with side chapels. Beyond the sanctuary and St. Edward's Chapel, with their paving of Italian marble mosaic and their royal and other tombs, the last of the pre-Reformation additions to the abbey is the great fan-vaulted chapel of Henry VII, unusual among such chapels in being aisled, with the late Perpendicular design of Robert and William Vertue, allowing for the inclusion of windows, akin to oriels, of a triangular projection. The tombs of Henry VII and of his mother Lady Margaret Beaufort are fine Renaissance achievements by the Florentine Pietro Torrigiano, and the altar, set up in the 1930s, reproduces Torrigiano's design.

The chapter house, now under the care of the Department of the Environment, was started about 1245. Octagonal in shape, above a crypt, it has trefoil-headed arcading whose spaces were later filled with striking wall paintings, while the five-light windows of a building of basically English Gothic character were an important anticipation of the 'geometrical' style. The splendid tiled floor largely survives, but much of the fabric, including the vault and its slim supporting pillar, dates from a painstaking restoration by Sir George Gilbert Scott.

St. Bartholomew's Priory, Smithfield This important priory of Augustinian canons was founded, in 1123, by Rahere, who was also the founder of St. Bartholomew's Hospital. Most of the nave was used by the local parish, but soon after the Dissolution this was exchanged for the crossing and presbytery. Under

109 London, Augustinian friary church (Dutch Church), destroyed in the war: nave

Mary I the eastern part of the church was used by the Dominican friars of a restored foundation. Not much now remains of the domestic buildings bar a heavily restored eastern range, but the church is London's finest piece of Norman Romanesque architecture; the western end has been much altered and restored, with some good late Victorian Gothic additions by Sir Aston Webb. The seventeenth-century Gothic tower, recalling that at Abbey Dore though it is of brick, was built over the easternmost bay of the south aisle of the nave.

The surviving portions of the church comprise the eastern bay of a ten-bay nave, the crossing of rectangular shape, the much altered and renovated transepts, the presbytery with its aisles, and the fifteenth-century lady chapel, built over a crypt and much renovated since its return to church use. The best-known part of the church is the excellent Norman presbytery, whose cylindrical pillars have scalloped capitals and, round the apse where they are closely spaced, some strongly stilted arches. The main triforium arches each enclose four smaller arches, and the clerestorey windows above them are late Decorated work. One bay of the southern triforium is now filled by Prior Bolton's attractive oriel window of about 1520. In the aisles groined vaults have been well restored between original Norman cross arches. The founder's tomb, now a fine canopied work of the fifteenth century, lies on the north of the sanctuary.

The Temple Church The important church, much damaged by wartime bombing but since renovated, which was, before the suppression of the Templars, the chief English church of this knightly order. Its round nave, still with its western porch, is an extremely important example of the early Gothic, with an extensive use of marble, also seen in the choir limb of Canterbury Cathedral; in the triforium stage the interlacing arches are of a much more Norman character. The original church was consecrated in 1185, but by 1240 its comparatively short apsidal choir limb had been replaced by the present Early English choir, three-aisled and architecturally important in that the equal height of its central space and aisles makes it a 'hall church', though without some of the features of German hall churches, and without the unique structural devices seen in the 'hall church' choir limb of Bristol Cathedral.

The fine marble effigies of knights, on the floor of

the circular nave, were badly calcined, and otherwise damaged by blazing debris which fell on them during the bombing.

St. John's, Clerkenwell The headquarters church of the Knights Hospitaller of St. John (the Baptist) of Jerusalem who eventually took over most of the Templars' English property. Founded, like the Temple Church, in the twelfth century, its original plan was also that of a round nave with an unaisled and apsidal choir limb; this choir was soon replaced by a much larger building, aisled and rectangular, like that later built in the Temple. The circular nave, destroyed by Wat Tyler's insurrectionists in 1381, was replaced by a rectangular nave which was itself demolished at the Dissolution.

The surviving parts of the mediaeval church are mostly in the attractive crypt of the choir, partly late Norman and partly early Gothic. Above it the present church is largely Georgian, while the fine gateway of the early sixteenth century also remains. The gateway and the church now make up the English headquarters of the order as revived, with an Anglican character in its religious observances, in the nineteenth century.

St. Helen's, Bishopsgate This is an important example of a church, subdivided down the middle by a central main arcade, which was partly that of a Benedictine nunnery and partly a parish church. The Benedictine priory was founded early in the thirteenth century, and considering its wealth and importance it is remarkable that its church seems never to have been extended beyond its original limits. The church's one side chapel, architecturally corresponding to the lady chapel of Lacock Abbey, was on the southern, or parochial side; the important late fifteenth-century tomb of Sir John Crosby, the builder of Crosby Hall, is under one of its arches.

Some Early English work, including a lancet window and a blocked doorway which led to the cloisters, remains in the wall of the north aisle, while in what was once the nuns' choir two windows in the wall are placed high to allow for domestic buildings abutting onto this side; those in the nave, now late Perpendicular, come lower down. The east window of the nuns' choir is Decorated, but nearly all the other windows in the church are Perpendicular, and the fine arcade between the nuns' and parish halves was built in the fifteenth century. The nuns' stalls, with well-carved elbow pieces, are now in the parish chancel.

Of the church's many post-Reformation monuments the most historic is the table tomb of Sir

110 Westminster Abbey: cloisters, south walk, fourteenth century

111 Clerkenwell, London: crypt of Hospitallers' church

Thomas Gresham, in whose nearby house Gresham College was founded.

KENT

Two of Kent's most important monasteries were cathedral priories, while little remains of some of the rest. Some of the most important remains are those at Canterbury, and of some nunneries.

St. Augustine's Abbey, Canterbury The second great Benedictine abbey in Canterbury is sadly ruined, and what remains is in some ways a parallel to what one finds at Bury St. Edmund's. As at Bury the best-preserved buildings are two excellent gateways in the western wall of the precinct. The Great Gate is mostly of the fourteenth century, the more southerly of the two being a century later. The ruins of the domestic buildings, which lay north of the church, are unimpressive, but of the church somewhat more survives. Apart from a stretch of the nave's Norman north aisle, and part of a finely arcaded Romanesque north-west tower, the remains are mostly at crypt level, but are important. A fair amount remains of the crypt which lay beneath the apsidal presbytery and radiating chapels of the Norman church which replaced a sequence of Anglo-Saxon predecessors. Below this level there are the foundations of two early Saxon churches, one of which contained the tomb of St. Augustine, also the foundations of the large building which was built, by Abbot Wulfric about 1050, to connect the two older churches. This was circular inside and octagonal outside, and was probably modelled on the rotunda at St. Bénigne at Dijon in Burgundy. Further east the ruined chapel of St. Pancras, perhaps of Roman origin and certainly containing much Roman brick in its fabric, is a separate building.

In the middle of last century a college for the training of missionaries was founded within the site of St. Augustine's. The new buildings of that time are convincingly collegiate and are scholarly work by Butterfield in his pre-polychrome phase.

Bradsole, St. Radegund's Abbey High up in the hill country just behind Dover this abbey has left some of the best ruins in England of a Premonstratensian house. Founded not long before 1200, it was never a rich abbey and seems to have been little changed after the early decades of the thirteenth century; the carved stonework which survives is nearly all of the twelfth or thirteenth centuries. The buildings well show how the lay-out of an abbey of White canons, where lay brothers were an unimportant factor and where there was hardly any lay population, was conditioned by the occupants' rule and way of life. At St. Radegund's the nave is so short that the northern gable of the western range is clear to the west of its western wall. The presbytery limb, unaisled but flanked by long chapels, was long enough to hold a lady chapel behind the high altar. Though the church was cruciform, there was no central tower, a somewhat curiously designed tower being sited against the north side of the nave. A fair amount remains of the domestic buildings, including the chapter house walls and three fine entrance arches. The refectory range was the portion of the buildings turned into a house in post-Reformation times. Further out there are the ruins of two gatehouses.

West Malling Abbey An important site both for the remains of the mediaeval abbey of Benedictine nuns and for its present-day occupation (see page 109) by an Anglican community of Benedictine nuns and for the modern church which they have recently built.

The original abbey was founded, late in the eleventh century, by Gundulf, Bishop of Rochester. It was a medium-sized community, dissolved in 1538. The lower stage of its imposing fifteenth-century gatehouse still stands; adjoining it is an attractive Decorated chapel. The church was unaisled and cruciform, with a square-ended presbytery probably extended in the thirteenth century. Much of its south transept remains also, with alterations at the level of its western doorway, the lower part of the western tower. This displays imposing Norman work, of the twelfth century, with arcading, zig-zag decoration, and corner turrets which have been considerably restored. The upper stage, octagonal and perhaps of the fourteenth century, recalls the arrangement seen in the west tower of Ely Cathedral.

The chief relic of the domestic buildings, altered to form a country house and now providing much of the accommodation used by the present community, is the southern range. Its main mediaeval feature is a very beautiful run of thirteenth-century cloister ar-

112 St. Radegund's Abbey, near Dover: tower of church

cading, trefoil-headed and with foliate capitals and dog-tooth decoration. The arches were never glazed and the alleyway behind it did not project but was built *into* the fabric of the refectory range.

The most modern buildings put up to serve the nuns' needs have been designed by Keith Murray and Robert Maguire. The most notable of these, on the site of the original crossing but to the north of its main alignment, is the church, whose inner structure, rectangular but with rounded ends, a high-pitched roof, and clerestorey lighting, rises above a rectangular outer structure which acts as an ambulatory. Of concrete blocks, with an almost unimpeded floor of quarry tiles, and with a simple altar and choir furnishings, it is a building of imposing austerity which ranks as one of England's most important conventual churches built in a totally modern idiom.

Minster in Sheppey On an upland site which must have been awkward both for water supply and the haulage of stone, the nunnery here had Saxon origins,

and there is still some Saxon masonry in the north wall of the church. The nunnery which existed at Minster after the Norman Conquest had a curious history of alternation between the Benedictine and the Augustinian rules, but at the Dissolution was a house of Augustinian canonesses. Only the gateway remains of the domestic buildings, but the church is a good example of 'parallel' subdivision between conventual and parish sections. The sturdy western tower, never finished to its designed height, stands at the west end of the nuns' section. Here and in the parish section a good deal of the architecture is Early English, with a

113   West Malling Abbey (Anglican Benedictine nuns): the new church

dividing arcade of the thirteenth century, but several windows, in each part of the church, are Perpendicular. An excellent wooden screen of the fifteenth century still stands in the nuns' part of the church.

The church is well known for its monuments, and for the early fourteenth-century brass of Sir John de Northwode and his wife.

Canterbury, Dominican Friary These remains are charmingly sited on each side of one of the branches of the river Stour. The guest house is on one side, while on the other the best survival of the main friary buildings is the bulk of the southern, or refectory range. The refectory is above an undercroft which has simple central pillars and vaulting in brick. In the refectory, whose screen remains at one end, the architectural features, below an original cradle roof, are of the thirteenth century, with two-light windows having plate tracery on a quatrefoil pattern. The western wall has lancets, while the archway for the

114 Aylesford, Kent: Carmelite friary, cloister walk, fifteenth century

reader's pulpit, and the stairway leading up to it, are still to be seen in one of the side walls.

Aylesford, Carmelite Friary Down by the Medway below Maidstone this is, perhaps, the most important site in England where conventual buildings of the Middle Ages are now, with appropriate additions, occupied by the order which was there before the suppression.

Founded in 1242, the priory at Aylesford was one of the first two Carmelite friaries established in England; unlike most of the country's friaries it remained in a comparatively rural location, and even when the original rectangular church was replaced in the fourteenth century the new church still had an unaisled nave. This church has disappeared, but its outlines, and that of its predecessor, are indicated in the pavement of the present shrine area.

Of the domestic buildings the south range and most of the western range still stand, having become a mansion after the suppression, with major alterations, in Charles II's reign, by the Bankes family. Much of the roofing was burnt in a fire in 1930. The structure of these two blocks is largely of the fifteenth century, with fine alleyways built into the structure as one frequently found them in friary buildings. What was once the refectory is now the library of the modern friary, while a small chapel is in the cellarium space below. The outer courtyard, with one of its blocks now a galleried dining hall for pilgrims and other visitors, is also mediaeval in its basic structure, some buttresses, doorways, and one-light windows being of the fourteenth century. The other main relic of the mediaeval friary is the gatehouse, of the fifteenth century but altered by the Sedleys in 1590.

Since the return of the Carmelite friars in 1949 various new buildings have been put up to serve the needs of what is now a major centre for pilgrimages, retreats, and conferences. The most important, disposed round the perimeter of an open-air worshipping space which is focused on a covered High Altar, contains a sequence of chapels. These buildings, designed by Adrian Gilbert-Scott, are in a modernised version of the Gothic idioms prevalent in the thirteenth century or soon after 1300. Artistically they are less notable than the large collection of fine modern glass and ceramic murals, altars, and Stations of the Cross by Adam Kossowski.

SURREY

Much impoverished by the almost total disappearance of such important religious houses as Benedictine Chertsey and Augustinian Merton, Surrey is not a good county for monastic remains. The ruins of Waverley Abbey, whose best fragment is part of the vaulted cellarium range of the thirteenth century, are

115 Bayham Abbey, Sussex (Premonstratensian): a general view

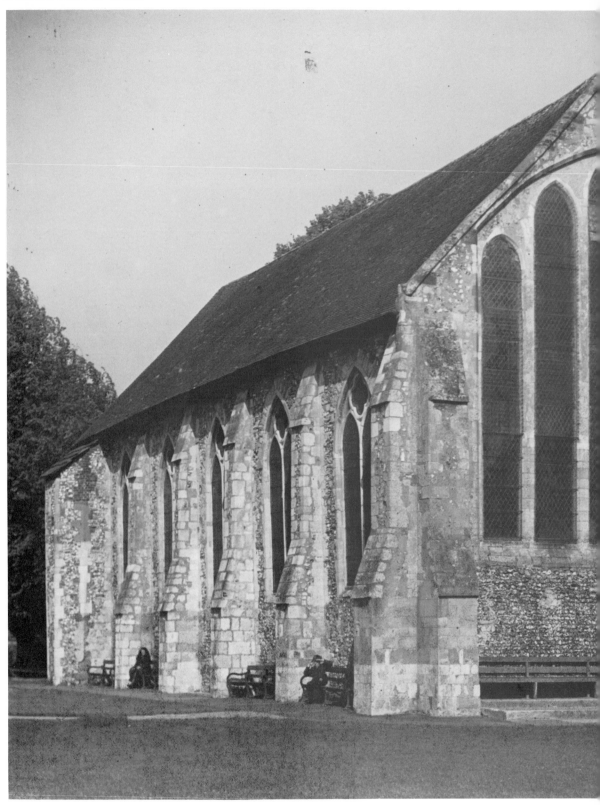

historically important, as this was the first Cistercian abbey in England, but they are not impressive. Nor are those of the Augustinian priory of Newark near Pyrford. In both cases, as is all too common in the southern and eastern counties, the robbery of worked stone has been so drastic as to leave little but the rubble core of the walling which still stands.

SUSSEX

Not many of the old religious houses of Sussex merit separate treatment. At Battle little remains of the Benedictine abbey except some much altered domestic buildings and the splendid gateway of the fourteenth century, while at Lewes the ruins of the chief Cluniac priory in England, much diminished in any case by the Victorian period, were still more destroyed when a railway line was driven through the site. Nothing substantial remains of the county's one Cistercian abbey at Robertsbridge.

Boxgrove Priory   A few miles from Chichester the church here is one of the most attractive in the country which started as an 'alien' priory of Norman foundation, in this case a cell of Lessay Abbey in the Cherbourg peninsula. It became 'denizen' late in the fourteenth century and continued as a small independent priory till 1536. The nave, whose north aisle was curiously interrupted by one of the cloister walls, was parochial before the Dissolution, but as at Pershore the parishioners happily exchanged it for the presbytery limb.

As it stands now the church consists of the two eastern bays of the Norman structural nave, the Norman transepts each of which has an unusual gallery, the crossing and a low Norman tower, and the presbytery limb which is a good example of eastward elongation early in the thirteenth century. The choir limb is the best part of the church. Early English work of high quality, it still has most of its lancets though some aisle windows were replaced in the Decorated period. Black Purbeck marble is mixed with freestone, and all the vaults are of a simple quadripartite design. The most important feature is the arrangement of the choir limb in four double bays, each one with a retaining arch covering two arcade arches; the same design occurs in the vaulted chancel of what is now Portsmouth Cathedral. The triforium stage has been eliminated, and the vault was decorated, in the

116   Chichester: the choir of the Franciscan friary

sixteenth century, with floral and foliate painting in the Renaissance manner like that in the choir vault at Chichester Cathedral. Other Renaissance design work occurs, along with a basically late Perpendicular design, in the chantry chapel installed in 1532 by Thomas, the ninth Lord De la Warr.

Bayham Abbey* Almost on the Kent border, the ruins here are among the best in England of a Premonstratensian abbey, located on its present site early in the thirteenth century. It was suppressed by Wolsey in 1525, against strong local protests, to help finance his colleges at Oxford and Ipswich. The original plan was typically Premonstratensian, with an unaisled nave (rebuilt in the fifteenth century) so short that, as at St. Radegund's, near Dover, the cellarium range stood west of its western wall. The most important remains, with walls still standing to a considerable height, are those of the eastern part of the church and of the eastern domestic range where two piers of the chapter house vault still stand. In the second half of the thirteenth century the presbytery limb was lengthened eastwards, with an eastern crossing and two more transepts with vaulted chapels projecting from them. The sanctuary was, unusually in an English monastic church, apsidal, and some corbels of its vaulting remain.

As at Fountains and Rievaulx the ruins at Bayham were treated as a fine 'picturesque' feature in a Georgian park, the abbey gatehouse by the river Teise becoming a waterside summerhouse.

Easebourne Priory* This was a small establishment, near Midhurst, of Augustinian canonesses, founded about 1248 but with its church incorporating much of a Norman parish church, including its western tower. The north aisle was widened to make a small new parish church, so that this was another example of a church where the nuns' chapel and the parochial church ran parallel to each other. Both sections still stand, with a modern chancel extending the parochial section.

Much of the eastern range also survives, with work of the thirteenth and fourteenth centuries and three chapter house arches. Part of the refectory range is now a parish hall.

Chichester, Franciscan Friary The choir of this friary remains substantially intact as a leading feature in a public park. Of five bays, and of the middle years of the thirteenth century, it has five eastern lancets, and attractive side windows of two lights with early plate tracery.

BERKSHIRE

Apart from the two great Benedictine abbeys of Abingdon and Reading Berkshire was not, before the Dissolution, a county with many religious houses. As the remains are scanty both at Abingdon and Reading the county is not well-off for monastic sites, and only one deserves separate treatment.

Hurley Priory This was a small Benedictine priory, founded about 1086 as a cell of Westminster, but later independent. When it was dissolved in 1536, however, its estates were granted back to Westminster for the great abbey's last four years. The nave was used by the parish and remains, while excavation has revealed traces of the crossing, and of an apsidal Norman presbytery which was lengthened eastwards, with a northern chapel, in the thirteenth century and again in the fourteenth. The long, narrow nave is still the parish church, with an excellent Norman west window, other windows of the same period, and some drastically renovated Norman doorways. There are some remains of a thirteenth-century chapter house, and other fragments of the eastern range, but the main relic of the domestic buildings (north of the church) is the refectory range, mainly Norman but heightened, with good Decorated windows, in the fourteenth century.

HAMPSHIRE

Beaulieu Abbey One of the most important Cistercian abbeys in southern England, founded in 1204 by King John, with one of the largest Cistercian churches in the country, and still keeping important surviving buildings, much visited both for themselves and as an accompaniment to the well-known transport museum.

The great church was unusual in that it was, in the manner of such French Cistercian abbeys as Pontigny, round-ended with an eastern ambulatory and with chapels leading off it as well as off the transepts. Except for some of the walls of the south transept, and for much of the outer wall of the southern aisle of the nave, preserved after the Dissolution to help enclose a farmyard or garden, the church has almost wholly disappeared; it was destroyed, down to its very foundations, to provide stone for Henry VIII's coastal castles on the Solent. Something remains of the eastern range, but the main survivals are on the south and west sides of the

117 Beaulieu Abbey, Hampshire (Cistercian): refectory pulpit

western cloister enclosure. Much of the range was preserved to serve agricultural and domestic needs after the Dissolution, so that one has some important work remaining from the thirteenth century. At the northern end the one-time cellarium has rectangular windows and very simple vaulting. Further to the south there are two bays, with fine vaulting and lancets, of the lay brothers' refectory. The monks' refectory remains intact as the local parish church. It is an excellent Early English building, lancetted and attractively restored and reconditioned in recent years. Up a stairway in its western wall it has one of the best of all refectory pulpits, now used for parish sermons, while the building's waggon roof, with excellent wooden bosses, is from late in the fourteenth century.

The great gatehouse of the abbey is now the main part of the present-day mansion.

Netley Abbey A late Cistercian foundation of 1239, never as important as Beaulieu not far away, but well-off for its picturesque remains. Most of the buildings were Early English, though with early traceried windows as well as grouped lancets, and there were also some Decorated windows of a slightly later period. The church had a nave of eight bays and an aisled eastern limb of four. Much of the outer walling still stands, with windows and vaulting shafts, but except in the south transept, whose chapels retain their vaulting and where the triforium arcading and the clerestorey windows still remain, the arcades have been destroyed.

The sacristy and the chapter house are both substantially preserved; also other parts of the eastern range. Most of the southern and eastern range of the cloister buildings have been destroyed, but the latrine block south of the monks' dormitory has been preserved, while to the east of the main buildings of the abbey a building which may have contained lodgings for visiting abbots has a thirteenth-century vaulted undercroft and much of its upper structure, including a vaulted chapel.

Christchurch Priory The finest example in England of a complete church of Augustinian canons regular preserved and still used for worship: the main modification in its structure was when the Norman central tower was removed during alterations in the fifteenth century. As at Waltham the Norman church was at first one of secular canons, but the college was refounded, about 1150, as a priory of canons regular. The domestic buildings have almost wholly disappeared.

The nave is an extremely fine Norman Romanesque structure, with moulded arches rising from scalloped capitals and an excellent triforium stage. The transepts and their chapels are also Norman, and the north transept's external turret has plain and interlaced arcading, and an exterior pattern of diagonal interlacing recalling work at Durham. In the nave the clerestorey and the vault are Early English, while the fine fifteenth-century western tower was built, as was that at Wimborne Minster not far away, to hold the parishioners' bells.

Behind an extremely fine pulpitum of the late fourteenth century, the choir of four bays was rebuilt, with a simply ribbed vault having pendants at the side like those in the Henry VII chapel at Westminster, late in the Perpendicular period. Its low arcades are largely masked by the excellent choir stalls of soon after 1500, while the east end, with no east window, is closed by a splendid reredos, whose canopied figures displayed the tree of Jesse. This choir at Christchurch particularly well shows how a monastic or collegiate choir was shut off from the rest of the church and occupied a small portion of the entire building. The eastern lady chapel, also late Perpendicular, has the rare feature of another chapel above it.

The chantries of the Countess of Salisbury (executed by Henry VIII in 1541) and of Prior Draper are admirable works of late Perpendicular Gothic, but with touches of Renaissance decoration.

Romsey Abbey The finest church of a mediaeval nunnery, in this case an important abbey of Benedictine nuns, remaining in England. The domestic buildings have almost wholly disappeared, and the lady chapel was pulled down soon after the Dissolution, but otherwise the church is intact except for the Perpendicular outer north aisle which was built for the use of the parishioners, and which became surplus to requirements when the rest of the

church was saved for post-Dissolution parish use.

The abbey was of Anglo-Saxon foundation, and the church still has two important masterpieces of pre-Conquest sculpture. One is the large rood, or crucifix now set in the western wall of the south transept, the other is the plaque, showing a Crucifixion group in low relief, now set in an altarpiece in one of the apsidal side chapels of the Norman church. Unlike the churches of some smaller and later nunneries Romsey Abbey was, like the even larger church of the Benedictine nuns of Barking in Essex, built with a central crossing, transepts, and a full array of side chapels. The present church is, for the most part, a splendid masterpiece of Norman architecture, never running to anything loftier than a squat Norman central tower but with particularly fine Norman Romanesque work in its arcades, in the two arches behind the high altar, in the triforium where the space above each pair of arches has a curious little pillaret, and in the clerestorey of the presbytery and transepts. In the nave the three western bays were finished in the Early English period, and most of the nave clerestorey was assimilated to an early Gothic design.

The pair of east windows displays very fine Geometrical work of about 1280. Another of this magnificent church's treasures is a painted reredos, with two tiers of figures, of about 1500.

WILTSHIRE

Though it contained some important nunneries, mediaeval Wiltshire had, on the whole, fewer monastic establishments than the other Wessex counties. There are few remains of some of those which did exist; there are, however, three monastic sites particularly worth visiting.

Malmesbury Abbey Wiltshire's one great Benedictine house, with origins going back to a Celtic founder and to the time of St. Aldhelm in the seventh and eighth centuries. During the later period of the great Benedictine reform King Athelstan was a major benefactor to Malmesbury as he was to other Wessex abbeys, and it was at Malmesbury that he was buried in 940. William of Malmesbury, one of the best early mediaeval historians, was a monk there in the twelfth century. Most of the present church, and much of what was destroyed at the suppression, is extremely

118 Malmesbury Abbey, Wiltshire (Benedictine): Norman crossing arches

119 Malmesbury Abbey: Romanesque sculpture in south porch

fine late Norman work, of high architectural and decorative quality and well displaying the good qualities of Cotswold stone.

Apart from its western arch only one other pier and one more arch of the central crossing survives, and there is hardly anything of the Norman presbytery, or of its eastward extension of the fourteenth century. What remains is the bulk of the magnificent nave, bought after the Dissolution by William Stumpe, a rich local clothier, and given to the parishioners to replace an older and much smaller parish church. The whole of the south aisle remains, along with the south porch and its outstanding Romanesque carvings of the middle decades of the twelfth century. But three bays of the main nave and of its north aisle collapsed with the fall of a western tower. The architecture of the nave is outstanding late Norman work, with round pillars, early pointed arches in the arcades and pointed cross arches in the aisles, and triforium units each of four small arches under a rounded retaining arch. These arches were filled with masonry to strengthen the structure when the fourteenth-century central tower was built. The clerestorey is mostly in the Decorated style, and the nave's beautiful ribbed vault is also of the fourteenth century. In the south aisle one notes how the Norman wall arcading was somewhat brutally interrupted when Decorated windows were inserted.

Athelstan's tomb, of about 1500 with a canopied effigy, is now in the nave; presumably it was moved from a place of honour in the presbytery.

Edington 'Priory' This was one of the two establishments in England of a group of regular clergy, perhaps only found in England, who were known as Bonshommes. They followed the rule of St. Augustine, and their life seems to have differed little from that of Augustinian canons. The head of each house was known as the Rector. Originally a small chantry college, in 1358 the church became that of a convent of Bonshommes, the change being made by the locally born Bishop Edington of Winchester. Except for the early sixteenth-century screen which still separates the choir from the crossing and the nave, the beautiful church, which is intact, dates from the first two decades after 1350. It is an unusually good example of the transition from Decorated to Perpendicular, with the chancel displaying more Decorated character than the nave whose idiom is more Perpendicular, though with Decorated windows, in the western walls of the aisles, flanking a fine Perpendicular west window of eight lights. The central tower, of no great height, is battlemented and without pinnacles.

Lacock Abbey A comparatively late foundation, of Augustinian canonesses, started by the Countess Ela in 1229 and still showing some of the country's best remains of the domestic quarters of a mediaeval nunnery. It is also one of the best examples of conventual buildings converted, with the minimum of alteration, into a country mansion. The Renaissance features remaining from the time of its adaptation are also of great architectural note, while the hall, on part of the site of the western range, is an extremely important Georgian Gothic building.

The church, rectangular and with a southern lady chapel, has disappeared except for its north wall. There are, however, extremely important remains of the domestic buildings, largely of the thirteenth century and less altered at ground level than in the upper floors. Much of the eastern range is particularly well preserved. The vaulted sacristy had two altars in its eastern section; next to it is the chapter house, a very fine Early English apartment, vaulted and with its doorway and two flanking arches intact. The eastern range ends with the vaulted subvault which lay beneath the canonesses' dormitory. Its vault ribs are simpler than those in the chapter house, while here and elsewhere in the buildings some of the windows are Victorian restorations, in the Early English style,

to replace Renaissance and Georgian alterations.

Some vaulted rooms, perhaps of the fourteenth century, remain in the western range which contained the abbess' quarters, while three of the beautiful cloister walks still stand, being of the fifteenth century with Perpendicular windows and lierne vaults.

Lacock Abbey, along with its great barn which now contains the Fox Talbot museum of science and photography, belongs to the National Trust along with the outstandingly attractive village. It ranks as one of the most-worth-visiting of all England's monastic sites.

SOMERSET

This was a county with many pre-Reformation religious houses, so dominated by the great Benedictine abbey of Glastonbury that their combined revenues did not equal the Glastonbury total. The remains of the principal monasteries are hardly commensurate with their one-time importance, while at Bath the 'Abbey' is in a somewhat anomalous position. In late Saxon times it was, indeed, a Benedictine abbey of the ordinary type, but from 1090 and for over a hundred years its church was Somerset's one cathedral. Then from the thirteenth century it was a co-cathedral, monastic in its régime, with Wells. Its almost complete replacement, on a smaller scale, was started in 1499 but was not finished by 1539 when the cathedral priory was dissolved, leaving Wells the only cathedral of a diocese which none the less kept the double title. The unfinished shell was eventually fitted out as the city's chief parish church, and is now known as the abbey. But in mediaeval terms it was intended to be a cathedral, so that it hardly falls within the scope of this book.

Glastonbury Abbey Vastly rich in its legendary and historic associations, this great Benedictine monastery became the wealthiest in the country, after Westminster, and the main fabric of its church was larger than the cathedral at Wells. The remains are, however, pathetically scanty; even the great gatehouse has lost much of its upper structure.

Excavations have revealed something of the Anglo-Saxon abbey which St. Dunstan knew, but its Norman successor perished in a great fire in 1184. The ruins, so scanty that a visit to the abbey can be a depressing experience, are those of the large church, for the most part of the transitional period between Romanesque and early Gothic, which was built soon

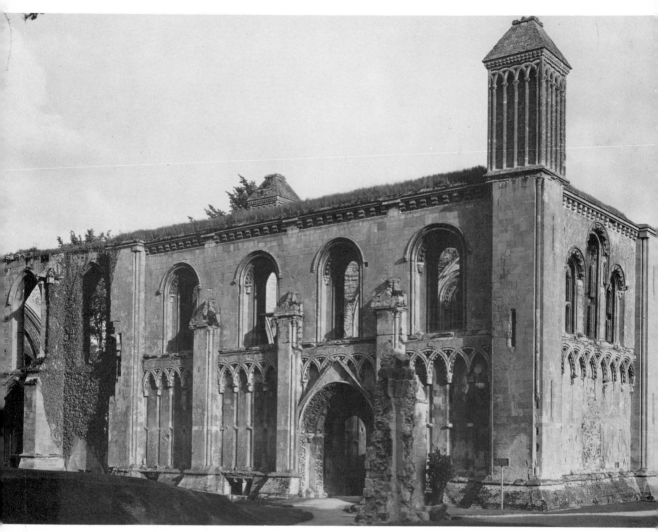

after the fire. The most intact part of it is the lady chapel, unusually and for special reasons at the extreme west end of the church, and linked to the main building by a vestibule of Early English work. It was sited in this position to replace one of the ancient wattle chapels which had, from a very early date and perhaps from the period of the Celtic monastery, stood on this particular spot. The present chapel is a splendid Transitional building, more Romanesque than Gothic in character, and its sculpture is akin to that in the great porch at Malmesbury.

Of the main church, also of the Transitional period but with a stronger Gothic character, the chief remains are the eastern crossing piers, and enough of the transept walling to show that the arcades and triforium arches were, in each bay, included within a larger arch. Further east the style of an extension of

120 Glastonbury Abbey (Benedictine): western lady chapel, late twelfth century
121 Glastonbury Abbey: abbot's kitchen, fourteenth century

the fourteenth century was closely assimilated to that of the earlier presbytery and nave. Enough carved stonework remains to show that the presbytery was given an inner casing of traceried stonework like that at Gloucester, and that the Perpendicular central tower had 'strainer' arches to support it.

Most of the domestic buildings show little but foundations, though a fair amount remains of the refectory's subvault. The one perfectly preserved building is the splendid abbot's kitchen of the fourteenth century, square but with an octagonal lantern supported by a stone roof of the same shape.

Not far away the abbey barn, now a museum of Somerset rural life, is a sophisticated piece of agricultural architecture of about 1300, altered some two centuries later.

Muchelney Abbey Sited on an 'ey', or island, of slightly rising ground in the low-lying country near Langport this was a moderate-sized Benedictine abbey of Anglo-Saxon origins, but rebuilt after the Norman Conquest. The excavated ruins of the church's foundations are of great interest as they include the foundations of the small apsidal pre-Conquest church as well as those of its much larger successor. The chief remains, all late mediaeval, are of the two-storeyed southern cloister walk, of the northern wall of the refectory, and of the abbot's house. This last is an excellent building, purely domestic in character, of the early years of the sixteenth century; it was long used as a farmhouse. Its upstairs parlour has transomed windows and a notably splendid panelled fireplace; also some original glass. A building, now separate from the rest and preserved because of its use as a barn, was the monks' latrine block.

The mediaeval priest's house (for a secular priest serving the parish church) is a well-known building in the village.

Stogursey Priory An attractive example of an 'alien' Benedictine priory church which remained as the local parish church after the suppression of the priory and the bestowal of its lands, like those of other similar cells of French monasteries, on Eton College. Stogursey was a cell of Lonlay in Normandy, and was founded about 1100. From this initial period one has an unaisled nave, remodelled and re-windowed and given some fine bench ends in the fifteenth century, and a simple central tower on plain arches with sculptured capitals. Late in the twelfth century the eastern end was rebuilt, with a square east end, on a much more splendid scale with elaborate arches in the two-arch arcades. The resulting side chapels were enlarged and re-windowed, and integrated into the transepts, in the fifteenth century. The destroyed domestic buildings lay south of the church.

Cleeve Abbey A late twelfth-century Cistercian foundation, always of moderate size and most important now in that its domestic buildings, which were long used as a farm, are the best preserved living quarters of any Cistercian abbey in England.

The church, an Early English building on the standard Cistercian plan, seems to have been little altered throughout the abbey's history. The only

substantial parts of it remaining are the southern wall of the south transept, and part of the south aisle wall of the nave. Far more impressive are the eastern and southern ranges, and a part of the two-storeyed western cloister alley which was rebuilt only a few years before the abbey's dissolution. Most of the eastern range is of the thirteenth century, with the sacristy, a book store, most of the vaulted chapter house, the parlour, and the calefactorium, or common room, which has lost its vault. Above these compartments the dormitory, with numerous lancets, is substantially intact (though with a post-monastic roof) and is one of the best-preserved monks' dormitories in England. The two-storeyed refectory range is now a building of the fifteenth century, with an east–west alignment replacing the normal Cistercian north–south direction of the previous refectory. Its lower storey was divided into private apartments for some of the monks, while the upstairs refectory is a splendid room, with good Perpendicular windows and a cradle roof like those in many West Somerset and Devon parish churches. It could have been available for use as the guest hall of the abbot whose quarters, along with a richly painted reception room, were fitted out in a three-storey block to the west of the refectory.

Hinton Charterhouse Priory Of the two Carthusian priories in Somerset, the one which preserves the most of the main buildings, as distinct from the lay brothers' quarters, is Hinton Priory. This was founded, about 1227 after a move from an earlier site in Gloucestershire, by the Countess Ela who also founded Lacock Abbey. The buildings still above ground are a part of the refectory and a three-tier building, also of the thirteenth century and with lancets. The lower storey, leading out of a small cloister, was the chapter house. There is a room above it, while the four-gabled top stage was a dove house. The plan of the great cloister, and of the cells leading off it, has been revealed by excavation.

Woodspring Priory A small priory of Victorine Augustinian canons, established early in the thirteenth century on a remote coastal site, with attractive remains now belonging to the Landmark Trust. The founder, William Courtenay, was a grandson of one of Becket's murderers, and a relic of the saint's blood made Woodspring a resort of West Country pilgrims honouring St. Thomas of Canterbury.

Nothing remains above ground of the original cruciform church, or of the shorter presbytery of the fifteenth century. But the fan-vaulted central tower and the short nave, both of the fifteenth century, still stand. They survive because they, and not the domestic buildings, were turned into a house after the Dissolution. A large northern chapel, with an arcade of three arches, is later in the Perpendicular period; as it has a separate outside door it may have contained the shrine which was visited by pilgrims. The chapter house doorway is finely cusped work of the fourteenth century, while to the south-east a fifteenth-century building could have been the infirmary; if so it was a large one for so small a community. Among the farm buildings a magnificent fifteenth-century barn is larger than the church.

Stavordale Priory Another small priory of Victorine canons, probably founded in the thirteenth century. It was always small and poorly endowed. Its independent existence ended in 1533 when it became a cell of the much larger Augustinian priory at Taunton. As at Woodspring it was the church which was partly subdivided to become a house; along with what was once the latrine block it is the chief survival of the priory buildings.

The church was simply planned as at Flanesford in Herefordshire with an unaisled nave, no transepts, and an unaisled choir limb. A thirteenth-century piscina remains in what was once the sanctuary, but most of the church was rebuilt in the fifteenth century; a projection to the south of the nave may have been a porch or a bell tower. Few of the fifteenth-century windows retain their mullions or tracery. The stone screen still stands across the lower part of the chancel arch, and the two halves of the church still have their original timber roofs. Off the north-east corner of the church is the beautiful fan-vaulted chantry chapel of John, Lord Zouche who lived in the priory buildings; it is a most accomplished late Perpendicular work of about 1525.

DORSET

The county had numerous pre-Reformation monasteries, with a heavy Benedictine dominance. At Abbotsbury and Cerne the remains, except for a gateway at Cerne and a barn (still half-roofed) of spectacular size at Abbotsbury, are not substantial. Dorset's only mediaeval Cistercian abbey, at Bindon, is of more note for the place which its ruins have in *Tess of the D'Urbervilles* than for the architectural importance of the ruins themselves, while its chief Cistercian remains came into the county as a result of a modern boundary change. At Shaftesbury, where the abbey of Benedictine nuns was the largest and richest mediaeval nunnery in England, almost nothing can be seen, while there are no substantial remains, at Tarrant Keynston, of what was the country's most important abbey of Cistercian nuns. As it happens, Dorset now has England's one modern Cistercian nunnery. This is at Stapehill, near Wimborne, with an Early English church of about 1850 by Charles Hansom, laterally subdivided, as were some mediaeval nunnery churches, between the worshipping places of the nuns and the laity.

Sherborne Abbey The present church was that of a Benedictine Abbey and is the successor of the monastic cathedral, of the Anglo-Saxon period, whose bishopric was moved, soon after the Norman Conquest, to Old Sarum. At the west end of the nave's north aisle a round-headed doorway of this church survives, and there are some other expanses of pre-Conquest masonry. It is also possible that the pillars of the nave, which is certainly shorter than the completely new naves of most large or medium-sized abbeys of the Norman period, are of Saxon masonry coated with Perpendicular panelling. The total structure was at one time considerably longer, and the west wall still has traces of the parish church of All Hallows which was added late in the fourteenth century and pulled down after 1540 when most of the abbey church was made over to the parishioners. Disputes between the monks and the parishioners, coming to a head in 1437 when a riot brought about the destruction by fire of much of the monastic church, caused its rebuilding as the beautiful structure, mostly Perpendicular, which is now the largest church in Dorset.

The south porch, the crossing arches, and much walling in the transepts are the main visible relics of the Norman abbey church. The upper stage of the somewhat stocky central tower is Perpendicular; so too is the short presbytery of three bays with its splendid fan vaulting which was the first in England to be put over the central space of any church of major calibre. The fan vaulting in the remodelled nave was put up later, almost certainly between 1486 and 1493. Thirteenth-century Early English architecture is in a chapel north of the presbytery, and in the first bay of the lady chapel. This chapel was long used, and altered early in Elizabeth I's reign, as the house of the headmaster of Sherborne School, but has now, with modern Perpendicular additions, been restored to church uses. North of the church, some of the monastic buildings remain among those of the school.

Milton Abbey This Benedictine house was of Anglo-Saxon foundation, but like others was rebuilt after the Norman Conquest. The Norman church was mostly destroyed by fire in 1309, but that which replaced it remains except for the lady chapel. Its plan is of great interest for the way in which some aspects of monastic church planning evolved in the last two pre-Reformation centuries. Milton Abbey church, now the superb chapel of a boys' public school established in the adjacent mansion and other buildings, is one of the most beautiful of all England's monastic remains. As at Fountains and Rievaulx the church survived as the great picturesque feature of a Georgian parkland. But it improves on such 'scenic' remains as Fountains, Bayham, and Rievaulx in that most of the church is still roofed and in use; in its wooded downland valley it ranks among the most rewarding of the sites covered in this section.

The present church, most of it built on the site once occupied by the western part of the Norman nave, has a crossing, transepts, and a presbytery limb. A nave, in the circumstances less necessary for a monastic church than its eastern parts, was clearly intended but seems never to have been built. Most of the building is Decorated of the fourteenth century, with the vaults in the choir and its aisles unusually simple for their date. The tower, like that at Sherborne comparatively low, is Perpendicular of the fifteenth century. A splendid fan vault covers the tower space, and the transepts have fine lierne vaults of about 1490. The choir limb lacks continuous arcades. Its first two pairs of arches start above the backing of the stalls, while further east stretches of blank walling alternate with arches to allow liturgical access to the aisles and sacristy. The Decorated east window is high above a towering reredos of canopied niches, while the sanctuary has the feature, very rare in England but found in mediaeval German churches, of a richly canopied wooden sacrament house.

The one important relic of the abbey's domestic buildings, north of the church, is the abbot's guest hall, with an original roof and an ornate wooden screen, which was built in the 1490s. The Georgian mansion, of 1771 onwards by Sir William Chambers, has a 'Gothick' exterior intended to sympathise with the mediaeval Gothic of the church.

Forde Abbey Originally in Devon, but since 1844 in Dorset and only some two hundred yards from the river Axe which divides the property from Somerset Forde, this was an important Cistercian abbey. It is notable now both for its monastic remains and for the seventeenth-century additions and alterations which made it a splendid mansion.

Founded on its present site about 1138 the abbey still has work of the twelfth and thirteenth centuries, but is specially notable for the lavish extensions to its domestic quarters built, by Thomas Chard the last abbot, a few years before the Dissolution. The church has disappeared, and the claustral buildings lay north of it towards the Axe; the monastic remains are from the northern half of those buildings. The vaulted chapter house, Transitional Norman and in two bays with a Perpendicular east window, is now, with a fine classical screen of the seventeenth century, the chapel of the mansion. North of it the Early English dormitory range has an excellent subvault and two rows of original lancets, while the refectory, running north and south in the usual Cistercian manner, was horizontally subdivided in the fifteenth century. The upper half, which has windows and an arch-braced roof of that period, was the 'misericorde' where the eating of meat was allowed on certain days.

The most spectacular changes were made by Abbot Chard and, as at Cleeve, they well showed how even a Cistercian abbot was expected, in the last monastic decades, to cut a figure in local society and to provide lavish hospitality. The one remaining walk of the cloisters is of this Tudor period and was once fan-vaulted west of the cellarium range; at right angles to it, the late Perpendicular abbot's guest hall, with transomed windows, has its own entrance beneath a splendid embattled gate tower which is dated 1528. To the west again were the abbot's lodgings; here, and in the remaining half of the cellarium range, the fittings completed in 1658 are of special magnificence.

DEVON

The mediaeval monastic buildings of Devon have been severely diminished by ruination since the Dissolution, with particularly heavy losses at Benedictine Tavistock and Augustinian Plympton which were the county's two richest monastic houses. So little is left of the original Cistercian buildings of Buckfast Abbey that this monastic site is best considered in the modern section. A fair amount remains of the Augustinian priory at Frithelstock, and at Plymouth there are some remains of the Dominican friary.

122 Milton Abbey, Dorset (Benedictine): choir limb, fourteenth century

Exeter, St. Nicholas' Priory This small Benedictine priory was founded, about 1087, as a cell of Battle Abbey and kept that status till the Dissolution. Some of the refectory range still exists, but most of the remains are those of the western, or cellarium range. A simply vaulted Norman undercroft lies below part of the building, while work of the fifteenth century has rooms which included the prior's lodging, a guest hall with an arch-braced roof, and a projecting western tower. The cloisters had the comparative rarity of a circular fountain, or *lavatorium*, projecting into the enclosure.

One of the post-Reformation uses to which the buildings were put was to serve as the Exeter Assay Office, where much plate by West Country silversmiths was brought to be stamped with the Exeter mark of a three-towered castle.

Buckland Abbey A Cistercian abbey, one of the last three founded in England, which was founded, in 1274, by Amicia (née de Clare), the dowager countess of Devon. Its later associations are with two of the most famous Elizabethan seamen, and its remaining buildings are notable in that most of the church, horizontally subdivided and otherwise fitted out as living quarters, became the main element of the mansion which is now an important branch of the city museum and art gallery of Plymouth.

Most of the claustral buildings, and other living quarters, were pulled down soon after the Dissolution, but one attractive separate building of the fifteenth century, with a slender battlemented tower, still stands and may have been the abbot's house. The church has lost its transepts, but most of the remainder, a late thirteenth-century building with some round windows in its low central tower, stands in a subdivided form. It had the usual short presbytery of a Cistercian abbey, a Perpendicular chapel to the north of that presbytery, and a short nave which suggests that, in the last decades before 1300, lay brothers were fewer and less important in a Cistercian abbey than they had been in the previous century. A room occupying the one-time sanctuary has a piscina, an aumbrey, and fine canopied sedilia of about 1400. The eastern wall had a pair of Geometrical windows, while five smaller windows, above a doorway, made an effective composition in the west front.

After the Dissolution most of the church was remodelled as a house by Sir Richard Grenville whose father obtained the property in the 1540s; a fine

123 St. German's Priory, Cornwall (Augustinian): the west front

fireplace of his time is dated 1576. Other changes were made, after he had bought the mansion in 1581, by Sir Francis Drake who used Buckland Abbey as his main country residence. Not far east of the church, in an unusual position for such a structure, a long, profusely buttressed barn of the fifteenth century is outstanding of its type.

Torre Abbey Within the boundaries of Torquay and with its remains now used for cultural and social purposes by the local municipality the Premonstratensian Abbey of Torre was one of mediaeval England's few important abbeys on a seaside site. Founded in 1196 it was a large establishment, and at the time of the *Valor Ecclesiasticus* in 1535 it was the richest abbey of White canons in the country.

The church was on a typically Premonstratensian plan, with an unaisled presbytery, transepts each with two chapels leading out to the east, a central tower, and a short nave to which a north aisle was added in the fourteenth century. Most of its somewhat scanty remains are of about 1200, the best-preserved portion being the south transept, and with great masses of the tower's masonry lying where they fell. The chapter house entrance has the usual doorway with lower flanking arches; as at Furness and Haughmond the doorway is round-headed but of a basically Gothic character. The site of the refectory is covered by the Georgian mansion built by the Cary family, but the western range is substantially preserved. It has a vaulted undercroft of the early Gothic period, while upstairs the abbot's hall and the guest hall include important reconstruction work of the fifteenth century. A projecting tower in the Perpendicular style recalls that at St. Nicholas' Priory at Exeter, while the great gateway of the abbey, also Perpendicular, stands close to the western range. A large monastic barn is another feature of the abbey buildings.

Polsloe Priory On the eastern outskirts of Exeter this was a small priory of Benedictine nuns. The western range of the conventual buildings still stands. Foundations have been exposed of what was probably an unaisled, rectangular church, also of the refectory range. But the chief remains are in the excellent Early English western range which has lancets along with other windows. Above the cellarium stage the upper floor has a guest hall which still has a simple wooden screen of the thirteenth century, and an original partition between the guest hall and the prioress' room. This has a hooded fireplace not unlike the one in the similar apartments at Lacock.

CORNWALL

Celtic monasteries, like those whose separate huts have been excavated at Tintagel, existed in Cornwall, and there were several mediaeval monastic foundations whose remains are not, however, impressive. At St. Michael's Mount the heavily restored mansion chapel was the church of a Benedictine cell of the abbey of Mont St. Michel, while at St. Anthony in Roseland the largely rebuilt chancel, and the crossing and central tower of the present church were the monastic half of a small cell of the great Augustinian priory at Plympton. Only one of Cornwall's three Augustinian priories has left important remains.

St. German's Priory Replacing the cathedral of the separate Cornish bishopric which came into being in the tenth century and continued for a little over a hundred years, the priory of Augustinian canons regular seems itself to have been the successor of a church served by secular canons. The conventual eastern half of the church has been destroyed, but much of the nave, which was parochial before the Dissolution, remains in use after a good deal of change and mutilation. Two Transitional Norman arches, and some of the clerestorey, still stand on its southernmost side, but the aisle was widened in the fourteenth and fifteenth centuries, with beautiful Decorated tracery in an eastern chapel. The finest part of the church is its splendid west end. The lower part of each tower is late Norman, but in the northern tower the upper stage is octagonal and Early English, while the square top storey of the southern tower is Perpendicular of the fifteenth century. Between the towers the west wall of the nave has good Norman windows; below them beneath a projecting gable is a great doorway of seven orders, elliptical in shape and, despite severe weathering, one of the most splendid late Romanesque doorways in the whole country.

Wales

Like Cornwall Wales had its Celtic monasteries, but those described here are all of the normal mediaeval type. Numerous though unevenly spread, they have, thanks to the remoteness of some of them, left important remains. But none of the Welsh religious houses were, by English standards, large or well endowed. Not one of them, at the time of the *Valor Ecclesiasticus* of 1535, had a clear income of as much as £200 a year. The Cistercians were much in evidence, but except for some 'alien' priories in Monmouthshire the houses of Benedictine monks were few. The largest, the priory at Brecon which was a cell of Battle Abbey, had a fine church which, as it is now a cathedral, falls outside the scope of this section. The Augustinian canons were sparsely represented in Wales, and there were very few nunneries.

As in the section on English monastic sites I deal with those in Wales under the old counties. Some counties have none for me to record here, and the South is better off, for my present purpose, than the North.

FLINT

Basingwerk Abbey* A Cistercian house near Holywell, founded in the twelfth century and with most of its ruined buildings of that period or Early English of the thirteenth century. It was on the standard Cistercian plan, with no eastward elongation of its church, but with some alterations, after their first construction, to its domestic buildings. The best remains of the church are in the west wall and in one of the crossing piers, but there is more to see of the monks' domestic buildings. There are considerable remains of the eastern range; they include two Early English arches which led to a vaulted extension of the chapter house. The refectory still has part of its reader's pulpit, also some good thirteenth-century arcading which adorned the inner side of a row of lancets along its western wall.

DENBIGHSHIRE

Valle Crucis Abbey A small Cistercian abbey in a beautiful valley near Llangollen, founded about 1200 by a Welsh prince. Much of the church, and of the buildings of the eastern range which were kept for farming purposes, still stands. Their architecture is for the most part very early Gothic, with stiff-leaf capitals and with a Romanesque reminiscence in the excellent round-headed doorway which led into the sacristy from the cloisters.

The nave of the church, of only five bays, was short by Cistercian standards. Most of its west wall remains, a charming little rose window of the thirteenth century being above three plate-traceried windows which stand over the western doorway. A great deal of the presbytery survives, and its east wall has an unusual composition of two lancets above a row of three larger ones below them. The two chapels off the south transept have kept much of their simple vaulting.

The best feature of the eastern range is the intact chapter house, beautifully reconstructed in the fourteenth century with three vaulted aisles, pillars without capitals, and Decorated windows; it is, perhaps, the best Cistercian chapter house anywhere in England or Wales. Above it, the dormitory is still roofed and has its lancets of the Early English period; adjoining it is a room, perhaps the sacrist's apartment, which had a window looking into the sanctuary.

ANGLESEY

Penmon Priory A small house of Augustinian canons, picturesquely sited at the far end of the island's north-eastern peninsula. Its early history is somewhat uncertain, but it eventually settled down as an Augustinian priory of the ordinary type.

The church is cruciform, with a Norman nave, a stone-capped central tower, and a south transept

which has some excellent Norman wall arcading; the north transept was rebuilt in the nineteenth century. The nave, which has an ornate south doorway, with a sculptured tympanum, is remarkable in that all its windows remain from the original building period, while the arch from the nave to the crossing is an ornate work. The modern presbytery is longer than the nave, but of the same size as its late mediaeval predecessor. The domestic buildings were unusual in that they lay south of the presbytery and not against the nave. The main remaining building, of the thirteenth century, is the refectory block which had a cellarium and may have had the dormitory above it. Another building of note is a splendid stone-roofed dove house, built shortly before the Dissolution.

124   Valle Crucis Abbey, Denbighshire (Cistercian): view looking east

125   Valle Crucis Abbey: chapter house

CARDIGANSHIRE

Strata Florida Abbey   A Cistercian abbey in the upper valley of the Teifi, founded in 1164 by an Anglo-Norman baron but later with a more purely Welsh character. The ruins, though not impressive in a major way, are in many respects of great interest. The church, mostly Transitional Norman, was on the usual Cistercian plan, with three chapels off each transept; the remains show that its presbytery was lengthened by one bay in the thirteenth century. Most of the ruins are those of the church, and they include a fine collection of mediaeval tiles; the foundations of the refectory are covered by the present farmhouse. The most striking survivals are in the nave, where one can see much of the solid walls which parted the lay brothers' choir from the aisles, and which formed a continuous, above-ground sleeper wall for the arcades. The western doorway, most happily intact, is a major architectural rarity with no equivalent elsewhere in England and Wales. Round-headed and with five continuous moulded orders, it has those mouldings interrupted, at regular intervals, by unbroken moulding, or banding, each course of which ends, outside the main composition of the doorway, in a whorl like an ammonite or the head of an abbot's pastoral staff.

PEMBROKESHIRE

Caldey Island   The small priory on the island (originally known as Ynys Pyr) was the successor to a Celtic religious community. The mediaeval priory was founded about 1113 and became a cell of the larger, and now far more drastically ruined abbey of St. Dogmael's in the same county. Both monasteries were houses of the reformed Benedictines of the order of Tiron. As the domestic buildings became a farm after the Dissolution they, like the church, are substantially intact, and this tiny group of monastic buildings may well be the smallest in England and Wales to remain in so good a condition. The refectory was almost square, and the monks of so small a priory seem to have dispensed with a chapter house, but otherwise all the usual buildings round a cloister garth were built and mostly seem to be Norman period or of the fourteenth century. The church, only 76 feet long, had a presbytery and an unaisled nave which served as the choir; also a western tower and spire only 47 feet high.

The old priory church is under the care of the

Cistercian monks of the modern abbey on the island, and Mass is still offered in it. The present-day monastery is covered in the section on modern communities.

CARMARTHENSHIRE

Talley Abbey*   Founded late in the twelfth century this was the only Premonstratensian abbey in Wales. Its domestic buildings have almost wholly disappeared, but though the ruins of its church are somewhat scanty they are of considerable interest. The plan, with a short presbytery flanked by three chapels on each side, and with a long aisled nave of eight bays west of the central tower, was much more typical of a Cistercian abbey than it was of a house of White canons. The best remains, apart from some walling of the presbytery and the chapels, come from the central tower; probably of about 1200. The eastern wall is nearly intact and the northern one considerably so.

One authority has suggested that the church was originally planned for Cistercians, but that it was later handed over to the Premonstratensians. Most of the nave was parochial before the Dissolution, and after that a much smaller parish church was contrived within the ruins. This was pulled down in 1772.

BRECONSHIRE

Brecon, Dominican Friary   Founded about 1250, this friary has left important remains, and its choir is the only choir of a mediaeval friary, in England or Wales, which is still used for worship. After its suppression the friary was continued, by the transfer of revenues from Abergwili near Carmarthen, as a collegiate church, and some of the domestic buildings were used as their main residence by several Bishops of St. David's. A grammar school was also founded in the buildings. This was revived, in the nineteenth century, as Christ College, which now uses the re-roofed and restored friary choir as its chapel.

The choir is Early English of the thirteenth century and has beautiful shafted lancets in its side walls, sedilia, and a restored double piscina. The east window, of five lancet lights under a retaining arch, must have been inserted later in the century. The nave is ruined, but some of its fourteenth-century northern arcade still stands. Large parts of the friars' domestic buildings are incorporated into those of Christ

College; they include a fine fourteenth-century room which has a window shaped as a convex-sided triangle.

Though just in Breconshire (now Powis) the remains of 'Father' Ignatius' monastery of Llanthony are dealt with along with the original Llanthony, lower down the same valley but in Monmouthshire (Gwent).

GLAMORGAN

Ewenny Priory One of the most attractive examples, anywhere in Britain, of a small Benedictine priory which was a cell, or dependency, of a larger abbey, in this case St. Peter's at Gloucester. Except for the north transept, and the chapels leading off both transepts, the church is intact, and though the site of the monks' domestic buildings is covered by a more recent mansion there are still two fine fourteenth-century gateways, and the perimeter walls, of a fortified manor, which adjoined the priory.

A church, now the Norman nave of the larger building, existed at Ewenny before 1141 when the priory was founded, well showing how small Benedictine monasteries, and other church property, in the Anglo-Norman lordship of Glamorgan often belonged to large English abbeys in the area under the influence of the powerful Earls of Gloucester. The monastic part of the church, with its central tower, transepts, and a short presbytery, was added to the older church, the two parts being separated by a solid screen. The nave, with its north aisle, is still parochial, while the eastern part of the building, long a private chapel, is now cared for by the Department of the Environment.

The south transept, the central tower with its post-Norman stepped battlements, and the presbytery are all of much architectural interest. The transept still has the two Norman arches which led into its chapels, also, in its western wall, an excellent run of triforium arcading. The tower arches rest on paired shafts, while the first two bays of the unaisled presbytery have the feature, very rare in British Romanesque buildings, of a barrel vault; the vault over the easternmost bay is groined. The presbytery is entered through the rare feature of a fourteenth-century wooden screen with Decorated tracery. Among various monuments the early thirteenth-century floriated grave slab of Maurice de Lundres, the priory's founder, is outstanding of its type.

126   Strata Florida Abbey, Cardiganshire (Cistercian): west doorway

Margam Abbey Of great importance, along with Holm Cultram, as one of the two Cistercian abbeys in England and Wales where part of the nave is still used for worship. The founder, in 1147, was Robert Fitzroy, Earl of Gloucester, the abbey being towards the western end of his Glamorgan lordship. The church, with an aisled presbytery, became one of the largest Cistercian churches in Wales, and the western six bays of its nave became a parish church soon after the Dissolution. The roof was lowered early in the nineteenth century, but traces of the clerestorey stage exist above the late Romanesque arcades with their squared piers and simple arches. The west front still has its trio of round-headed and shafted windows and, below them, a fine doorway of three moulded orders and traces of the roof of a galilee porch. The wheel window (modelled on that at Robert of Gloucester's other foundation of St. James' Priory, Bristol) and the turrets are neo-Norman work of the Regency period.

Inside the church the tombs of the Mansels, who obtained the property and preserved the nave, are of high Renaissance quality. The ruins of the eastern part of the church, and of the domestic buildings, are on private land. Their best features are the magnificent Early English entrance arch, and a vaulted vestibule, which led to a beautiful polygonal chapter house whose vault and central pillar were still intact in 1780.

193

MONMOUTHSHIRE (Gwent)

Abergavenny Priory A Benedictine cell to an abbey at Le Mans in France; it continued, after the suppression of the 'alien' priories, as a small independent priory, of importance as the burial place of several families of note in the surrounding area. The whole church survives in parochial use, but most of the present nave is modern. The central tower with its vaulted tower space, the presbytery with its side chapels, and the unaisled eastern lady chapel are mostly of the fourteenth century, but have some Perpendicular windows. The choir stalls, with a continuous cove and cresting rather than individual canopies, survive from the monastic furnishings.

The mediaeval tombs, from about 1273 to the early sixteenth century, are outstanding. The families of Cantilupe, de Braose, Hastings and, particularly, the ap Thomases and Herberts are all represented; their memorials make Abergavenny Priory as important for its own area as Tewkesbury Abbey is for the lower Severn valley.

Chepstow Priory The castle here, started by Richard Fitzosbern in 1068, was the earliest of the great castles built in South Wales to establish Anglo-Norman lordships. The Benedictine priory was founded soon afterwards, and was, till the fifteenth century, a cell of the Norman abbey of Cormeilles which was the family abbey of the Fitzosberns. The five western bays of the nave survived the Dissolution as the parish church, and in 1841 and at the end of the Victorian period the building was enlarged to regain its cruciform plan and something of its original dimensions.

The Norman nave has lost most of its aisle walls. Above its simple arcades with their square piers the triforium is of two arches in each bay on the southern side and of single arches on the north; the clerestorey is of plain single windows. The finest Norman work is in the west front which was built late in the Norman period, with three west windows and, below them, a magnificent doorway of five orders of rolled moulding, zig-zag work, star pattern, and other decoration. Above the west front the tower is of Queen Anne's time.

Tintern Abbey One of the most famous and impressive of all ruined abbeys, in a particularly beautiful site in the Wye valley where the situation is, however, thanks to the modern road (authorised in 1824) and the numerous visitors which it can easily

127 Margam Abbey, Glamorgan (Cistercian): the nave

bring, less of a 'wild secluded scene' than it was when the poet Wordsworth came to Tintern in the summer of 1798. The abbey was Cistercian, and was notable for the way in which the first, comparatively small and unaisled church of the abbey founded in 1131, was wholly replaced, late in the thirteenth century and shortly after 1300, by the stately church, with its comparatively short nave, whose ruins now stand between the road and the river to the north.

The church is much better preserved than the domestic buildings, and were it not for the loss of its northern nave arcade it would be the best preserved ruined monastic church in the country. It has an aisled presbytery limb of four bays and a structural nave of six. There was never any triforium stage. The style, late Geometrical merging into early Decorated, is

much the same all through the church, but the arcade arches in the presbytery and transepts (i.e. in the monks' part of the church) are more richly moulded than those in the nave. Many shafts have been robbed from pillars and doorways in the eastern part of the church. In each of the four gables a large upper window was placed, as in the choir at Selby, to light the space between the vaults and the timber roof. The church's most notable stylistic feature, with most of its tracery intact, is the early Decorated west window of seven lights.

The original domestic buildings were replaced earlier than the church so that the ruins of the refectory, which are better preserved than those of the eastern and western ranges, have windows, with early plate tracery, of the first half of the thirteenth century. A watergate, which led to the slipway built for the ferry across the Wye, is a building of much interest and character.

Llanthony Priory In a wild, deep, and romantic valley in the Black Mountains the site of Llanthony is what one would normally expect for a Cistercian abbey. The priory was, however, one of Augustinian canons regular, but its austere remoteness was so little to the canons' taste that its dependent priory at Gloucester eventually became much the richer and the more important of the two. The ruins of *Lantonia Prima* are, however, of great merit and beauty, making it one of the most attractive monastic sites in the whole country.

A group of hermits (in the literal sense of dwellers in a wilderness) settled at Llanthony early in the twelfth century, living by no particular rule but recognised, not later than about 1117, as a community of Augustinian canons. After many of the inmates had left, in 1136, for Hereford and then Gloucester, the original priory remained numerically small. Soon after 1175 an attempt was made to revive it, and the ambitious church, whose splendid ruins are still admired, was started about that time. Except for a Decorated or Perpendicular east window the church changed little after its completion about 1200.

The church had an unaisled presbytery with large flanking chapels, transepts and a central tower of moderate height and a nave of seven arcaded bays with another between its pair of finely arcaded western towers. Much of the presbytery, of the central tower, and of the south transept is left, all Transitional Norman with some windows round-headed and with trumpet-scalloped capitals for the vaulting shafts. The nave, whose north arcade remains intact, had continuous pointed arches, without capitals, and a low triforium and clerestorey whose units were combined, in each bay, under single arches. This sophisticated design seems to be related to the late twelfth-century work at Wells Cathedral and possibly, in addition, to the church of Llanthony's daughter priory just outside Gloucester.

The remains of the domestic buildings include a slype whose vaulting is still intact, and the ruins of an apsidal chapter house. A little is left of the refectory undercroft, but the main domestic survival is the undercroft of the western range which, along with the south-western tower, forms part of the present hotel.

A few miles up the valley, at the end of a road which is passable by cars but not by such large vehicles as motor coaches, the Victorian monastery and church built by 'Father' Ignatius Lyne is at Capel y Ffyn just over the Breconshire border. 'Father' Ignatius' first plan had been to buy and restore *Lantonia Prima*, but when he could not do this he built *Lantonia Tertia* in an even remoter situation. His scheme was to build a church almost as large as the original Llanthony, and the style which he chose, including trumpet-scalloped capitals, was that of the ruined church of 1175–1200, his architect being Charles Buckeridge. The choir was finished in 1882, but the nave was never built. The choir, roofless but now tidied up and with Lyne's tomb before the site of its high altar, remains as a remarkably convincing monastic ruin of the last century. The simple Gothic monastery buildings do not adjoin it, though they must have been meant, in the manner of mediaeval monastic buildings, to connect directly with the projected nave. They are now a guest house, and the long, narrow room used as a chapel, in the 1920s, by Eric Gill and his community of artists has painting and lettering by Eric Gill on its roof beams and elsewhere.

Lantonia Prima and Tertia make this valley of the Honddu a *pièce de résistance* for monastic enthusiasts.

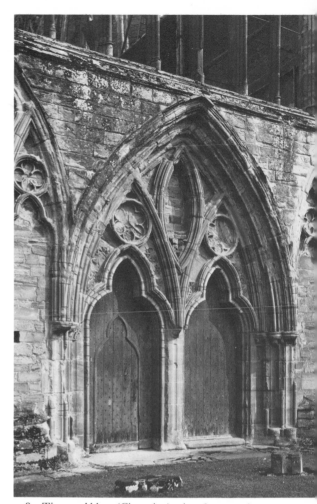

128   Tintern Abbey (Cistercian): view from south-east

Usk Priory   This was a small, aristocratically recruited house of Benedictine nuns, well known in the region for its shrine of St. Radegund which became a place of pilgrimage. Of Norman foundation it had an apsidal presbytery and semi-circular chapels off its transepts. All these have been destroyed, but the central tower remains, and the groined space below it is now the chancel of the church. The nave and its north aisle, which were the parish church before the Dissolution, still serve that purpose and are mainly of the fourteenth century; at their eastern end the delicately cusped and traceried screen is about a hundred years later. The nave also has, at its west end and as a northern entrance, two attractive rib-vaulted porches of the late fifteenth century.

The gatehouse is the only important survival of the domestic buildings.

Some Modern Communities

I here give a small selection of present-day religious houses. Some such convents, particularly those of Anglican religious orders, have already been mentioned in some detail. As all of them are now the homes and worshipping places of existing religious communities they obviously differ from the preserved or ruined buildings on old monastic sites where some of the churches are now parish churches of the Church of England, or where the ruins of all sections, including those of buildings which were once private quarters like dormitories, parlours, kitchens, and refectories are freely open to outsiders in a way that would have been impossible in the days of their intact pre-Reformation use. While the churches of modern communities, particularly those of orders which serve schools and lay people from outside, are many of them easier to visit, and more free for circulation, than their mediaeval equivalents this ease of access naturally does not apply, unless one is expected, to their domestic buildings.

In the more strictly enclosed and contemplative convents the churches, except for the extern chapels provided for lay visitors, are not normally seen except by those with special business. Though some of these conventual churches, particularly those of some Anglican women's communities, are important as modern church architecture I have not normally described them in this section. A few, however, are briefly mentioned, the first two because of their special historic position among the communities which arose, at first on the Continent, in the 'penal' period of English Catholicism which was also the time of the Counter Reformation and the Teresian reform.

England
CO. DURHAM

Darlington, Carmelite convent Best known for its great place in England's railway history Darlington is also a vintage town for contemplative communities,

of early origins and now existing side by side. One of them, indeed, came to Darlington only five years later than the opening of the railway to Stockton-on-Tees.

The origins of the Darlington Carmel go back to 1648, when the community was founded at Lier near Antwerp. In 1794 the nuns migrated to England, first to London and then to a house near Bishop Auckland. They moved again in 1804 and in 1830 came to Darlington where they bought a large late-Georgian house, set in ample grounds on the rural outskirts of what was still a fairly small town. A large room, now the refectory, was the nuns' first chapel, but additions to the house were made at various dates. The most important of these, finished in 1859, was a spacious stone-built chapel, Early English in character with five eastern lancets and a reredos of trefoil-headed niches whose statues have been cleared away as part of the chapel's redecoration and reordering. A small extern chapel lies north of the sanctuary.

The Carmelite community which had, since 1875, been at Wells was, in 1972, amalgamated with that at Darlington.

Darlington, Abbey of Poor Clares Next to the Carmelites, and further south along Nunnery Lane the buildings of the Poor Clares' Abbey are wholly Gothic, and more obviously conventual as the Victorians understood such groupings. This convent too is of seventeenth-century origin; its community has existed a little longer than that of the adjacent Carmelites. It was founded at Rouen in 1644, from the pioneering post-Reformation convent of English Poor Clares at Gravelines. In 1793 the convent was suppressed by French Revolutionaries, and in 1794, after some months in a French prison, the nuns returned to England. For the next six decades their history was that of a series of moves typical, after flight from the Continent, of many English religious communities. For a time they were in a country house in Northumberland, and then at Scorton near Catterick in Yorkshire. From there, in the 1850s, these Poor

Clares moved to Darlington, buying the site of their present abbey from the Carmelites whose grounds were large enough for such a subdivision.

The buildings, designed by Joseph Hansom, were finished in 1857. In red brick with stone dressings and decoration, they include an outer lodge, while the chapel has, at its north-western corner, a turret with an attractive stone cap. A porch has a niche with a statue of St. Clare. The style of the buildings is early Decorated, the chapel being unaisled with an extern chapel on its sanctuary's northern side. The stalls, from Scorton, are simple late-Georgian woodwork, and the screen is an attractive early Decorated work corresponding to the building itself. More typically Victorian elaboration is in the sanctuary, with an east window of six lights and below it a rich altarpiece and a throne for use at Benediction.

YORKSHIRE

Ampleforth Abbey   The largest community in the English Benedictine congregation was founded in 1608 when some English monks of other congregations started conventual life, at Dieulouard in Lorraine, in what had been the secular collegiate church of St. Laurence. The monks and the school remained at Dieulouard till 1793, when the school was disbanded and the community temporarily dispersed. After a time at Acton Burnell and then in Lancashire (from which county, with numerous Benedictine parishes, many Ampleforth monks have come) the Laurentians moved, in 1802, to a late-Georgian house built, on the hillside at Ampleforth, to accommodate the Benedictine chaplain of the Fairfax family of the nearby Gilling Castle. This house, altered but still standing and with its later top storey recently taken down for reasons of safety, remains the nucleus of the monastic and school buildings which arose, on a largely linear plan unlike that of a mediaeval monastery, along the hillside and below the road between Ampleforth and Oswaldkirk.

The original house was soon extended at each end, and in 1818–20 a new block, containing a downstairs refectory subdivided by two rows of Greek Doric columns, was run out at the back. A chapel was fitted out in one wing, but its successor, like Ampleforth's later nineteenth-century buildings, was purpose-built and in revival Gothic. Designed by Charles Hansom and finished in 1857, it was more like a parish church than most mediaeval priories or abbeys. It had an unaisled nave and chancel and a south transept and

was in the Decorated style. Just east of the enlarged Georgian house the main buildings of the College, mid-Victorian Gothic by Joseph Hansom, went up early in the 1860s, and in 1893 an architect named Bernard Smith made plans for wholly new monastery buildings and for a large cruciform church, with a spire, which would have absorbed the site of the old buildings and of Charles Hansom's church. What was actually built, by 1898, was the present late-Victorian Gothic monastery block of study bedrooms. Its position, and that of the preserved Georgian buildings, determined the modest length of the present church which arose on the site of Charles Hansom's building.

The church is the most important, and the most visited of Ampleforth's buildings. Its architect was Sir Giles Gilbert Scott, who also designed some excellent boarding houses, and other buildings, for the College. His church is aisled and cruciform, with a simple central tower of an early Gothic type, a single compartment on each side of the crossing, and vaulting in three saucer domes modelled on those of St. Front at Périgueux and other churches, of Byzantine inspiration, via St. Mark's at Venice, in western France. The arches of the short arcades are not, however, rounded as at Périgueux, Cahors, Angoulême, and elsewhere.

The new church was built in two stages. The western limb, with the monks' choir which has the abbot's throne against the middle of the west wall, was started in 1922. Its arches, windows, and doorframes, early Gothic and with finely carved capitals, are all rendered in a beautiful greenish blue stone. The high altar, under the western crossing arch and with a single-arched canopy in an Arts and Crafts Gothic more distinctively Scott's own, are of the same material. But the crossing piers, and the eastern nave of the church, with its short projection and a deep gallery, to give more seating for the boys of the College, have their brick arches more simply detailed and faced with whitish plaster. The work was done, at a time of post-war financial stringency, in 1958–61. A large crypt, with many chapels, runs under the nave and below much of the southern, downhill side of the church; its use has been lessened by the frequency, upstairs, of concelebrated Masses.

The choir stalls (from Scott's designs) and much other woodwork in the abbey were made by the famous craftsman Walter (or 'Mousey') Thompson of Kilburn not far from Ampleforth. His whimsical little rebus of a climbing mouse can here, as in such other places as Bridlington Priory, be spotted by observant visitors. The extensive buildings of the school, which lie east of the church and monastery, include some new blocks by the well-known modern architects Arup Associates. Of buff-coloured concrete, they include classrooms, common rooms, dormitories, and study bedrooms.

LEICESTERSHIRE

Mount St. Bernard Abbey The history of Mount St. Bernard's Abbey belongs to that of the reformed, or Trappist Cistercians since the upheaval of the French Revolution. England's first post-Reformation Cistercians had been the mainly French community which was, for a few years, at Lulworth in Dorset. Some years after these monks' return to a Cistercian monastery at Melleray in Brittany most of the English and Irish monks in the community were forced to leave France and founded the new abbey of Mount Melleray in Ireland. From there, in 1835, the daughter house of Mount St. Bernard was established, on land in the Charnwood Forest country of Leicestershire bought for the monks by Ambrose Phillips de Lisle. Its buildings, started to designs by Augustus Pugin and with the church put up in two main stages, are those of the present abbey. The domestic buildings, with a cloister court somewhat small in relation to the church, and with numerous small and narrow lancets typical of Pugin's Early English designs, recall conventual buildings which Pugin designed in Ireland and elsewhere. They include a polygonal chapter house (not by A.W. Pugin) while the guest house, now mainly used for retreats, is more mid-Victorian in character and is only partly by him.

The most important of the present abbey buildings is the church, over two hundred feet long and with its western half, now the monks' choir and not the nave as was intended when, in 1840, Pugin made his designs, completed in 1844. Its simple Early English style, with round pillars, chamfered arches, no triforium, and a steeply pitched timber roof, is like that of Pugin's Nottingham Cathedral, a few miles away, which was built at the same time. The choir stalls are truly Cistercian in the simplicity of their woodwork, and were designed by Eric Gill.

For nearly a hundred years the church remained unfinished. When, in 1935–37, the eastern part was built its layout differed much from what Pugin had envisaged. His drawings, and a ground plan of 1869, show that his original ideas were for a short eastern presbytery of a traditional Cistercian type. But the actual eastern limb, in style very similar to Pugin's work and used as a nave for visiting laity, is of six bays and not much shorter than the western limb in which the monks have their choir. The architect, also the designer of the present central tower which is higher than the central tower, with a broach spire, which Augustus Pugin designed, was Albert Herbert of Leicester. The tower space is vaulted, and the simple dignified High Altar lies below its eastern arch. The sanctuary was planned for the liturgy as this was celebrated before the second Vatican Council and has not been adapted to serve more recent needs.

STAFFORDSHIRE

Hawkesyard Priory Close to the Gothicised mansion now known, from its association with the potting family of the Spodes, as Spode House and a much frequented conference centre, the priory of Hawkesyard is the most conventual, or rather collegiate, in character of England's present-day Dominican friaries. The Dominicans came there in 1894 and soon started the church and friary buildings. The church was finished in 1899 and the domestic buildings, round two sides of a quadrangle which was to have had a third range and a polygonal chapter house, were built in the following years. The architect was Edward Goldie, and the priory buildings, whose cloister walks project into the quadrangle, are in an undistinguished late-Gothic style. But the brick and stone church, though simpler than it appears in its architect's designs, is of considerable merit; I have mentioned it elsewhere as 'a convincing Oxbridge chapel'. Of nine bays and late Perpendicular, it has a choir of five bays and an antechapel of four. Its blank east wall is largely filled, as in the chapel of New College, Oxford, by three tiers of statues in canopied niches; above them a Crucifixion group is flanked by mural paintings. The chapel has a simple hammerbeam roof, canopied stalls in the collegiate manner, a fan-vaulted chantry chapel on one side and, unexpectedly, a splendid Baroque organ case of 1700–1 which was originally in the college chapel at Eton.

HEREFORDSHIRE

Belmont Abbey This Benedictine abbey near Hereford is interesting for two reasons: its church was not originally built for monastic use, and it is England's one example, among modern Catholic churches, of a one-time cathedral no longer having that status.

Francis Wegg-Prosser, a local gentleman who in 1850 became a Roman Catholic, owned the Belmont estate and there built an almshouse and a school. In 1854 he started a more ambitious church to designs by the young Edward Pugin who had recently taken over his father's practice. With transepts and a short chancel this was first meant as a parish church, with no precise arrangements for its staffing. But the Benedictines soon took over the church, putting up monastery buildings both to serve this community and as a general novitiate for their English congregation. The church, enlarged to meet monastic needs and with its central tower finished in the 1880s, became the cathedral priory church of the Catholic diocese of Newport and Menevia. Its cathedral status lasted till 1920 when Cardiff became that bishopric's sole headquarters. Since then Belmont has been an abbey of the ordinary English Benedictine type.

The church, of modest size and with its tower arches somewhat intrusively parting the nave from the choir and sanctuary of the 1860s, clearly shows its parochial origins and later monastic use. The nave, of three bays with a full clerestorey and various neo-Decorated windows, is more spacious than the attractive, but somewhat cramped eastern limb which has side chapels but no real clerestorey; its upper windows, concave-sided triangles of early fourteenth-century character, lie beneath projecting gables. The north transept holds the chantry chapel and the elaborate polychrome Gothic tomb of the Benedictine Bishop Brown, while that of Bishop Hedley, who died in 1915, is of Renaissance character and is now in the nave.

The Victorian Gothic monastic buildings are in a plainer Gothic style than that of the church; they have some good sculptured features. Some school buildings, of the 1950s and later, are 'contemporary' in character.

WORCESTERSHIRE

Stanbrook Abbey This is the largest community, in the English congregation, of Benedictine nuns. Founded at Cambrai in 1625 the community was there till the French Revolution. After nearly two years in prison the nuns came to England, and like other 'refugee' penal communities they moved more than once before the property at Stanbrook near Worcester was bought for them in 1835. Alterations and additions included a simple late-Georgian chapel which later became a chapter house; its architect was Charles Day of Worcester who also designed the Roman Catholic churches at Hereford and Bury St. Edmund's.

The abbey's main buildings are Victorian Gothic. The church, by Edward Pugin, was finished in 1871. It was logically designed for the needs of a modern nuns' community, and though it has side chapels its main fabric comprises an unaisled nave (used as the nuns' choir) and a sanctuary equivalent to a parochial chancel. The stalls are not in continuous rows but in groups in the window recesses. The architectural style is ornate Geometrical Gothic, while instead of the bellcote shown in Edward Pugin's drawings the church has a tall north-western tower with one pinnacle higher than the rest.

A large domestic block was started in 1878, and another block, forming an L-shaped building for this large community, is of the 1890s. Both are Gothic by Peter Paul Pugin.

GLOUCESTERSHIRE

Prinknash Abbey This beautifully sited, much visited Benedictine abbey of the Subiaco congregation has had a varied history since, in 1928, its community moved from Caldey Island. The old house, with its chapel enlarged by a Victorian Gothic sanctuary and again, in 1955, by a laity chapel designed by H.S. Goodhart-Rendel, served for over forty years as the monastery. It has its own earlier Benedictine history as it was once part of the estates of St. Peter's Abbey, Gloucester. Though some of the building is early mediaeval, it was largely rebuilt, in the 1520s, by William Parker, the last abbot, who used it as a country retreat.

In the 1930s the late Abbot Upson conceived a scheme for a vast abbey church, and ambitious domestic buildings, which were to be built on a sloping site commanding a superb view over Glouces-

129 Prinknash Abbey, Gloucestershire (Benedictine): church below, monastery block above

130 Prinknash Abbey: a monk's cell

ter and the lower Severn valley; this was nearly a mile from the old buildings. The style of the church, to be about as large as Gloucester Cathedral and for which Mr. Goodhart-Rendel got out designs, was to combine Byzantine and Norman Romanesque features. The steep site made it necessary to plan a double crypt, and work on the lower tier started in 1939. This lower crypt was finished in twenty years, but it later became clear that the abbey as first planned could never, for financial and other reasons, be finished.

What eventually happened, after some controversy with the planning authorities, and a public enquiry, was the building by 1973, from designs by Mr. F.G. Broadbent, of an abbey whose present buildings are mainly domestic and whose plan, bar the refectory block projecting to the north, corresponds to the cruciform plan of the church of the earlier scheme. The monks wished to use the existing sub-crypt, so this, with some art metalwork and beautiful modern glass made in the abbey, is now the monastic church. It is somewhat low inside, but is reasonably capacious and has the three altars which are all that seem necessary now that concelebration has become frequent. Above it, the space planned for the upper crypt has become the library, while higher still a four-storeyed block of study bedrooms, faced with yellowish Cotswold stone and in a simple 'contemporary' style uses, as its main supports, the foundation piers meant for the pillars of the crypt and presbytery of the church of which Abbot Upson dreamed. A transeptal section, which perpetuates that church's cruciform plan, contains the abbot's quarters, an infirmary, and a house chapel, while a long western limb corresponds to the proposed nave and contains the long *ambulacrum*, or passageway, between the monastery block and a wing, contains guest-rooms, offices, and a parlour, whose plan recalls the *westwerk* of some great mediaeval Benedictine churches.

The crypt church is open to visitors, while the well-known pottery, the shop, and tearooms are a little way up the hill. The old manor, now known as St. Peter's Grange, has become a Retreat House. Its programme, with visits by Quaker, Baptist, and United Reformed groups as well as by Roman Catholics, is markedly ecumenical.

OXFORDSHIRE

Oxford, Dominican Friary (Blackfriars) The Dominicans returned to Oxford late in the 1920s. Their well-known church and priory are in the Broad, next to the High Anglican stronghold of Pusey House. The architect was Doran Webb of Salisbury and the church, of somewhat unusual dimensions and orientated west and east, is in a late Perpendicular style. Both the nave and the choir are unaisled and wide for their length, and their broad timber roofs are of some constructional virtuosity. No solid screen divides the two component parts. A large 'east' window of seven lights is devoid of coloured glass. In the nave a series of small chapels, each in its own recess, leads off one

side. The domestic buildings, south of the church, are in a simple Elizabethan or Jacobean idiom.

LONDON

Ealing Abbey In 1897 a small Catholic parish was established here, the first priest being a monk of Downside. A small priory, dependent on Downside, was later set up, and the Benedictine presence in London was thus re-established. The running of a large parish, the serving of convent chapels and the conduct of a large boys' day school are now the concern of a medium-sized community. In 1947 the priory became independent, and in 1955 attained the rank of an abbey. Alone among the monastic churches of the English Benedictines the one at Ealing was badly damaged by wartime bombing; one now sees it in a rebuilt and slightly extended form.

The first part of the church, designed by F.A. Walters who also worked for the Benedictines at Downside and Buckfast, was opened in 1899. It was later extended by Edward Walters to form a long nave, in the early Perpendicular style, understoreyed and with a hammerbeam roof of East Anglian character; East Anglian references are also in the dignified west front, with flush work and a large nine-light window, whose fine glass fortunately survived the bombing, above the three entrance doorways.

The 'eastern' part of the church was that which got destroyed, and two demolished side chapels have not been replaced. What was done, in an ecclesiastical phase which one can call post-war but pre-Vatican II, was the building, in a style like that of the church's unbombed portion, of two transepts and a crossing which supports the short lower stage of a tall intended central tower. The architect, who had taken over the Walters practice, was Stanley Kerr-Bate. His scheme of 1954, for an ambitious eastern limb, with a presbytery of six bays and an apsidal lady chapel, was never carried out, and the church now ends, just behind its High Altar, in a temporary flat wall. In the nave there are, off the 'south' aisle, arched recesses for side altars. One of these was fitted up, as a chapel of St. Boniface and as an act of reparation for the destruction of 1940, by the West German Government. A large, well-equipped parish centre also adjoins the church. In the sanctuary the monks' stalls are post-war woodwork of Gothic character.

The original monastery block, brick and stone early Tudor by F.A. Walters, lies to one side of the church; it contains a chapter house with a set of pseudo-mediaeval stalls. The recent extension, finished in 1975 and by the Coventry architects Hellberg, Harris, and Rayner, is in a wholly contemporary style. The new monastery block has triangular projections, as at Douai, along its front wall, with an attractive blend of warm red brickwork and tile hanging, while the new refectory is a single-storey building. The school, now with over seven hundred boys, has its varied buildings well to the other side of the church, while a lay community has been established in a nearby suburban house.

Ealing Abbey has recently set up a small daughter house at Montreal in Canada.

KENT

St. Augustine's Abbey, Ramsgate* This is a Benedictine abbey, of the Subiaco congregation and with its attendant school now, at Westgate on Sea, elsewhere in the Isle of Thanet, in buildings formerly used by the canonesses of St. Augustine. Its church, of moderate size and not at first built for monastic use, is most important as a building by Augustus Pugin, with the architect's tomb in a chantry chapel in the south transept which has no north transept to balance it.

Augustus Pugin bought the cliff-side site in 1841 and there, by 1844, built The Grange, a brick-and-stone Tudor-style house with a tower and a private chapel on its eastern side. The house was Pugin's main home till his death in 1852. His church of St. Augustine, cruciform and with its nave and chancel three-gabled in a typically Kentish manner, was built just east of the house in 1845–50. The broach spire designed to cap its unpinnacled central tower was never built, and the tower windows are not as they appear in one of Pugin's drawings. The building of this church, one of the few where the architect was his own patron and encountered no restrictions or complaints from clients, was largely financed by Pugin's earnings from his superb decorative work in the Houses of Parliament.

The church was not monastic in Augustus Pugin's time, and the Benedictines first came there in 1856. The monastery buildings, across the road from the church, and reached by an underground tunnel, were put up in 1860–61. The church and The Grange are the buildings designed by Augustus Pugin. The church is smaller than some others designed as abbey churches, and is in the early Decorated style particularly favoured by its designer. The nave and presbytery are each of two bays, and the chamfered

tower arches are notably fine. The presbytery's side arches, moulded and with foliate capitals, are more elaborate. Re-ordering, to meet current liturgical requirements, has had some effect on Pugin's furnishings. The presbytery screen has been moved to the lady chapel, while the choir stalls have been re-arranged so that some are now placed along the eastern wall. This means that Pugin's High Altar and its tabernacle have been dismantled, but the removal of the tall canopy once over the tabernacle and the Benediction throne has produced a much improved view of Pugin's beautiful east window.

SUSSEX

Worth Abbey This Benedictine abbey was founded, as a dependent priory of Downside, in 1933, and Downside's Junior School was there for a few years. The property, with its large Victorian Gothic mansion of various dates, had been known as 'Paddockhurst' and was, immediately before its purchase, the property of the second Viscount Cowdray whose father made many alterations still seen in the house. A simple monastery block, of temporary construction, was soon built, but some of the mansion's rooms are still used by the monks, among them the refectory which has rich pseudo-Baroque decorations and a striking stucco frieze, by Walter Crane, which shows aspects of the history of transport. A long, narrow late-Gothic winter garden was at first used as a geometrically inconvenient church for the monks and the boys of the school. But Worth Abbey's most striking feature is the new church, completed in 1975 though not as originally planned early in the 1960s.

Designed by Mr. Francis Pollen, the church at Worth is certainly England's most important monastic church in so strikingly 'contemporary' a style. Square, but with the interior impression of a circle created by the shallow concrete dome over its sanctuary and congregational space, its detailed planning, and its relationship to the other monastic buildings, have been affected by the fact that Worth is a smaller community than was once envisaged and by liturgical changes during its building, temporarily interrupted for financial reasons. The monastery blocks, which were to have enveloped it on two sides, are not yet needed, while concelebration has removed the need for lateral chapels and for a crypt full of altars. What has happened, in an impressive interior whose concrete structure is masked by beautiful buff-coloured brickwork, is the fitting out, behind screen walls

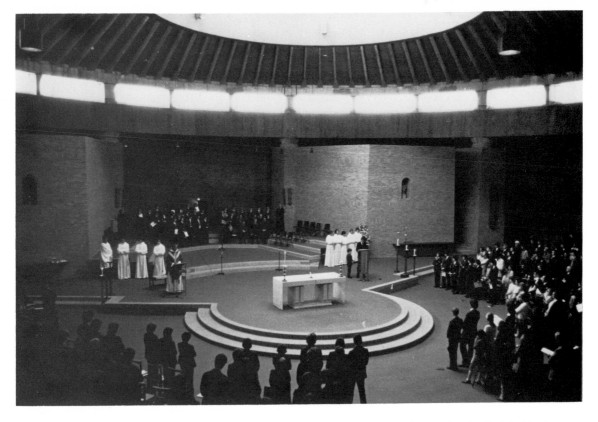

132 Worth Abbey, Sussex (Benedictine): inside the new church

which severely mask them from the main worshipping space (consisting of the sanctuary, the choir and the 'nave'), of two chapels which are, when one gets inside them, serenely devotional. The church's most striking feature, with a silhouette like that associated with 'flying saucers', is the concrete dome whose supporting piers are clad with brick. A massive concrete ring beam runs below a series of horizontal windows whose eventual glazing should give colour to the church's interior. The choir space has yet to be permanently furnished, and an entrance narthex has still to be built. Proposals for this, for two more side chapels, and for conference rooms, have recently been put forward, and money is being raised for the task, essential in view of the condition of the monastery block of 1933, for its replacement by new buildings which may be pleasantly grouped round a three-sided court.

A pioneering and interesting aspect of life at Worth Abbey is the lay community whose activity is centred in a house, of about 1830 with additions, elsewhere in the grounds. The abbey also has a small dependent priory at Lima in Peru, for which purpose-built buildings have been erected; there are also hopes for Peruvian recruitment.

Parkminster Priory* England's one present-day priory of Carthusian monks was founded, at Cowfold in Central Sussex, by monks who came from France, in 1873. A French architect named Normand designed the buildings which arose between 1876 and 1883; their layout can best be appreciated from aerial photographs. The traditional Carthusian plan has generally been followed, though the cottage-like 'cells' are sited more closely than their equivalents in mediaeval Charterhouses. The buildings include the Victorian mansion which was already on the site. The courtyard facing the church's west front seems larger than the 'little cloisters' of mediaeval Carthusian priories, while the façade of the church is a fairly elaborate composition in the French Gothic of about 1200. The church has the curious feature of a tower and spire, far-seen over a low-lying countryside, *beyond* its eastern end.

131 Ramsgate Abbey (Benedictine) by Augustus Pugin: in the church

BERKSHIRE

Douai Abbey This Benedictine community started, in 1615, in Paris. After two moves a monastery
and a church were built, and St. Edmund's Priory
remained in Paris till the French Revolution.
Members of the Stuart royal house were frequent
visitors and patrons. James II, the Duke of Berwick,
and one of the King's daughters were buried in the
church and Dr. Johnson, in 1775, was among the
visitors, staying in the monastery during his visit to
Paris. Unlike the monks of Douai and Dieulouard the
community did not, after imprisonment by the
French Revolutionaries, migrate to England. Some
stayed in Paris, but as they could not recover their
conventual buildings their school was re-started, in
1818, in part of what had been St. Gregory's Priory at
Douai. The monastic community followed, a Gothic
chapel was built to Augustus Pugin's designs, and the
monastery and school remained at Douai for the rest
of the nineteenth century. But in 1903, on the
suppression by the French government of teaching
religious communities, these English Benedictines
and their pupils moved to England, settling at
Woolhampton in buildings which had been those of a
diocesan school in the Roman Catholic diocese of
Portsmouth; they were now relinquished for the
purpose which, with important additions, they have
since served. A Catholic parish church was already
available, but this has now been superseded, for
monastic and school purposes, by the eastern fragment of a large, but incomplete abbey church designed in the 1920s.

Of Douai's present buildings some (particularly an
aisled Gothic church of 1848) are from the Catholic
mission which went back to penal times. Some are the
academic buildings put up, between 1883 and 1894,
for the diocesan school. The rest, including important
work of the 1960s, were built by the Benedictines for
the monastery and the school.

The diocesan school's buildings, of mellow red
brick with stone dressings, are in the early Tudor style
once much favoured for educational buildings. They
include work by F.A. Walters; their best feature,
recalling some similar entrances at Cambridge, being
an attractive gate tower aligned, at an angle to the
adjacent blocks, to command the road approach.

Monastic buildings, including a long cloister with
gabled windows, were by Sebastian Pugin Powell and
were put up soon after 1906. Before the First World
War schemes were worked out, by various architects,
for a large cruciform abbey church to serve the monks

and the school. More projects for a new church, one
by Sir Giles Scott for a great rectangular building with
a row of saucer domes, were evolved in the 1920s. The
architect actually chosen, for a church started in 1928,
was J. Arnold Crush who had been Lutyens' pupil and
had worked with Sir Giles Scott. His design was for a
large cruciform church, with an apsidal lady chapel
and in a style, late Decorated and early Perpendicular,
akin to Sir Giles Scott's nave at Downside. The lady
chapel (now the monks' choir) and a bay and a half of
the intended presbytery were built by 1933. The outer
rendering is mostly in warm red brick, but the
interior, as at Downside, is of stone.

In 1963 a scheme was announced, with Sir
Frederick Gibberd as architect, for the extension of
the church in 'contemporary' style, and for new
monastic buildings whose completion would free
older monastery blocks for more school accommodation. The church has still to be extended, but its re-
ordering is soon to be taken in hand. What was
finished by 1966, and can now be seen, is the first
section of the new monastic buildings. An access
cloister and a calefactory are among them. But of
greater interest, and well showing that what present-
day monks need is the provision of up-to-date blocks
of study bedrooms, are the two new monastery blocks.
Built of red load-bearing brick which tunes in with
that of the church, their serrated profile screens rooms
whose walls are angled to give views and catch good
light, and which recall modern buildings in some
historic 'Oxbridge' colleges.

HAMPSHIRE

Farnborough Abbey These buildings now belong
to a small English Benedictine community of the
Subiaco congregation, but they have had an unusual
history, and were not first built for monastic use. They
are also, in any English setting, even more of an
architectural exotic than Westminster Abbey was
under Henry III.

In 1881, after moving from Chislehurst to
Farnborough, the Empress Eugénie started the
church, and an adjacent house for its priests, so that it
could contain the tombs of Napoleon III, herself, and
the Prince Imperial. The first religious community to
care for the tombs and pray for Bonapartist souls was
of French Premonstratensian canons, but in 1895 they
were succeeded by French Benedictines from
Solesmes who were followed, in 1946, by Subiaco
Benedictines from Prinknash.

133   Quarr Abbey: the refectory

The abbey's main feature is its conspicuous hilltop church, of modest size and finished in 1888. It was designed by a French architect, Gabriel Hippolyte Alexandre Destailleur, who had designed a side chapel at Chislehurst and whose larger works included the restoration of several French Renaissance châteaux and, for the Rothschilds and others, of pseudo-Renaissance mansions, including Waddesdon in Buckinghamshire. His church at Farnborough, cruciform with an unaisled nave, an apse, and a somewhat exotic Gothic dome, is in the rich flamboyant Gothic style current in France about 1530. Beautifully vaulted and a gem of its type it has a wheel window, with rich flamboyant tracery, in the apse above the sepulchral crypt. It is certainly among the country's most exciting modern Catholic churches.

Quarr Abbey, I.O.W.* Another place where modern monks have reoccupied a mediaeval monastic site, in this case that of the Cistercian abbey of Quarr, first founded in 1132 as a Savigniac house. The present buildings are, however, some distance from the mediaeval ruins; they include a mock-Tudor

mansion whose fabric contains some stone from the older abbey. The buildings of this century are, however, some of the most striking modern monastic buildings put up in England.

The return of monasticism to Quarr was in 1907, when the French Benedictines of Solesmes, who had left France owing to anti-clerical laws and were already elsewhere in the Isle of Wight, bought the property and started the present monastery and its church. Most of the French monks went back to France in 1922, and the present community, though still in the Solesmes congregation, is mainly English. As at Farnborough the new buildings were by a French architect, but their brick-built Gothic is not closely imitative but of challenging originality. Their architect was a member of the community, Dom Paul Bellot, trained in Paris and with a deep knowledge and appreciation of the use of brick, in the Flemish or North German manner, in modern churches. His monastery buildings, on a quadrangular plan and with

207

134 Alton Abbey, Hampshire (Order of St. Paul): architect's sketch 1928

effective Gothic cross arches in the cloisters, refectory, and chapter house, were finished in 1907, while the church is of 1911–12. Despite a large porch or narthex, it is comparatively small as it has to provide for no lay congregation. The monks' choir is in the structural nave, while a stocky tower, with corner pinnacles, rises over the sanctuary. A notably beautiful corner turret, in its style recalling a period about 1200, marks the church's south-west corner, while there and elsewhere in the abbey the brickwork's external patterning is most effective.

St. Paul's Abbey, near Alton* The Anglican Order of St. Paul started in the East End of London, in 1889, and was at first wholly engaged in work for seamen's welfare. In 1895 the community bought land a few miles from Alton and there combined life of a more monastic character with the running of a home for retired seamen. The abbey, now Benedictine in character, still has an attractively built seamen's home, and a guest house, among its buildings. The church is among the most traditionally monastic of those used by any Anglican men's community. Its five-bay nave and transepts, with Percy Green as their

architect, were started about 1900 and were finished in five years. Beyond a massive screen the central tower and the choir, by Sir Charles Nicholson, were built after the First World War. Early Gothic in style the buildings are, in the manner of the Wessex chalklands, of flint rubble with arches outlined in brick.

SOMERSET

Downside Abbey The oldest community in the English Benedictine congregation was founded, in 1607, at Douai in what was then the territory of the Spanish Netherlands. The monastery and church of St. Gregory's Priory were soon built and the school duly followed. Douai, with its English College for training secular clergy, was an important Continental centre of 'penal' Catholicism, and the English Benedictines stayed there till the French Revolutionary army occupied the town. After a spell in prison the monks came to England in 1795, going at first to the Smythes' mansion at Acton Burnell in Shropshire. In 1814, when the mansion of Mount Pleasant, in the Mendip village of Stratton-on-the-Fosse, was for sale they bought the property; the house still stands as the oldest element in the complex of abbey and school buildings, which present a *multorum gatherum* of architectural attributions.

The oldest building used by the Downside Benedictines forms part of the school. Next to the original mansion the old chapel, and the adjacent buildings, were finished in 1822 and are England's oldest post-Reformation monastic buildings of a recognisably conventual type. By the versatile Bath architect H.E. Goodridge, they are in an Early English idiom which was pre-ecclesiological yet sufficiently 'correct' to be praised by Augustus Pugin who himself got out ambitious, unexecuted schemes for a new church and monastery at Downside. When the time came for new school buildings the Gothic blocks of 1853–4, which still stand, were by Charles Hansom.

Downside's most important monastic buildings are those started in the 1870s to designs by Edward Hansom (Charles' son and an old boy of the school) and his partner A.M. Dunn. They are richly adorned, and partly in a high-Victorian polychrome style. The impressive refectory is mainly used by the school, while the architects' plans for other buildings, nearer the church, allowed for a quadrangle whose elements are not used exactly as their mediaeval equivalents would have been. The monastery, as at Ampleforth and other modern abbeys, is a block of study bedrooms with a somewhat later western wing. Its best feature, continued along the church's southern side, is a fine vaulted cloister, built not as working space but as a passageway. A long cloister (the Petre cloister) links the monastery with the school refectory and with another passageway, of Edward Hansom's time but now surmounted by new buildings fulfilling his idea of a two-tiered link, for monks above and boys below, between the church and the school and some of the monastic buildings.* What he planned above the Petre cloister was never built, so the church looks south over an open-ended court which allows fine distant views of the church and its lofty tower.

The abbey church, two and a half bays shorter than its proposed length, is none the less Downside's great glory. Larger than Truro Cathedral it is one of the great achievements of England's Gothic Revival, while Downside Abbey and St. John's church at Norwich (now a cathedral) are the Roman Catholics' two most ambitious modern Gothic churches in England. Hansom and Dunn designed the church in 1872; their plans, including a tall spire above a southern tower, were for a church with shallow

*The latest buildings, by Mr. Francis Pollen, include a new refectory and a floor of guest rooms above it. The same architect's new library, polygonal on a square base, lies out to the east.

transepts, and apsidal with radiating chapels in the manner of a French *chevet*. What was built to these designs can easily be distinguished from the work, in a more English tradition, of later architects. The transepts, ornate in the late thirteenth-century manner though with some capitals still uncarved, were finished, along with one bay each of the choir limb and the nave, in 1882. The apsidal lady chapel, the choir's northern aisle wall, and three chapels were finished according to the Dunn and Hansom plans. But on the southern side two large chapels, square-ended and Perpendicular, marked an abrupt departure from the first scheme. Most of the tower is by Dunn and Hansom, but the topmost stage, designed by Sir Giles Scott, was not finished till 1938.

The choir limb, now re-ordered so that the stalls lie east of the High Altar, which has been sited closer to the nave, was splendidly fashioned, between the outer walls planned for it, by Thomas Garner who had been G.F. Bodley's partner, but who practised alone after joining the Roman Catholic church. What he built was a choir of six and a half bays, with arcades of an early Decorated type and three eastern arches creating a squared east end, of similar type. There is no triforium stage, and above the arcades the large clerestorey windows are in the style of the late fourteenth-century transition from Decorated to Perpendicular, which was favoured by Bodley. The noble trio of eastern windows, glowing with Comper's glass, make a feature also found in Bodley's churches and in Gothic ones by Bentley. But the simple quadripartite vault is more in the French manner envisaged by Edward Hansom.

The nave was built, after the First World War, with Sir Giles Scott the architect of a building which is of a somewhat chilly whiteness. Scott's first ideas, including giant arches, no triforium or clerestorey, and narrow passageways, had been akin to those he exploited in Liverpool's Anglican cathedral. But the community preferred a nave essentially harmonising with the choir. So Scott designed them a splendid if less enterprising nave, in the early Perpendicular manner and with a triforium, but with its vault as simple as that in the choir.

Another architect who worked for Downside was F.A. Walters (already the designer of Downside's daughter priory church at Ealing) from whose designs, in 1913, the large Perpendicular sacristy was started. He also designed some of the church's numerous tombs of bishops and abbots. But the finest tomb, with its exquisitely detailed canopy an Arts and Crafts Gothic achievement by Sir Giles Scott, is that

of Cardinal Gasquet, a prior of Downside who later became the Vatican Librarian.

DEVON

Buckfast Abbey Another well-known, much visited Benedictine abbey, now part of the English congregation and with a school as well as the monastery. It is another instance of the reoccupation by monks of an important pre-Reformation monastic site. The original abbey, following an earlier Benedictine house, was founded in 1136 as a Savigniac monastery; like other Savigniac abbeys it became Cistercian in 1147 and so remained till the Dissolution. Since the building of a late Georgian Gothic mansion on part of the site of the western range, very little remains of the old abbey bar a late mediaeval tower which probably formed part of the abbot's house. The present Buckfast Abbey, re-using much foundation work of the mediaeval church as the foundations of the present buildings, is almost wholly a creation of the last hundred years.

Monks came back to Buckfast in 1883, when French Benedictines of Pierre Qui Vire, who had been exiled in 1880, bought the property. New monastic buildings were soon started; they were Romanesque from F.A. Walters' designs and with the unusual feature, in the refectory, of a row of arches running down the middle of the room. The community later became largely German. The present church, whose nave, crossing, transepts, and presbytery rest on mediaeval foundations and recreate much of the plan of the old Cistercian church, was started in 1907 with Walters as its architect. Only at its east end did it differ, somewhat unhistorically, from the plan of its predecessor. Excavations revealed that the mediaeval choir aisles were prolonged, as at Abbey Dore, to allow for an eastern ambulatory and four projecting chapels, and that a lady chapel, unusually in a Cistercian church, ran out some thirty-six feet further east. But the present church, as first built, had six eastern chapels and a T-headed east end, recalling those at Fountains and Durham, which never existed at Buckfast before the Dissolution.

The style of the church, with slightly pointed arches and vaults whose Bath stone ribs are pleasingly infilled with local red sandstone, is that of the transition from Romanesque to Gothic; the church may, in essentials, resemble that built in the twelfth century. Walters, somewhat unhappily, included a triforium stage in a church whose internal height is really too little for a three-tier elevation. The exterior, uniform in style except for its eastern chapel, is of much dignity, but the central tower, all in an early Gothic idiom, has been carried up to a height more that of the fifteenth century; it looked much better, as I first saw it, when it was incomplete.

The most modern part, finished in 1966, and a courageous departure from mock-Romanesque, is the Blessed Sacrament chapel. This runs out beyond the eastern chapels, covering the site of the mediaeval lady chapel and of the one which Walters proposed. It is, however, wider than either of these. By the Plymouth architects Walls and Pearn, it is markedly modern, with excellent windows designed and made in the abbey. The main church is also of note for its works of art. These include splendid mosaic pavements, an abbot's throne which incorporates late mediaeval woodwork, and a High Altar with its retable and a sanctuary corona of a strongly Rhenish Romanesque stamp. Better still are the candelabra and the memorial plaque to Abbot Vonier, fine modern bronze work by Benno Elkan.

Abbotskerswell, St. Augustine's Priory One of the more remarkable sets of buildings specially put up for the use of a contemplative community, in this case canonesses regular of St. Augustine. The community was that of St. Monica's at Leuven (Louvain) in the Spanish Netherlands, founded in 1609 and with many nuns drawn from well-known English Catholic fam-

ilies of the penal period. The French Revolutionaries drove the nuns from the Netherlands and having had various homes in England the community was, for some sixty years, at Spettisbury in Dorset. In 1860 the nuns moved to the comparatively new house of 'Abbotsleigh' at Abbotskerswell near Newton Abbot. Conventual buildings, and a church whose sanctuary was designed for the perpetual adoration of the Blessed Sacrament, were finished by the end of 1863. The architect for most of the work was Joseph Hansom. The main domestic block has a striking tower, octagonal on a square base and with a spire of Germanic appearance, half way along its southern side. More striking is the nuns' church, with an extern chapel on its northern side. The principal stalls, as at Stanbrook, are in a series of recesses beneath the windows of the 'nave' (actually the choir); each recess has its own gable. The church is richly decorated with shafts and corbels, and its unusual sanctuary, on an octagonal plan with a complete set of pillars and attached columns, is surmounted, and lit, by an octagonal tower with arcading and a cap of German Romanesque type. The elaborate altar composition, and a spirelet, above the exposition throne, rising almost to the tower vault, were by Benjamin Bucknall, another Roman Catholic architect of the 1860s.

Wales

PEMBROKESHIRE

Caldey Island (the modern abbey) The present-day abbey is unusual in that the buildings first put up for Anglican Benedictines have now, for nearly half a century, been used by Roman Catholic Cistercians. The Anglican monks, under Abbot Aelred Carlyle, came to Caldey in 1901, occupying a house near the remains of the mediaeval priory (see page   ). After a few years in Yorkshire they returned to Caldey, and the present buildings, a somewhat sprawling group whose architect was Coates Carter, were built between 1906 and 1911. Their style can be described as Romantic Romanesque, with one tall circular tower not unlike a minaret and with pointed caps, on this and other towers, recalling those which gave romantic silhouettes to some ancient or renovated German castles. The interior woodwork is more lavish than one would find in a monastery built for Cistercians, but the rectangular church, rebuilt after a fire in 1940, is of an austere simplicity appropriate to the community whose choir offices and Masses are sung here.

Bibliography

This list includes only works of general application to monasticism as a whole, to religious orders as these have worked, or still work, in England and Wales, and to particular aspects of the subject, e.g. granges and the Dissolution under Henry VIII. Works on individual monastic houses have been omitted. Valuable information on these can be obtained from the appropriate volumes of the Victoria County History.

A great quarry of information, including the text of many charters and other documents, is Sir William Dugdale, *Monasticon Anglicanum*, ed. in 6 vols., 1817–30.

No present-day student can overlook the classic works, by their scholarship and judgment superseding much that went before them, of the late Professor David Knowles, himself a Benedictine monk. A short but valuable work, covering many other countries as well as England and Wales, is *Christian Monasticism*, 1969. More detailed, with a purely English and Welsh relevance, are his *The Monastic Order in England*, 2nd edn. 1963, reprinted 1966, 1976, and *The Religious Orders in England*, 3 vols., 1949–69. See also David Knowles and R.N. Hadcock *Mediaeval Religious Houses in England and Wales*, 1953, and Lionel Butler and Christopher Given-Wilson, *Medieval Monasteries of Great Britain*, 1979.

Earlier works on the general subject are Abbot (later Cardinal) F.A. Gasquet, *English Monastic Life*, 1904; A. Hamilton Thompson, *English Monasteries*, 1913; D.H.S. Cranage, *The Home of the Monk*, 1926; R. Liddesdale Palmer, *English Monasteries in the Middle Ages*, 1930; R.E. Swartwout, *The Monastic Craftsman*, 1932; Geoffrey Beard and Allen Billington, *English Abbeys* (on a gazetteer system), 1949. More recent are F.H. Crossley, *The English Abbey*, revised, with additions by Bryan Little, 1962; Hugh Braun, *English Abbeys*, 1971; and George Zarnecki, *The Monastic Achievement*, 1972. See also R. Gillyard-Beer, *Abbeys*, H.M.S.O., 1958; the companion volume on Scottish Abbeys is by Stewart Cruden, 1961. Also of value are J.C. Dickinson, *Monastic Life in Mediaeval England*, 1961, and Dom Denys Rutledge, *The Complete Monk*, 1966.

For the Dissolution and kindred topics see Geoffrey Baskerville, *English Monks and the Suppression of the Monasteries*, 1937; C.W.O. Woodward, *Dissolution of the Monasteries*, 1966; Joyce Youings, *The Dissolution of the Monasteries*, 1971.

For nunneries, of all orders, see Eileen Power, *Mediaeval English Nunneries*, 1922.

For individual orders see, for the Cluniacs and Grandmontines, Rose Graham, *English Ecclesiastical Studies*, 1929; E.M. Thompson, *The Carthusian Order in England*, 1930; J.C. Dickinson, *The Origins of the Austin Canons and Their Introduction into England*, 1950; H.M. Colvin, *The White Canons in England*, 1951; Rose Graham, *St. Gilbert of Sempringham and the Gilbertines*, 1903; J.R.H. Moorman, *The Franciscans in England*, 1974; A.R. Martin, *Franciscan Architecture in England*, 1937; A.F.C. Bourdillon, *The Order of Minoresses in England*, 1926; Bede Jarrett, *The English Dominicans*, 1921; Aubrey Gwynn, *The English Austin Friars in the Time of Wyclif* (including other material), 1940; Launcelot Sheppard, *The English Carmelites*, 1943; Canon J.R. Fletcher, *The Story of the English Bridgettines of Syon*, 1933.

For one aspect of the mediaeval subject, see Colin Platt, *The Monastic Grange in Mediaeval England*, 1969.

For more recent developments see Dom Basil Whelan, *Historic English Convents of To-Day*, 1936; Peter Anson, *The Religious Orders and Congregations of Great Britain and Ireland*, 1949; *Directory of Religious Orders etc. of Great Britain and Ireland*, publ. John S. Burns and Sons, Glasgow; Marcelle Bernstein, *Nuns*, 1976, paperback edn. 1978; ed. Daniel Rees, *Consider Your Call, A Theology of Monastic Life*, 1978.

For Anglican Communities see Peter Anson, *The Call of the Cloister*, 2nd edn., 1964 and A.M. Allchin, *The Silent Revolution*, 1958.

Index